International Political Economy Series

General Editor: Timothy M. Shaw, Professor and Director, Institute of International Relations, The University of the West Indies, Trinidad & Tobago

Titles include:

Leslie Elliott Armijo (*editor*)
FINANCIAL GLOBALIZATION AND DEMOCRACY IN EMERGING MARKETS

Robert Boardman
THE POLITICAL ECONOMY OF NATURE
Environmental Debates and the Social Sciences

Jörn Brömmelhörster and Wolf-Christian Paes (*editors*)
THE MILITARY AS AN ECONOMIC ACTOR
Soldiers in Business

Gerard Clarke and Michael Jennings (*editors*)
DEVELOPMENT, CIVIL SOCIETY AND FAITH-BASED ORGANIZATIONS
Bridging the Sacred and the Secular

Gordon Crawford
FOREIGN AID AND POLITICAL REFORM
A Comparative Analysis of Democracy Assistance and Political Conditionality

Matt Davies
INTERNATIONAL POLITICAL ECONOMY AND MASS COMMUNICATION IN CHILE
National Intellectuals and Transnational Hegemony

Martin Doornbos
INSTITUTIONALIZING DEVELOPMENT POLICIES AND RESOURCE STRATEGIES IN EASTERN AFRICA AND INDIA
Developing Winners and Losers

Fred P. Gale
THE TROPICAL TIMBER TRADE REGIME

Meric S. Gertler and David A. Wolfe
INNOVATION AND SOCIAL LEARNING
Institutional Adaptation in an Era of Technological Change

Anne Marie Goetz and Rob Jenkins
REINVENTING ACCOUNTABILITY
Making Democracy Work for the Poor

Andrea Goldstein
MULTINATIONAL COMPANIES FROM EMERGING ECONOMIES
Composition, Conceptualization and Direction in the Global Economy

Mary Ann Haley
FREEDOM AND FINANCE
Democratization and Institutional Investors in Developing Countries

Keith M. Henderson and O. P. Dwivedi (*editors*)
BUREAUCRACY AND THE ALTERNATIVES IN WORLD PERSPECTIVES

Jomo K.S. and Shyamala Nagaraj (*editors*)
GLOBALIZATION VERSUS DEVELOPMENT

Angela W. Little
LABOURING TO LEARN
Towards a Political Economy of Plantations, People and Education in Sri Lanka

John Loxley (*editor*)
INTERDEPENDENCE, DISEQUILIBRIUM AND GROWTH
Reflections on the Political Economy of North–South Relations at the Turn of the Century

Don D. Marshall
CARIBBEAN POLITICAL ECONOMY AT THE CROSSROADS
NAFTA and Regional Developmentalism

Susan M. McMillan
FOREIGN DIRECT INVESTMENT IN THREE REGIONS OF THE SOUTH AT THE END OF THE
TWENTIETH CENTURY

S. Javed Maswood
THE SOUTH IN INTERNATIONAL ECONOMIC REGIMES
Whose Globalization?

John Minns
THE POLITICS OF DEVELOPMENTALISM
The Midas States of Mexico, South Korea and Taiwan

Philip Nel
THE POLITICS OF ECONOMIC INEQUALITY IN DEVELOPING COUNTRIES

Pia Riggirozzi
ADVANCING GOVERNANCE IN THE SOUTH
What are the Roles for International Financial Institutions in Developing States?

Lars Rudebeck, Olle Törnquist and Virgilio Rojas (*editors*)
DEMOCRATIZATION IN THE THIRD WORLD
Concrete Cases in Comparative and Theoretical Perspective

Eunice N. Sahle
WORLD ORDERS, DEVELOPMENT AND TRANSFORMATION

Benu Schneider (*editor*)
THE ROAD TO INTERNATIONAL FINANCIAL STABILITY
Are Key Financial Standards the Answer?

Howard Stein (*editor*)
ASIAN INDUSTRIALIZATION AND AFRICA
Studies in Policy Alternatives to Structural Adjustment

William Vlcek
OFFSHORE FINANCE AND SMALL STATES
Sovereignty, Size and Money

International Political Economy Series
Series Standing Order ISBN 978–0–333–71708–0 hardcover
Series Standing Order ISBN 978–0–333–71110–1 paperback
(*outside North America only*)

You can receive future titles in this series as they are published by placing a standing order.
Please contact your bookseller or, in case of difficulty, write to us at the address below with
your name and address, the title of the series and one of the ISBNs quoted above.

Customer Services Department, Macmillan Distribution Ltd, Houndmills, Basingstoke,
Hampshire RG21 6XS, England

World Orders, Development and Transformation

Eunice N. Sahle

First published 2010 by
PALGRAVE MACMILLAN

Palgrave Macmillan in the UK is an imprint of Macmillan Publishers Limited, registered in England, company number 785998, of Houndmills, Basingstoke, Hampshire RG21 6XS.

Palgrave Macmillan in the US is a division of St Martin's Press LLC, 175 Fifth Avenue, New York, NY 10010.

Palgrave Macmillan is the global academic imprint of the above companies and has companies and representatives throughout the world.

Palgrave® and Macmillan® are registered trademarks in the United States, the United Kingdom, Europe and other countries.

ISBN 978-0-230-22107-9 hardback

This book is printed on paper suitable for recycling and made from fully managed and sustained forest sources. Logging, pulping and manufacturing processes are expected to conform to the environmental regulations of the country of origin.

A catalogue record for this book is available from the British Library.

Library of Congress Cataloging-in-Publication Data
Sahle, Eunice Njeri.
  World orders, development, and transformation / Eunice N. Sahle.
    p. cm. — (International political economy series)
  Includes bibliographical references and index.
  ISBN 978-0-230-22107-9 (hardback)
  1. World politics—1945–1989. 2. World politics—1989–
  3. Hegemony. 4. Neoliberalism. I. Title.
JZ1310.S24 2010
341.2—dc22   2009048531

Printed and bound in Great Britain by
CPI Antony Rowe, Chippenham and Eastbourne

For Professor Micere Githae Mugo with love:
thank you for making the power of ideas visible, and a life of
ideas imaginable

Contents

List of Table

Acknowledgements

I would like to thank the following institutions for their contributions to this project. First, the University of North Carolina at Chapel Hill (UNC-Chapel Hill) for a research leave and a Junior Faculty Award that enabled the drafting of a preliminary outline for this book. Many thanks to Queen's University, the International Development Research Centre in Canada and University of North Carolina for financial support for research in Malawi. At Palgrave Macmillan, I would like to thank Dr Philippa Grand whose quick and generous response to earlier versions of this project made the long labour of revising not only bearable but also interesting. I cannot thank Alexandra Webster, Associate Director and publisher for International Relations, IPE and Development, and Professor Timothy Shaw, Editor, IPE series, enough for their support. Their interventions at crucial junctures, insightful comments and encouragement throughout the many moons of revisions made this project possible, and for that, I will forever be grateful. I thank Renée Takken too for her patience and support during the final stages of the project.

Several individuals have in different but complementary ways contributed to my life during the writing of this book. I particularly would like to thank Professor Micere Githae Mugo, Archbishop Emeritus Dr David Gitari and Kamoji Wachiira for being a fundamental part of my intellectual journey. At UNC-Chapel Hill, I extend special thanks to Julius Nyang'oro, Professor and Chair, Department of African and Afro-American Studies, for his tremendous support throughout this process. Further, I would like to thank Adam Versenyi, Professor and Chair, Curriculum in International and Area Studies for supporting my work and being a great source of encouragement. Finally, thanks to the following colleagues for their support: Ann R. Dunbar, Deborah Crowder, Travis Gore, Mark Driscoll, Judith Blau, Arturo Escobar, Alphonse Mutima, Tanya Shields, Chris Nelson, Perry Hall, Jonathan Weiler, Trevaughn Eubanks, Ann Schaff, Bereket Selassie, Karla Slocum, John Pickles, Kenneth Janken, Kia Caldwell, Tomeko Ashford-Carter, Barbara Anderson, Reginald Hildebrand, Joseph Jordan, Michael Lambert and Karen Booth. I am also grateful for the encouragement of the following colleagues at other institutions: Wisdom Tettey,

Kwasi Ofori-Yeboah, Patrick Bond, Wiseman Chirwa, Wangui wa Goro, Alfred Nyasulu, Ngugi wa Thiong'o, Joseph Mensah, Ollen Mwalubunju, Michael Byers, James Tully, Korbla Puplamplu, Walter Mignolo, Paul Haslam, John Kapito, Abigail Bakan, Seodi White, Richard Sandbrook, Charlotte Maxwell, Molly Kane, Vera Chirwa, Oloo Onyango and Diane Nelson. Thanks to Glen Williams, former Chair, Department of Political Science, Carleton University, Canada, for 1999–2002. Very special thanks to Professor Emeritus Colin Leys, for his tremendous support when I worked with him at Queen's University many years ago. Revised elements of work that he read during that period appear here in parts of Chapters 3 and 4. I thank him for all the lessons and inspiring discussions in Kingston, London, Ottawa and Toronto. In the midst of working on this project, a group of us lost a close friend and intellectual collaborator, the late Edward Osei-Kwandwo Prempeh of Carleton University in Canada. Those of us who knew him miss his wit, grace, intellectual rigour and commitment to social justice projects in Canada and elsewhere.

For love and much more, I thank my family and dearest friends, and their families: Anne-Marie, Nazik, Almuth, Suzanne, Karen, Gamal, Tesfai, the Tetteys, Poet Jay, Patrick, Irene, the M'kwendas, Haileab, Trudy, Freda, the Chimimbas, Elizabeth, Thomson, no.2-Barbara, *Papa* Fit. Tewelde Tedla, *Mama* Lemulemu, the Msimatis, Lucretia, Luther and Colman. Special thanks to Wathira Kamoji for years of Sunday updates and sisterhood. I am particularly grateful to my parents and grandparents for their love and encouragement, and my wonderful aunt Jacinta for the early days and beyond. I extend my deepest thanks to Nade, Pahtea, Ann-Roberta and Wizzy for always being there during the vicissitudes of this project. Thanks to my nieces and nephews especially, Beth, Elizabeth, Nathan, Michael and Machi, and my sister Ruth for their humour and wonderful mischief. Finally, yet importantly, with much love, I thank Ben and Nia for infinite contributions to everything I do. While I deeply appreciate their contributions to this project, none of these individuals and institutions is responsible for the analysis I make here.

List of Abbreviations

ADMARC	Agricultural Development and Marketing Corporation
AFRICOM	US Africa Command
AGOA	African Growth and Opportunity Act
BOC	Brazilian Organizing Committee
CDC	Commonwealth Development Corporation
CHS	Commission on Human Security
COMECON	Council for Mutual Economic Assistance
CSS	Critical Security Studies
DFID	Department for International Development
EPB	Economic Planning Board
FDI	Foreign Director Investment
FOCAC	Forum on China Africa Cooperation
GATT	General Agreement on Tariffs and Trade
GDP	Gross Domestic Product
HIPC	Heavily Indebted Poor Countries
IC	International Council
IDS	International Development Studies
IMF	International Monetary Fund
IPE	International Political Economy
IR	International Relations
ISI	Import Substitution Industrialization
KPR	Korean People's Republic
KRB	Korean Reconstruction Bank
MCP	Malawi Congress Party
MDC	Malawi Development Corporation
MDGs	Millennium Development Goals
NAFTA	North American Free Trade Agreement
NGOs	Non-government organizations
NIEO	New International Economic Order
ODA	Official Development Assistance
ODC	Oriental Development Company
OECD	Organization for Economic Cooperation and Development
SEZ	Special Economic Zones
TDHB	Transnational development historic bloc

TT   Tobin Tax
UN   United Nations
UNDP   United Nations Development Programme
WSF   World Social Forum
WTO   World Trade Organization

1
Introduction

From the push for 'Third World' modernization to the current human security development discourse, there has been no scarcity of ideas and practices claiming to represent the blueprint for the march towards cultural, political and economic capitalist modernity for social formations in the global South (South). Overall, in the post-1945 period, ideas embedded in shifting development discourses have emerged as the 'common sense' (Gramsci, 1971) through which this process is imagined and mapped out in policy. This development has made questioning the underpinning philosophy, aims and effects of development discourses in a prevailing conjuncture an act of pure folly in the eyes of most people in the global North (North) and the South. Thus, despite the fact that the history of the last several decades has indicated the limitations of these discourses, the promise of development in the South along Euro-American lines continues to 'gain acceptance everywhere' even though 'the moral duty is fulfilled in the very act of proclamation rather than in any actual success' (Rist, 2004: 215).

While the manner in which development discourses translate a given social formation in the South is mediated by local conditions, including resistance by social forces, historical experiences, religious traditions, and social relations such as gender and class, the influence of these discourses cannot be ignored. At the subjectivity level, for instance, these discourses have generated a 'profound ideological shift' (Pigg, 1992: 492) on how political, cultural and economic processes are perceived (Ferguson, 1994; Escobar, 1995a; Mitchell, 2002). In Nepal, for example, the embedding of development discourse by international development institutions and the state has transformed 'the way in which people . . . conceptualize national society and differences within it', and, in the process, changed 'the meaning of the village in Nepalese social imagination' and the approach to 'social identities' and processes of social change (Pigg, 1992: 491–492). Overall, as Rist (2004: 214) argues, development discourse 'being eminently social, this belief is *a product of history*... but it is also an instance that *produces history*..."Development", like any other belief, has become a historical agent... Everywhere it wins acceptance' (Rist, 2004: 214–215). As a 'historical agent' development discourse has had significant effects on politico-economic processes in the South as we will argue and demonstrate in various parts of this book. Yet, despite its profound effects, proponents of this discourse have represented it relentlessly as a neutral scientific tool that explains and facilitates understanding of past and future politico-economic processes in the South, and as a set of ideas, that enables the transition of traditional societies to the linear path of universal modernity.

This book has two objectives. The first one attempts to re-think post-1945 development discourses in an effort to move beyond their technocratic and ahistorical representation and to highlight their core sources of power. The book argues that, in the context of shifting world orders (Cox, 1981; 1987), these ideas and other elements of a given world order have greatly influenced politico-economic processes in the South. In addition, it is argued that they have shaped the international development policies of dominant metropolitan states in the world politico-economic order and those of institutions of global governance, from Third World modernization to the current human security development discourse that informs the Millennium Development Goals (MDGs) framework.[1] We discuss the preceding issues in the chapters that form the first section of the book. Following this introductory chapter, the next one discusses the relevance of the neo-Gramscian tradition and Anibal Quijano's 'coloniality of power' (2007; 2008) perspective to our central concerns. Chapter 3 demonstrates the deep embedding of orthodox development ideas in the geopolitics and socio-economic modalities of the post-1945 world order and the politico-economic effects of these ideas. With a specific focus on the role of the state in the economy in Malawi and South Korea, Chapter 4's concern is highlighting the analytical poverty of orthodox development perspectives in the study of politico-economic processes in the South.

While a discussion of orthodox development ideas and their effects is a thread that runs throughout the book, our analysis takes a dialectic and ethical approach to the study of politico-economic processes. Thus, its second objective – the focus of the chapters comprising the second part of the book – is to tease out developments and debates that are currently calling for or are considered to signal the transformation of the core features of the prevailing neo-liberal and securitizing world order. Utilizing insights from the theoretical traditions underlying this project, Chapter 5 examines debates in International Political Economy and International Relations, and institutions of global governance concerned with the question of the transformation of global governance in the contemporary era. In Chapter 6, we discuss developments in China and Russia in the era of a neo-liberal world order, in addition to the nature of China's involvement in contemporary Africa. The focus of Chapter 7 is an examination of the rise of the human security development discourse and its adoption by institutions of global governance and dominant metropolitan states in the context of neo-liberal development ideas and securitization of development and security. Focusing on the World Social Forum, Chapter 8 traces the rise, contributions and tensions of a global phenomenon, which some scholars refer to as 'counter-hegemonic globalization' (Santos, 2008: xix). The Epilogue's concerns are the implications of the current crisis of the global liberalized financial system and the ascendancy to power of President Barack Obama in the USA to the world order.

Overall, the book hopes to enrich the field of international development studies (IDS) in four ways. The first is by indicating the ways in which the constitutive elements of the post-1945 world order have influenced politico-economic processes in the South. In this respect the book demonstrates how shifts in world orders have generated powerful ideas which, coupled with other elements of a given order, have influenced these processes in the South, including facilitating the reproduction of the power asymmetry between the North and the South in the world politico-economic system and other manifestations of coloniality of power. Such an approach to the study of politico-economic processes in the South interrupts the tendency in dominant approaches in IDS to ignore the influence of global political, economic and intellectual developments on these processes and, importantly, it historicizes the rise of development discourses. Ignoring the influence of the interplay of local and global conditions and representing orthodox development ideas in neutral terms is not only an analytically flawed approach, but also it has marked socio-economic, political and ideological effects. For instance, it enables the de-politicization of the rise of the capitalist world system and the power asymmetry that underpins this system and its conjunctural world orders. Moreover, such an approach treats the South as a marginal rather than a constitutive geopolitical-economic formation underpinning the emergence and evolution of the world politico-economic order. Overall, as Enrique Dussel (1996) has posited in his critique of what he calls the 'developmental fallacy' embedded in development discourses, the latter's tendency is to ignore the double process that has characterized the rise of the world politico-economic structure: the dominance of Northern metropolitan social formations and the marginalization of the South. Thus, for a comprehensive understanding of the political economies of the South to emerge, at the least, analysts need to recognize that 'since 1492 the periphery [South] is not a "before," but an "underneath": the exploited, the dominated, the origin of stolen wealth, accumulated in the dominating, exploiting "center" ' (ibid.: 5). Consequently, from a neo-Gramscian perspective we suggest that politico-economic processes in the South or elsewhere are better examined 'not as a sequence or series of discrete events or moments which when aggregated equal a process of change' but rather as influenced by 'the ensemble of social relations' (Gill, 1993: 24) involving the interplay of local and global economic, ideological and political developments in a given historical moment.

Second, we conceptualize orthodox development ideas through a power analytic in an effort to destabilize the technocratic and apolitical pretensions that have always marked development discourses. In this respect, our analysis departs from the 'positivist methodological individualism'[2] of orthodox development discourses that represent them as being neutral. Third, and at the level of theoretical formation, this project highlights the relevance of the neo-Gramscian critical theory tradition to the study of politico-economic processes in the South. However, even though this tradition forms the analytical foundation for this project, we contend that it is limited. To address some of its analytical gaps, we incorporate insights from the coloniality of power approach. Further, drawing on insights from critical feminist analysis, in Chapters 3, 5 and 7, we provide brief examples indicating the gendered foundations and effects of orthodox development discourses, and other elements of shifting world orders in the post-1945 period. While our focus in this respect is orthodox approaches in IDS, our premise is that the neo-Gramscian and the coloniality of power perspectives also ignore their gendered foundations and the gendered effects of ideas and world orders.[3] Fourth, the book contributes to IDS by discussing the question of transformation. Departing from the positivist and 'problem-solving theory' (Cox, 1981) framing orthodox development perspectives, we engage with the question of transformation of core features and other politico-economic conditions characterizing the contemporary neoliberal and securitizing order. Such an approach we suggest opens up discursive and political spaces that enable critical reflections of normatively grounded questions, such as the 'emancipatory potential' (Santos and Rodríguez-Garavito, 2007: xxi) of contemporary developments such as the World Social Forum (Chapter 8) and the ascendancy to power of President Barack Obama (Chapter 9) in the USA.

Part I

World Orders and Development Discourses

2
Analytical Framing

In analytical terms, our premise is that the neo-Gramscian critical theory contributes to an examination of the central concerns of this project in several ways, two of which mark our entry point: its framework of world orders and dialectical approach to world orders and other power structures. In this chapter, we discuss the ways in which analytical insights from these dimensions of the neo-Gramscian tradition and other concepts from Gramsci's work, such as hegemony, organic intellectuals and historical bloc contribute to this project. Nonetheless, as we suggested in the last chapter, even with its robust analytical insights, this tradition can only lead to partial understanding of politico-economic processes in the South. Thus, in an effort to enrich the field of IDS and to broaden the neo-Gramscian approach, our project draws on analytical insights from Quijano's coloniality of power perspective. The first four sections of the chapter provide a discussion indicating the neo-Gramscian analytical framing of this project. In the last section, we highlight the contributions of the coloniality of power approach to the study of political and economic processes in the South.

World orders, development discourse and hegemony

The neo-Gramscian framework of world orders provides an important analytical entry point enabling us to develop one of our underlying claims: that in the post-1945 period, shifts in world orders have generated ideas that have influenced politico-economic processes in the South. In his articulation of the framework of world orders, Robert W. Cox argues that a prevailing world order (1981: 135–136) is characterized by a 'configuration of forces' comprising ideas, institutions and material capabilities (ibid.: 138). Nonetheless, his work does not assume

9

that this configuration of forces influences political and economic processes in a mechanistic way at a given juncture. As he states, 'no one-way determinism need be assumed among these three; the relationship can be assumed to be reciprocal.... The question of which way the lines of force run is always an historical question' (ibid.: 136) that can only be answered through an examination of politico-economic imperatives and developments of a given world order, and responses from social forces.

Though neglected in development discourses, we argue and demonstrate in Chapters 3, 4 and 7 that the rise of these discourses in the post-1945 juncture is linked to broader developments at the global level, especially shifts in ideas of a given world order. Further, moving beyond the technocratic and neutral representation of development discourses, we consider the latter as embodying the three elements of power articulated in a different context by Stephen Gill and David Law: overt, covert and structural (1988: 73–80). These elements of power in different but complementary ways enable development discourses to influence political, cultural and economic debates and practices in the South. Development discourses are thus considered here as embodying structural and ideological power with significant, cultural, political and economic effects. While characterized by contradictions and tensions at a given conjuncture and mediated by a range of social forces and conditions at the local level, these ideas delineate, for example, the terrain of debate concerning questions of democracy, the organization of economic production and struggles for gender equality.

Given their analytical and other shortcomings, the question remains as to what generates the power and resiliency of orthodox development discourses. We contend that a core source of their power lies in their being a constitutive feature of a given world order in the post-1945 period and the normalization and de-historicization of Euro-American transition to capitalist politico-economic modernity. The embedding of these discourses in a given world order provides dominant actors in this order enormous discursive space and other capabilities that enable them to construct 'consent'[1] and gain hegemony for their vision of politico-economic practices. For Antonio Gramsci, hegemony represents a process through which a dominant class or its elements, in a national context manages to make its interests accepted by other classes. Describing the characteristics of a hegemonic struggle, Gramsci states:

Previously germinated ideologies become 'party', come into confrontation and conflict, until only one of them, or at least a single combination of them, tends to prevail, to gain the upper hand, to propagate itself throughout society—bringing about not only a unison of economic and political aims, but also intellectual and moral unity, posing all the questions around which the struggle rages not on a corporate but on a 'universal' plane, and thus creating the hegemony of a fundamental social group over a series of subordinate groups.... [Thus] the development and expansion of the particular group are conceived of, and presented, as being the motor force of a 'universal expansion'. (1971: 181–182)

For Gramsci, ideas articulated by 'organic intellectuals' linked to a dominant politico-economic order play a significant role in the struggle for hegemony. In his view, 'every social group, coming into existence on the original terrain of an essential function in the world of economic production, creates together with itself, organically, one or more strata of intellectuals which give it homogeneity and an awareness of its own function not only in the economic but also in the social and political fields' (ibid.: 5). The success of organic intellectuals stems from their ability to present the ideologies, ideas and political and economic interests of dominant social forces as necessary, natural, inevitable and universal. In the context of shifting world orders in the post-1945 period, leading organic intellectuals have generated hegemonic ideas about politico-economic processes in the South. The ascendancy and embedding of these ideas, for instance, those that underpin the neo-liberal development discourse's self-regulating market doctrine (Chapter 3), has been facilitated by organic intellectuals situated in major sites of hegemonic knowledge production such as dominant universities in the North who are also closely linked to ruling elites in the North and the South. For instance, the introduction and implementation of neo-liberal policies by 'the Chicago boys' in Pinochet's Chile was closely tied not only to the writings of Milton Friedman and his close links with Chilean economists trained at the University of Chicago, but also to his personal ties to President Pinochet. Writing to President Pinochet on the question of neo-liberal 'shock-therapy' Friedman, for instance, advises him as follows: 'if this shock approach were adopted, I believe that it should be announced publicly in great detail, to take effect at a very close date. The more fully the public is informed, the more will its reactions facilitate the adjustment' (Milton Friedman in a letter to General Augusto Pinochet, 21 April, 1975, quoted in Klein, 2007: 91).

Overall, the hegemonic status of development discourses and their being strongly intertwined with other features of a prevailing world order act as vital sources of their power, enabling them to influence and shape politico-economic processes in the South. Peter Hamilton's seminal observation about the workings of hegemony brings into focus the powerful effects of these discourses given their hegemonic status: 'it is the sheer taken-for-grantedness of hegemony that yields its full effects—the "naturalness" of a way of thinking about social, economic, political and ethical issues' (1986: 8). Essentially, building on early colonial epistemologies and images, development discourses have in the post-1945 period constituted a powerful hegemonic 'representational system' (Hall, 1997: 5) that has historically, and in the contemporary era of securitization (Chapter 7) of development, played a central role in the articulation by dominant metropolitan states and other key actors in the world order of what they consider as the necessary political, economic and cultural trajectory in the South. On the whole, these discourses have come to form a powerful lens through which the South is imagined and acted upon by a range of social forces in the world politico-economic order. Thus, the power of these discourses and the sources of this power need to be illuminated. For while 'the discourse of development, the forms in which it makes its arguments and establishes its authority, the manner in which it constructs the world, are usually seen as self-evident and unworthy of attention' it does 'not arise in a social, institutional or literary vacuum ... [it is] assembled within a vast hierarchical apparatus of knowledge production and consumption sometimes known, with metaphorical precision, as the 'development industry' (Crush, 1995: 6). Overall, as Arturo Escobar posits, in Michel Foucault's sense of discourse, hegemonic development discourses establish 'a space in which only certain things [can] be said and even imagined' and in the main they generate a 'process through which social reality comes into being, ... [and] the articulation of knowledge and power, of the visible and the expressible' (1995a: 40).

For over 60 years hegemonic development discourses have set the parameters of debates and practices concerning a range of issues pertaining to core areas forming the 'web of life' (Harvey, 2006: 88)—economy, politics, environment and culture—in the South, and with powerful effects. Though mediated by domestic social forces and conditions, and structural, political and economic factors that underpin the 'uneven geographies of capitalism' (ibid.: 69–116) that have emerged in the rise of the world politico-economic order, the language and concepts of these discourses represent and facilitate the reproduction of national and global power asymmetries. Yet, even with their significant effects hegemonic development discourses continue to be portrayed in technical and neutral terms as being geared solely to aiding the process of economic and political progress and to containing, in the age of the global war on terror (Chapter 7), the various threats to national and global security posed by the South's 'underdevelopment'. To be sure, the nature and extent of the influence of the elements of power underpinning hegemonic development discourses and other features of a prevailing world order on a given social formation in the South is an empirical question, but historically, prevailing world orders have generated political and economic ideas that cannot be theorized away, ignored or passed off as neutral or universal scientific forms of knowledge. As Cox has argued, theories or ideas are 'always for someone and for some purpose.... The world is seen from a standpoint definable in terms of nation or social class, of dominance or subordination, of rising or declining power, of a sense of immobility or of present crisis, of past experience, and of hopes and expectations for the future' (1981: 128).

This project's focus on the nature and power of the hegemonic development discourses, however, does not mean that social forces in the South have no agency in their encounter with these discourses and other elements of a prevailing world order. Thus, while we use the concept of hegemony to illuminate the power of orthodox development discourses, we do not claim that these discourses and the drive for their global embedding by dominant actors in the world order and their allies in the South is total, that is, it leaves no room for alternative ideas and counter-consensus movements to emerge. This kind of claim would be a misinterpretation of Gramsci's dialectical thinking in his formulation of hegemony and other concepts. For Gramsci, the struggle for hegemony among political forces is dialectical, thus the possibility always exists for the formation of counter-hegemonic discourses and practices. Further, as Cox argues in relation to ideas characterizing a given world order, 'different groups of people ... [hold] differing views as to both the nature and legitimacy' of these ideas and other constitutive features of such an order. He goes on to argue that 'rival collective images' of a given world order offer 'evidence of the potential for alternative paths' (Cox, 1981: 136). Arguing along these lines we suggest that examples do exist of states and social forces in the South challenging the world economic and political order. In the 1970s, for instance, a bloc of Third World states attempted to challenge the world order by calling for the establishment of a New International Economic Order (NIEO).[2] Further, in the contemporary world order underpinned by neo-liberal ideas and securitizing logics, 'new social movements' (Escobar, 1995b; 2008) and movements and organizations linked to the World Social Forum (Chapter 8) are contesting core practices of this order and the nature and effects of its hegemonic development discourse. Further, these movements and other new social movements are seeking alternatives to hegemonic politico-economic ideas and practices, and defending their views of the social.

Institutionalizing world orders and development discourse

The post-1945 world order has emerged as a major source of power for hegemonic development discourse in other ways. For instance, the evolution of this order has seen the concentration of power not only in social formations in the North but also in the institutions of global governance that have emerged during this period. Like other processes of institutionalization, the rise of these institutions has been aimed at providing 'a means of stabilizing and perpetuating' (Cox, 1981: 136; 1987; see also Arrighi, 2005) the post-1945 world order. As the architectural core of the world order, these institutions play a pivotal role in the production and embedding of hegemonic ideas about state formation, human security, economy production and democratization in the South. The leading institutions of the post-1945 world order—the World Bank, the International Monetary Fund (IMF), the United Nations (UN) and since 1994 the World Trade Organization (WTO)—have over the years not only appropriated development ideas generated by leading organic intellectuals of the world order such as Deepak Lal (1985) in the contemporary era of neo-liberalism and Samuel Huntington (1967 and 1968) in the era of Third World modernization discourse, but also they have emerged as key producers of hegemonic development knowledge. These institutions are the primary avenue through which the hegemony of the world order is constituted and consolidated post-1945, for 'they [a] embody the rules which facilitate the expansion of hegemonic world orders... are themselves the product of the hegemonic world [b] ideologically legitimate the norms of the world order [c] co-opt the elites from peripheral countries and [d] absorb counter-hegemonic ideas' (Cox, 1993: 62).

The material capabilities they command as providers of loans and their being a constitutive feature of the post-1945 world order are key features that have enabled institutions of global governance to play a major role in politico-economic arenas in the South. Further, their role as producers of development knowledge has contributed to their emergence as key actors in the framing of international development policy. As a core institution of the contemporary world order for instance, the World Bank is a pivotal actor in the training of potential advocates of the neo-liberal ideas marking this order. The Bank does not shy away from identifying itself as a key player in this respect, as the following quotation from one of its training seminars on contemporary neo-liberal inspired environmental economic discourse for participants from various African countries, Russia and Chile indicates:

> The purpose of this training seminar is to try to create an epistemic community in Africa so that you can have more power with your governments when negotiating for institutional reform. You won't feel alone. We'll help you set up networks and share information. You will be able to say to your bosses: 'Hey, but that's how they're doing it next door, and look how successful they are.' We are prepared to offer you support.... And when you return home after this workshop, we would like you to initiate your own training workshops on environmental economics. This way we can change decision-making in your countries. (World Bank, 1995, cited in Goldman, 2005: 1–2)

Given their positioning in the world order, these institutions constitute the central pillar of the post-1945 global development knowledge production and dissemination apparatus. For the past six decades, these institutions have played an important role in the evolution of an internationally linked 'epistemic community' that includes development experts in leading ministries such as finance and economic planning; central banks in the South and their counterparts in the North; private actors, especially those involved in global finance; owners of multinational corporations; and, increasingly, non-governmental organizations involved in functions that have historically been the preserve of the state. In their discussion of 'epistemic communities' Emanuel Adler and Peter M. Haas argue that these communities are engaged not only in the production of intellectual innovations but also in their dissemination:

> under specified conditions, we can view international politics as a process by which the innovations of epistemic communities are

diffused nationally, transnationally, and internationally to become the base of new or changed international practices and institutions and the emerging of a new world order.... Once the expectations and values injected by epistemic communities into the policy process are internationally shared, they help coordinate or structure international relations (1992: 373).

Essentially, the structural power that institutions of global governance command has facilitated the formation of a global development epistemic community and made these institutions central producers and controllers of development knowledge, a social reality that has significant consequences in, for instance, the current promotion of a human security development discourse (Chapter 7). Because of their positioning in the world order, they are key actors in the global development knowledge apparatus, for while 'knowledge is power' these institutions have enormous power in the world order and 'power is also knowledge' for 'power decides what is knowledge and what is not knowledge' (Alvares, 1992: 230). Discussing the World Bank's power and effects in the global development epistemic community under neo-liberal conditions, Michael Goldman states:

> To drum up continuous business in a circumspect world, the Bank depends on its capacity to generate the ideas of new global problems as well as on its own global expertise, new mechanisms for intervention as well as new reasons for countries to borrow, new development subjects and subjectivities as well as new forms of its own legitimation. The Bank works hard to create its own demand through the production of new transnationalized institutions, networks, norms, beliefs, and professionals (who have become a class in itself). In this odd space of 'transnational society,' some government agencies and civil servants can participate in a potentially lucrative neoliberal agenda even while their peers in governments and society do not. (2005: 34)

World orders' material capabilities and transnational development historical bloc

As well as from ideas and institutions, hegemonic development discourses derive their power from the material foundation of shifting world orders. The conjunctural world orders that Cox theorizes, and which form an important analytical entry point for this project, are underpinned by a world capitalist system whose emergence most scholars trace to historical developments in the fifteenth and sixteenth centuries and its global expansion to the period of Europe's industrial revolution and colonial projects in the rest of the world.[3] Given its fundamental logic, the 'capitalist world economy' has over the centuries 'expanded to cover the entire globe, absorbing in the process all existing mini-systems and world empires' (Wallerstein, 2000: 140). As an earlier analyst of global capitalism states, this process is marked by a continual search for pathways to expansion: 'the need of a constantly expanding market for its products chases the bourgeoisie over the whole surface of the globe. It must nestle everywhere, settle everywhere, establish connections everywhere' (Tucker, 1978: 476). While presented in a linear, apolitical and neutral manner in hegemonic IDS perspectives, the rise of the capitalist world system has been marked by violence and the exploitation and marginalization of the majority of social forces in the world. For instance, this development has seen the emergence of a racialized international division of labour characterized by unequal exchange (Quijano, 2008: 184). In the main, the evolution of this system has historically and in the contemporary conjuncture set significant structural limits for economic projects of states and social forces in the South. A core source of these structural limits is a range of economic 'distortions' that have emerged in the making of a world capitalist system (Amin, 1976: 200). For instance, capitalist development in social formations in the South is typically based on export-led economic strategies for international markets (ibid.).

Overall, hegemonic ideas derive their powerful materiality from their being a core feature of the capitalist world order and adoption by dominant states and institutions of global governance. Through the deployment of vast financial resources, military capabilities and knowledge production and dissemination capacity, these states and institutions exert a powerful influence on politico-economic processes in the South and the capitalist world system in general. In the post-1945 period these dominant actors in the world order have come to form a transnational politico-economic complex with the capacity to construct and consolidate hegemony in the world politico-economic order. Thus, while Gramsci then used the concept of hegemony to demonstrate the important role that ideas and material power play in national politico-economic processes, we situate hegemony at the level of world politico-economic order.[4] The concept helps us illuminate the central role that hegemonic development ideas and other features of a prevailing world order—ideas, institutions and material capabilities—play in political and economic structuring in the South. In addition, since the notion of hegemony subsumes political, economic and ideological elements, as an analytical tool it 'avoids reducing everything either to economics (economism) or to ideas (idealism)', thus enabling the incorporation of the core elements of a prevailing world order into the analysis (Cox, 1993: 56). Discussing the nature of hegemony at the level of world politico-economic order, Cox writes:

> [This] is not merely an order among states. It is an order within a world economy with a dominant mode of production [capitalist] which penetrates into all countries and links into other subordinate modes of production. It is also a complex of international social relationships which connect the social classes of the different countries. World hegemony is describable as a social structure, an economic structure, and a political structure; and it cannot be simply one of these things but must be all three. World hegemony, furthermore, is expressed in universal norms, institutions and mechanisms which lay down general rules of behaviour for states and for those forces of civil society that act across national boundaries—rules which support the dominant mode of production. (Ibid.: 61–62)

For present purposes, and in recognition of the power asymmetry that underpins the world politico-economic order and its governing institutions, we conceptualize dominant states in the post-1945 world order and institutions of global governance as constituting a hegemonic transnational development 'historical bloc' (Gramsci, 1971: 377) (TDHB). We draw the concept of historical bloc from Gramsci's writings. Its analytical strength stems from its attempts to show the close link between material capabilities and hegemonic ideas on politico-economic processes. According to Gramsci, at the level of a national social formation, the power of a historical bloc stems from the ways in which the material power of such a bloc is intertwined with its ideologies. Consequently for Gramsci, in the struggle for hegemony, a historical bloc's 'material forces are the content and the ideologies are the form, though this distinction between form and content has purely didactic value, since the material forces would be inconceivable historically without form and the ideologies would be individual fancies without the material forces' (ibid.).

The hegemonic power of the post-1945 TDHB and its attendant development discourses, in addition to its powerful positioning in the world order, have been aided by the structural realities of social formations in the South. Even though all social formations are dependent on the modalities of the world capitalist system, the South, though not monolithic, has historically been marked by deeper forms of structural dependency—a development generated by the asymmetric manner of their incorporation into the world capitalist system and the dominance of metropolitan states and institutions of global governance in this system.[5] Thus, while all states face constraints and influences arising from the nature of the world politico-economic system at a given juncture, the power asymmetry between the North and the South leads to distinct forms of structural dependency and constraints. Commenting on these structural realities in the context of a rising neo-liberal world order, Gill observes:

> [This order] has created a new force-field of constraints, opportunities and dangers, i.e. new conditions of existence for all states, groups and classes in the system.... To continue the Orwellian metaphor, some are more constrained than others in this world-order system. Not only does this new order coincide with a decisive change in the productive powers and balance of social forces within and between the major states, but also state structures in the major capitalist countries have been transformed into different variants of a neoliberal form ...; at the same time, peripheral economies have become more tightly geared to the economic activity of the core. (1993: 31)

World orders, development discourse and transformation

In the preceding discussion we have attempted to demonstrate the analytical relevance of the neo-Gramscian critical theory framework of world orders to the central concerns of this book; especially important here is how the ideas central to a given world order and its other constitutive features shape politico-economic processes in the South. Beyond this framework we suggest that the dialectical approach that underpins neo-Gramscian critical theory's approach to the study of world orders offers crucial analytical insights into the question of transformation, which is a core concern for this project. From this perspective, alongside the structuring power and effects of a given world order and its constitutive features, the possibility for transformation exists. Thus, while local–global structures such as states and world orders set political and structural limits for politico-economic changes in the South, collective action and other political projects of various social forces influence the modalities of these structures. Overall, at a given conjuncture the balance of political forces plays an important role in the process of state formation, the material and political practices of the state, and the nature and transformation of a prevailing world order (Cox, 1981: 138). The balance of social forces at a given conjuncture is, of course, a result of historical developments that may involve changes in the terrain of economic production and its attendant contradictions, new ideologies, material and political practices of the state, social movements and 'political opportunity structures'[6] emerging from various sites.

Historically, and in the contemporary era, social forces have utilized existing or emerging political opportunity structures to push political projects aimed, for instance, at the transformation of state practices or the re-imagining of the world order. The nature of such transformation, however, and the resulting political and economic structures are contingent on and shaped by the 'limits of the possible' (Gill, 2003) at a given conjuncture. From a neo-Gramscian perspective, the limits of the possible 'are not fixed and immutable, but exist within the dialectics of a give social structure (comprising the inter-subjective aspects of ideas, ideologies and theories, social institutions, and a prevailing socio-economic system and set of power relations)' (ibid.: 17). Overall, what the neo-Gramscian analysis of world orders brings to the study of politico-economic processes and to the question of transformation in particular, is an emphasis on the need to pay attention to the nature and effects of a given world order and other power structures in a given historical moment. At the same time, this approach stresses the need to beware of reifying the features of such an order or state forms or assuming a priori the nature of the results of struggles for transformation. Neo-Gramscian critical theory conceives of world orders in conjunctural and dialectic terms signalling the role of human political agency and the contingent nature of the possibility and nature of transformation, and the ethical implications of developments considered to be signals of transformation (Cox, 1981: 136–137).

Generally, while containing an element of utopianism, a neo-Gramscian's approach to the question of transformation leans towards realist projects by limiting 'the range of choice to alternative orders which are feasible transformations of the existing world' in a prevailing historical juncture (ibid.: 130). Thus, while it 'allows for a normative choice in favour of a social and political order different from the prevailing order...it is constrained by its comprehension of historical processes [thus] it...reject[s] improbable alternatives just as it rejects the permanency of the existing order' (ibid.). In addition, and as previously mentioned, the project's focus on the question of transformation is underpinned by ethical implications of politico-economic processes, a concern which is neglected in hegemonic IDS approaches. Like other social science perspectives situated within the positivist tradition whose hallmark is the claim of being 'value-free' (Cox, 1981: 130), hegemonic frameworks in IDS ignore the ethical dimension of analytical inquiry. The incorporation of an ethical dimension in our analysis is shown not only in our efforts to indicate the effects of hegemonic development discourses and other constitutive features of a given world order, but also in our attention to whether developments said to be signalling the possibility for the transformation of core features of the current world order embody 'emancipatory potential' (Santos and Rodríguez-Garavito, 2007: xxi) or represent openings for their restoration.

Broadening Gramsci: coloniality of power

While neo-Gramscian critical theory forms the primary analytical entry point in our effort to enrich the field of IDS, our conclusion is that the utilization of this theory can offer only partial insights into the study of politico-economic processes in the South and in particular the central concerns of this project. Consequently, we argue that the incorporation of insights from the coloniality of power analytical framework fills some of the analytical gaps marking this theory. To begin with, while the neo-Gramscian approach considers the influences of colonialism on economic and political processes following the end of formal colonial rule, it nonetheless has a tendency to focus mainly on the structural legacies of colonialism and to ignore the myriad strategies from the colonial past that are utilized by the TDHB to generate 'the colonial present' (Gregory, 2004: 5–15).[7] For Derek Gregory 'while they may be displaced, distorted, and (most often) denied, the capacities that inhere within the colonial past are routinely reaffirmed and reactivated in the colonial present' (ibid.: 7). We contend that while neo-Gramscian critical theory foregrounds the role of ideas in politico-economic processes, its profound silence on the ways in which colonial racial thinking and other features of the colonial system of 'producing knowledge and meaning' (Quijano, 2007: 169) have informed the evolution of the capitalist world system, including its racialized international division of labour and shifting world orders in the post-1945 period, limits its analytical power in the study of politico-economic processes in the South.

The coloniality of power approach complements the neo-Gramscian theory in one essential way: it takes as its analytical entry point the different but complementary ways in which colonial strategies—ideas, political and economic practices—have been rearticulated in the post-1945 period to serve the political, economic and ideological imperatives of the colonial present. In the main, departing from the neo-Gramscian tradition, in its interrogation of the making of the world politico-economic and cultural order, the coloniality of power perspective's entry point is the argument that a dual process has marked this development. Thus, their historical approach to the study of this development, which also takes the concept of race seriously, leads theorists of coloniality of power to contend that it is better articulated and understood through the analytical lens of a 'modern/colonial system' (Mignolo, 2000: 35–38). From this perspective, capitalist cultural-political-economic modernity is dialectically linked to coloniality of power. At the analytical and emancipatory level, 'once coloniality of power is introduced into the analysis, the "colonial difference" becomes visible', and this enables the embedding of 'border epistemologies emerging from the worlds of colonial histories, memories and experiences [for capitalist] modernity, let me repeat, carries on its shoulders the heavy weight and responsibility of coloniality' (ibid.:37).

In terms of ideas underpinning the modern/colonial system that Mignolo theorizes (ibid), Quijano argues that in the colonial past, the notion of 'race' was central to the rise of the world capitalist system. In this process, there emerged 'the new social classification of the world population…"whites", "Indians", "Negroes", "yellows" and "olives", using physiognomic traits of the peoples as external manifestations of their 'racial' nature. Then, on that basis the new geo-cultural identities were produced: 'European, American, Asiatic, African and much later, Oceania' (2007: 171). This racial social order 'pervaded and modulated the basic instances of the Euro-centered capitalist colonial/modern world power' (ibid.). Further, he contends that even though colonialism as an explicit politico-economic and cultural order has ended, 'coloniality is still the most general form of domination in the world today' (ibid.: 170). For Quijano, strategies of coloniality of power in the epoch of informal colonialism '[have] proved to be longer lasting than Euro-centred colonialism'; a political, economic and ideological reality that continues to have significant effects on political, economic and cultural processes in the South (ibid.: 171). As far as racial thinking is concerned, the 'racial axis' that underpinned the colonial order (Quijano, 2008: 181) has been reproduced after the dismantling of this order. Thus, while taking seriously the structural realities and effects of the post-1945 capitalist world order as the neo-Gramsican critical theory does, with its inclusion of the role of racial thinking in the making of the post-1945 colonial present, the coloniality of power framework provides richer analytical insights in the study of the ways in which colonial economic, political and cultural logics, including the attendant knowledge systems, have been reproduced during this period. For Quijano,

> [The colonial structure of power] was, and still is, the frame-work within which operate the other social relations of classes or estates.... If we observe the main lines of exploitation and social domination on a global scale, the main lines of world power today, and the distribution of resources and work among the world popu-lation, it is very clear that the large majority of the exploited, the dominated, the discriminated against, are precisely the members of the 'races', 'ethnies', or 'nations' into which the colonized popula-tions were categorized in the formative process of that world power, from the conquest of America and onward. (2007: 168–169)

Regarding the core concerns of this book, we suggest that the mate-rial, ideas, military and institution capabilities underpinning the TDHB have in the name of development, enabled the making of the colonial present. These social realities characterizing the post-1945 coloniality of power have been important factors in the emergence and evolution of hegemonic development discourses and their attendant structural, overt and covert forms of power. In the case of the nexus of racial think-ing and hegemonic development discourses, we contend that while a celebratory and 'messianic' (Escobar, 1995a: 25) language claiming, for instance, that the South will eventually catch up with social formations in the North permeates these discourses, essentially what has occurred in the post-1945 era of development is a reconfiguration of racial think-ing. As Ann Laura Stoler (1995: 61) posits in her seminal discussion of Michel Foucault's work on racism, the latter as an idea and practice is usually 'recovered, modified, encased and encrusted in new forms' at dif-ferent historical moments to serve new cultural, political and economic projects.

We contend that in the post-1945 period, colonial racist imagery has emerged as the underbelly constituting the covert representational power of hegemonic development discourses and the development poli-cies of the TDHB. Thus, the racial register of the colonial past has been reproduced in this period through hegemonic development discourse to serve the political, economic and cultural projects of the post-1945 colo-nial present; a colonial present whose manifestations and practices are

informed by the constitutive projects of the TDHB and their collaborators in a given historical moment in the South. In terms of core features
of colonial knowledge structures and approaches and their reproduction
during this period Quijano states:

> The European paradigm of rational knowledge [which is marked by a
> subject-object 'radical dualism: divine reason and nature'] was not
> only elaborated in the context of, but as part of, a power struc-
> ture that involved the European colonial domination over the rest
> of the world. This paradigm expressed in a demonstrable sense,
> the coloniality of that power structure... Since the Second World
> War, the formation and the development of certain disciplines,
> such as Ethnology, Anthropology [and development studies] have
> always shown that kind of 'subject-object' relations between the
> 'Western' culture and the rest. By definition, the other cultures are
> the 'object' of study. Such studies about the Western cultures and
> societies are virtually non-existent except as ironic parodies. ('The
> ritual among the Nacirema'—a anagram of 'American'—is a typical
> example) (2007: 174)

Thus, although formal colonial projects have ended, the manifestation of their coloniality of power including racial thinking and other
elements—although taking a new form—remain. As for racial thinking,
hegemonic development discourses and other features of the prevailing world order have enabled its re-articulation. For as Sarah White
argues, like the colonial racialist logics of 'self/other, subject/object'
development discourse as it pertains to the South 'rests fundamentally
on notions of difference, between here and there, now and then, us and
them, developed and developing' (2002: 413). In the post-1945 period,

> Certain terms in development discourse, such as 'tribalism', 'ethnic-
> ity', 'tradition', 'religion', and perhaps pre-eminently culture, may
> do some work at times in standing in for race [but] race as a socio-
> historical construct...operates simultaneously as an aspect of identity
> and as organizing principle in forging social structure. In the end, it
> is not national background, ethnicity, sex or skin colour but geopo-
> litical interests, interests of nation states, international capital and
> regional blocs that are at issue in development [nonetheless] the
> means employed to achieve these ends are deeply implicated in
> tactics drawn from the imagery and practice of race. (Ibid.: 408)

Thus, as Chapters 3 and 7 will demonstrate, notwithstanding its apparently humanistic claims, hegemonic development discourses have facilitated the reproduction of colonial racial imagery. Essentially, in its conceptualization of the South, this discourse embodies 'a regime of bio-politics that generically divides humankind into developed and underdeveloped species-life. As such, it is intrinsic to racial discourse' (Duffield, 2007: 16). The racial classification of humanity—that forms the foundation of hegemonic development discourse—enables the reproduction of a sense of cultural, political and material superiority that upholds the attitude that social formations in the South are in need of perpetual tutelage from the TDHB and leading organic intellectuals of a prevailing world order. It is this sort of view that causes 'students and other inexperienced people who would not be given the time of day in their own countries to feel that they can come to a country such as Malawi and demand to see the most senior ranking and experienced government officials and proceed to tell them how to run their country' (Kuppens, 2006). We now turn our discussion to the rise and effects of hegemonic development discourse in the context of shifts in the post-1945 world order.

3
World Orders, Development Discourse and Coloniality

This chapter focuses on the constitutive elements of two hegemonic development discourses that have emerged in the context of shifts in world orders: modernization and neo-liberalism. The analysis demonstrates the influence of shifts in world orders in the post World War II period on the emergence and nature of these discourses. The chapter has five sections. The first section focuses on two key features of the world order that emerged following World War II. The second section discusses core elements of modernization development discourse while the next one provides highlights of the rise of a self-regulating market doctrine as a constitutive feature in the making of a neo-liberal world order from the 1970s onwards. The fourth section shows the influence of this doctrine on shifts in development discourse. The last section, discusses the politico-economic effects of hegemonic development discourses. Such an approach to the study of these discourses challenges their technocratic and ahistorical representation for, at minimum, it signals the covert, overt and structural forms of power underlying them.

World order and rise of modernization development discourse

As argued in the last chapter, hegemonic development ideas do not emerge or operate in political or economic vacuums. Rather, they are constitutive features of a given world order and other political and economic processes. In this respect, the rise of a hegemonic modernization development discourse was embedded in political, economic and intellectual developments that emerged in the interwar period, and especially with the rise of a new world order. The central features of this order that influenced the rise and nature of modernization development discourse were the rise of the USA as a hegemonic power, the emergence of institutions of global governance, anti-communist ideas and global Keynesianism. Due to space limitations, our focus here is on the emergence of institutions of global governance and the core ideas of the world order that emerged after World War II.

As discussed in Chapter 2, processes of institutionalization are a central aspect of a given world order. Thus, in response to the capitalist accumulation crisis that generated the economic depression of the 1930s and political developments generated by World War II, the dominant states in the world system instituted a process aimed at the emergence of new institutions to govern global capitalism. While the economic and military power of the Western alliance and the hegemony of the USA played a key role in the making of these institutions, a group of organic intellectuals able to articulate this alliance's political and economic views aided this process. The success of these organic intellectuals stemmed from their ability to present the ideas and political and economic interests of the alliance as universal, solely geared to the achievement of the global public good. While organic intellectuals from other parts of the Western alliance, for instance John M. Keynes, played a major role in this process, the core group was mainly drawn from American intellectual and business circles. The detailed study of the evolution of the Council on Foreign Relations (hereafter the Council) by Laurence H. Shoup and William Minter describes the formation of such a group of intellectuals, who because of their close ties to leading American capitalists and ruling elites, played a powerful role in shaping the post-war world order (Shoup and Minter, 1977).[1] In the case of the establishment of international financial institutions, the Council's interest in their emergence was proposed in 1941 and 1942 by its War and Peace study groups, who argued that these institutions were vital for 'stabilizing currencies and facilitating programs of capital investment for constructive undertakings in backward and underdeveloped regions' (quoted in ibid.: 166). They continued: 'it might be wise to set up two financial institutions: one an international exchange stabilization board and one an international bank to handle short-term transactions not directly concerned with stabilization' (quoted in ibid.: 168). These efforts laid the foundation for the later collaboration between the American economist, Dexter White, and John Maynard Keynes in the negotiations leading to the 1944 Bretton Woods Agreement. The latter paved the way for the creation of the International Monetary Fund (IMF) and the International Bank for Reconstruction and Development (later the World Bank) (Clarke, 1988: 249).

The UN and its specialized agencies emerged during the same period and also came to play a central role in the world order and politico-cultural-economic processes in the South. The Council advocated the creation of the UN to the US government, arguing that since the latter had to 'avoid conventional forms of imperialism' (quoted in ibid.: 170) an international body was needed that would provide the necessary political and security framework for American interests and those of its allies. Between 1943 and 1944 the Informal Agenda Group, whose membership was dominated by Council members, designed the UN framework, including its Charter. The design process culminated with the holding of the Dumbarton Oaks and the San Francisco Conferences in 1944 and 1945 respectively (ibid.: 170–172) that saw the creation of the UN and its agencies. While social formations from the South were constructed as equal members of the UN system, as in the case of the establishment of the World Bank and the IMF, the power asymmetry between the North and the South meant that states at the core of the world system were the dominant social actors in the modalities of the UN's emergence and evolution.

In terms of international trade, the General Agreement on Tariffs and Trade (GATT) emerged to facilitate agreements on this process. Like other institutional arrangements underpinning the world order, the GATT framework enabled the reproduction of the power asymmetry marking the world system. Essentially, this framework reproduced for the development age, the unequal trading arrangements that had characterized the incorporation of the South into the international division of labour from the era of slavery to that of colonialism (Amin, 1976). The asymmetrical nature of this trading regime was during this period highly criticized by scholars from the South, particularly the Argentinean economist Raul Prebisch and others affiliated with the United Nations Economic Commission for Latin America. Prebisch and his Latin American colleagues held that, contrary to the comparative advantage to be gained in facilitating international trade and national economic development as preached by the classical liberal economic argument, in fact Latin America's primary commodity specialization had resulted in declining terms of trade (Larraín, 1989: 13). To some extent, these criticisms contributed to the establishment of the United Nations Conference on Trade and Development in 1964 (with Raul Prebisch as its first Director). This institutional body effected limited success in generating fundamental change in the global trading arrangements during the period under review, and in the era of a neo-liberal world order underpinned by the WTO's trading regime since 1994.

Beyond the establishment of major institutions of global governance, ideas contributed to the formulation of modernization development discourse. During the period under review, anti-communism, authoritarianism in the South and global Keynesianism were the core politico-economic ideas underpinning the new world order. In the case of anti-communism, the geopolitics of the Cold War and the decolonization process—which increased the number of so-called Third World countries—provided the political context for the emergence of a concerted effort by the TDHB to influence political and economic processes in the South along anti-communist lines. The USA, as the hegemonic power in this order, to a large extent influenced other members' policies towards the South. The rhetoric of the American ruling class and that of other members of the TDHB indicated that aiding economic development in the South was its central goal. As President Harry Truman stated in his 1949 inaugural speech, 'more than half the people of the world are living in conditions approaching misery.... We must embark on a bold new program for making the benefits of our scientific advances and industrial progress available for the improvement and growth of underdeveloped areas. The old imperialism—exploitation for foreign profit—has no place in our plans' (quoted in Rist, 2004: 259–260).

Nevertheless, rather than facilitating emancipatory politico-economic processes in the South, the TDHB had a core political agenda. As Fred Halliday has argued, while Western Europe and Japan had distinct areas of influence after 1945, 'no such delimitations were stabilized' in the South; thus they became zones of intense East–West rivalry (1989: 11). Consequently, and as Marianne H. Marchand has pointed out, the effects of this on the TDHB's approach to the South was the subordination of the latter to the post-1945 'East–West security concerns' (1994: 290). Further, in line with political modernization theorists (to be discussed shortly) who claimed that authoritarianism was a necessary stage in the modernization of the emerging nations, during the period under review the TDHB backed authoritarian state forms in the South as a matter of course. In South Korea, members of the TDHB—the USA in particular—supported the rise and entrenchment of an authoritarian state as part of its strategy of containing the spread of communism in East Asia. As Chapter 4 will illustrate, during this period South Korea received high levels of foreign aid without any demands from the USA or any other member of the TDHB that it respect basic human rights. In Chile, US covert and overt support for the rise of the Chilean military dictatorship in the 1970s is another example of efforts by members of this bloc to influence the political practices of states and processes of state formation in the South along anti-communist lines. For the US

Salvador Allende's regime had to be contained because, according to Henry Kissinger, the USA National Security Advisor: 'I don't see why we need to stand by and watch a country go communist because of the irresponsibility of its own people' (quoted in Robinson, 1996: 146). William Robinson provides a detailed analysis of how, following the assassination of Allende during the 1973 military coup, the US 'propped up' a dictator whose years in power were marked by some of that era's pervasive violations of human rights, until a shift in the world order in the 1980s and 1990s saw the TDHB embark on a procedural democracy promotion agenda in the South and the former communist bloc (ibid.). The USA was not the only member of the TDHB supporting the rise of authoritarian states in the South. In the case of the French ruling elites, as long as dictators in Africa demonstrated a deep sense of 'Frenchness' and maintained their political and economic dealings with France, their authoritarian practices were considered insignificant. It is no wonder then that Jacques Foccart, a leading figure in the country's foreign affairs establishment, following the military coup in the Central African Republic that resulted in the emergence of the brutal despotic rule of 'Emperor' Jean-Bedel Bokassa, could declare that 'after all [Bokassa] was a very pro-French military man' (Schraeder, 2004: 278) who could count on France's support for his regime.

Authoritarianism in the South and anti-communism were not the only ideas characterizing the world order that emerged after World War II. Following the Great Depression, economic ideas and practices inspired by the work of John Maynard Keynes become the reference point for debates concerning national and global economic processes. Keynes, who had written extensively on economic issues in Britain, appeared on the world stage in the 1930s. While not calling for the dismantling of market capitalism, his ideas concerning the role of the state in the economy challenged some core assumptions of classical and neo-classical liberal economic thought. For liberal economic thinkers, state intervention in the economy had a suffocating effect on private capital and in the smooth working of the market mechanism, which left on its own would ensure economic growth and stability. From a liberal economic perspective, the self-regulating market was the natural organizing idea and practice of all societies (Polanyi, 2001: 144–148). Thus, state intervention geared to the 'self-protection of society' was unnecessary because, in the long run, the market would resolve whatever 'difficulties' a society faced (ibid.: 148). Overall, 'all protectionism' from the state was 'a mistake' generated out of 'impatience, greed, and shortsightedness' by advocates of such policies (ibid.).

For Keynes, core assumptions of liberal economic thought offered a limited understanding of economic processes. In his view, economic processes such as investment in the financial market were marked by uncertainty about expectations and by ignorance (Keynes, 1936: 153–158), and thus the representation of market capitalism as a process that would follow in an unproblematic manner the economic models mapped by economists provided only partial insights. Further, Keynes offered new insights on the nature of the emergence of money as a constitutive feature of capitalist economies. In contrast to liberal economic theory, which viewed money as a natural and rational instrument for economic exchange, Keynes conceptualized it 'as a symbol of value' leading to the emergence of 'a systematic monetary system' (Clarke, 1988: 235). While Keynes made significant contributions to economic debates, it was his views on the role of the state in the economy, the managing of the world economy through institutions of global governance, especially the World Bank and the IMF, that would have a significant influence on the consolidation of the post-1945 world order and constitutive ideas of hegemonic development discourse.

In terms of the role of the state in the economy, Keynes argued that the uncertainty of the market mechanism and the psychological features of human behaviour that influence savings, investment and consumption had led him to conclude that the state was an institution well positioned to take 'an ever greater responsibility for directly organising investment' (Keynes, 1936: 164). Increased investment by the state through borrowing to invest in major public works would stimulate the economy through the generation of employment. From a Keynesian perspective, such a policy would have multiplying effects. For instance, investment in public works would generate opportunities for related industries in the private sector and both developments would lead to employment and openings for consumer spending. Thus, rather than having a stifling effect, state intervention to stimulate the economy through public works would establish favourable conditions for private capital and workers. Thus, in addition to advocating and pushing for states to have more power in regulating monetary policy, especially the movement of capital across national borders, he strongly viewed public investment as the way forward out of the social and economic nightmare of the 1930s: 'direct state intervention to promote and subsidise new investment' was the sole 'means of escape from prolonged and perhaps interminable depression' (Skidelsky, 1996: 71). His views on the state's role in stimulating the economy, even in the context of significant economic crisis, saw him support Lloyd George's public works proposal in Britain in 1929. The project called upon the state 'to play a significantly increased role in the economy through various infrastructure schemes, such as an expansion of the public transport network, which would be financed through government borrowing' (Cord, 2007: 75). Keynes also expressed his support for President Franklin Roosevelt, who, departing from his 'Pittsburgh Pledge' in which he had indicated his commitment to rolling back the 'size of the federal government', ended up asking for and receiving US$3.3 billion from Congress for investment in public works in 1933 (ibid.). This initiative saw the reduction of unemployment in the two years that followed (ibid.).

Given our contention that ideas of a given world order are influenced by historical and politico-economic conditions, it is important to note that Keynes, writing at the height of a period of high levels of unemployment, global economic crisis and severe social dislocations, was concerned with generating theoretical foundations for public economic policy that would address these matters. These social realities also provided a significant opening for the adoption of Keynesian ideas by ruling elites in the dominant social formations in the North and theorists of modernization development discourse, as we will see shortly. At any rate, the economic realities of the Depression had led Keynes to shift his focus to advocating monetary policy reform as the main tool for public economic policy. Beyond the Great Depression, the existence of socialism as an alternative model for politico-economic arrangements was also a social reality that influenced his thinking. For Keynes, state-regulated capitalism had a socializing capacity in the employment and other sectors, and thus calls for socialism were unjustified. As he contended:

> The State will have to exercise a guiding influence on the propensity to consume.... I conceive, therefore, that a somewhat comprehensive socialisation of investment will prove the only means of securing an approximation to full employment; though this need not exclude all manner of compromises and of devices by which public authority will co-operate with private initiative. But beyond this no obvious case is made out for a system of State Socialism which would embrace most of the economic life of the community. It is not the ownership of the instruments of production which is important for the State to assume. If the State is able to determine the aggregated amount of resources devoted to augmenting the instruments and the base rate of reward to those who own them, it will have accomplished all that is necessary. (Keynes, 1936: 378)

By the 1960s, then, when most countries in the South had gained formal independence, a new world order underpinned by anti-communist,
Keynesian ideas and support for authoritarianism in the South was in
place. While the TDHB was not monolithic in its political and economic
approaches to the South, it nevertheless shared an interest in main-
taining the prevailing global, ideological, political and economic order
since it facilitated the TDHB's reproduction as a power bloc, and that of
the capitalist world order. Thus, while political actors in the South had
agency and used it to push their politico-economic projects, as the next
chapter will show in the case of the state in Malawi and South Korea, the
ideas and other constitutive features of this world order set the parameters within which their agency operated. In the case of development
policies, the prevailing modernization discourse provided the ideas for
both the TDHB and allied ruling elites in the South. It is a discussion
of the core elements of modernization development discourse that we
turn to next.

Modernizing the Third World

Modernization development discourse emerged out of and was influenced by the developments discussed above that underpinned the post
World War II world order prior to the ascendancy of a neo-liberal world
order in the late 1970s. The historical conditions of the 1940s saw an
increased interest in economic and political processes in the South, not
only by the TDHB but also by intellectuals. In the immediate post-war
period, but increasingly in the 1950s and 1960s, scholars formulated
a network of ideas concerning political, social and economic change
in the South—a body of work that came to constitute the hegemonic
modernization development discourse. In its various mutations, this discourse concentrated on generating ideas that its proponents represented
as providing scientific explanations of the social realities characterizing 'traditional' societies, and blueprints for these societies to follow in
their march to capitalist modernity along the same trajectory travelled
by the North.

The constitutive elements of modernization development discourse
came from various disciplines, but mainly from sociology, psychology,
economics and political science. In the field of sociology, Talcott Parsons formulated his famous 'pattern variables'[2] to indicate not only
the differences between traditional and modern societies, but also
the socio-cultural practices and institutions that needed transformation to enable the transition to modernity in traditional societies. For
psychologists such as David McClelland (1966: 76), the transition to

capitalist modernity in the North had been enabled by an understanding at the individual level of 'the need to do well, not so much for the sake of social recognition or prestige, but to attain an inner feeling of personal accomplishment' (quoted in Larraín, 1989: 94). This 'achievement factor' was lacking in the emerging nations, and for the latter to modernize, this variable was necessary and could be cultivated through education systems that pushed students at a very young age to hunger for achievement (ibid.).

Despite being situated within different disciplines, scholars affiliated with modernization discourse shared a linear view of history. This approach to social change was not new, steeped as it was in European evolutionary theories articulated by scholars such as Auguste Comte. For Comte, development was a process that combined both order and progress (Cowen and Shenton, 1996). Further, his evolutionary view of social change—which would greatly influence hegemonic development discourses—claimed that 'humanity was subject to laws of "development" analogous to those pertaining in the natural world that could be discovered and understood.... To reconcile order with progress, humans needed to comprehend the applicability of these laws and to implement them as they provided a clear path for their historical journey towards progress' (Cowen and Shenton, 1995: 34).

While other disciplines contributed to the making of modernization theory, ideas from economics and political science had (and continue to have) significant influence on the constitutive elements of modernization discourse and its effects on politico-economic processes in the South; thus we highlight claims from these disciplines. Like other proponents of modernization discourse, economists working within this discourse had a linear view of political-economic change. For instance, Walt Rostow's influential framework of stages of economic growth epitomized this linear view of history. Articulating his evolutionary view of social change, Rostow declared: 'it is possible to identify all societies, in their economic dimensions, as lying within one of five categories: the traditional society, the preconditions for take-off, the take-off, the drive to maturity, and the age of high mass-consumption' (1990: 4). According to this schema, rudimentary economic structures heavily dependent on agriculture and limited use of technology in economic production characterized traditional societies such as those in the South. These features resulted in economic stagnation and limited savings and investment for economic development. The transition to modernity began when, in the second stage of social change, traditional societies established the preconditions for economic modernization. For modernization theorists, colonialism in the South was considered as contributing to the preconditions stage of the modernization process: the colonizing powers filled 'a vacuum; that is...organize[d] a traditional society incapable of self-organization (or unwilling to organize itself) for modern import and export activity, including production for export' (ibid.: 109). Without colonialism, the modernization of traditional societies would have taken a much longer period given the stagnation of these societies and the lack of political actors committed to propelling them towards modernity (ibid.: 28).

With the end of formal colonialism, the political and economic elites who had emerged in the orbit of the colonial political economy were considered in modernization discourse as the pivotal players in the modernization of their societies. A core strategy in this process was for these elites to present modernization along the lines of the Western model as the central objective and end goal of their societies (see Rostow generally). In addition, these elites had to be anti-communist, for Communism could easily take root especially before the consolidation of preconditions for take-off to capitalist modernity; Communism was 'a kind of disease which [could] befall a transitional society' that had failed to create the necessary conditions for the modernization project (ibid.: 164). Nonetheless, actions of the TDHB and non-communist ruling elites in the South through the establishment of the necessary preconditions for take-off to modernization and progress along the lines of the North could avert such a development (ibid.). Further, Southern elites were to commit themselves to instituting public policies and other measures that would lead to the next stage of the modernization process. In their drive to establish the preconditions for modernization, elites would push for the establishment of state forms that facilitated the centralization of their societies and created the necessary institutional arrangements for their modernizing efforts (ibid.). For Rostow, the state had 'essential' roles to play in the modernization process, and pushing an argument similar to Keynes' as far as the nature of the role of the state in the economy is concerned, he stated 'there is no need for the government to own the means of production; on the contrary. But the government must be capable of organizing the nation so that unified commercial markets develop' further, 'it must lead the way through the whole spectrum of national policy—from tariffs to education and public health—toward the modernization of the economy and the society of which it is a part' (ibid.: 30).

Overall, from a modernization perspective, the linchpin of modernization for all societies was industrialization and the adoption of modern technology in economic production. States in the South then were to establish the institutional machinery, mobilize labour and establish other conditions that would facilitate rapid industrialization and diffusion of new technologies in economic production. The TDHB was to play a major role in this process by providing loans and technical assistance to fill the financial and technological gaps in the South (ibid.: 142–143). For advocates of modernization development discourse, the effects of industrialization on pre-existing political, cultural and economic processes was irrelevant; the goal was to achieve economic growth and ensure the transformation of so-called traditional societies into industrialized ones. From this perspective, 'the organizing premise was the belief in the role of modernization as the only force capable of destroying archaic superstitions and relations, at whatever social, cultural, and political cost. Industrialization and urbanization were seen as the inevitable and necessarily progressive routes to modernization' (Escobar, 1995a: 39–40).

The preceding discussion has highlighted the core elements of modernization discourse as far as the arguments concerning economic change are concerned. While economists such as Rostow contributed greatly to the emergence of modernization theory, political scientists were also at the forefront of this development. For instance, in his call for the emergence of centralized modernizing states dominated by modernizing anti-communist elites in the South, Rostow's ideas dovetailed well with those of political scientists engaged in the 'political development' discourse. A core assertion of such scholars was that the establishment of strong one-party authoritarian, anti-communist state forms in the South was the main route to politico-economic modernity. In their support for these state forms, they put forward a number of claims, some of which we highlight here. First, the emerging nations in Asia, Africa, the Middle East, the Caribbean and Latin America lacked the preconditions for liberal democratic state forms and, in general, democratic politics. According to this discourse, the establishment of liberal democracy would hinder economic development in the South, and thus it had to be postponed for a later conjuncture following economic modernization, for democracy could emerge and be sustained only if a country had achieved high levels of economic development (Lipset, 1981: 31). Second, the cultural frameworks of societies in the South were considered as obstacles to the establishment of liberal democratic states. According to Gabriel Almond, those advocating the establishment of liberal democracy in the emerging nations were naive, since the complex and culturally embedded Western forms of democracy would not work in these countries given their diverse cultural traditions (1970: 223).

Third, the manner in which social change was occurring in the South was creating conditions that hindered the emergence and consolidation of democracy. For Samuel Huntington, the governing elites in the emerging nations were confronted with problems of centralization of authority, national integration, social mobilization, economic development, political participation and social welfare—problems that had arisen, not sequentially as in the Western world, but simultaneously—and this was not a promising picture for liberal democracy (1967: 238–277; see also Almond, 1970: 228–233). Given the multi-faceted nature of the modernization project in the South, elites in the emerging nations needed to contain the expansion of political participation since the majority of citizens lacked the necessary political socialization, class and cultural attributes, and such a lack could lead to political instability (Huntington, 1967: 224).[3] Quoting John Johnson's (1964: 98–99) work on Latin America, Huntington argued that this scenario had emerged in countries of this region with disastrous political results when, starting in the 1930s, 'age requirements were lowered, property and literacy requirements were reduced or discarded, and the unscrubbed, unschooled millions on the farms were enfranchised in the name of democracy' (ibid.).

Given the lack of preconditions for the establishment of liberal democracy in the South, modernization discourse proposed that the establishment of strong-handed, anti-communist one-party state forms which would ensure the ability of governing elites to control citizens, ensure stability and engender economic growth along capitalist lines as the way forward. Beyond the geopolitical considerations, the premise underlying this proposal was the notion that, like other late industrializing societies such as Germany, authoritarian state forms were the only option for the emerging nations. This claim—informed by the linear view of history that underpinned modernization discourse—was that historically, state despotism had been a key feature of all societies in their early stages of transition to modernity. For proponents of the political development doctrine, the emergence and consolidation of authoritarian states, commonly referred to as 'developmental dictatorships', would be enabled by the existence of a united politico-economic elite committed to containing Communism, stability and modernizing its society. The emergence of strong one-party anti-Communist state forms could be achieved with the support of the post-1945 TDHB working closely with ruling elites in the Third World (Huntington, 1967: 240–241).

To sum up this section, for almost three decades following World War II, the ideas embedded in modernization development discourse gained hegemony and greatly influenced the development practices of the TDHB and allied ruling elite projects in most of the South, as some examples discussed later and in Chapter 4 will show. As the preceding discussion indicates, a linear view of history, anti-communism, Keynesianism and authoritarian managerial-elitism were the core features of modernization development discourse. The emergence of this discourse dovetailed well with the ideas and other constitutive features underpinning the world order and the politico-economic projects of governing elites in the South, and with ideas articulated by organic intellectuals closely linked to the TDHB such as Rostow and Huntington. While the core assumptions of modernization development discourse, such as its linear view of history, continue to influence development discourse, some of its constitutive ideas about the state were by the late 1970s dislodged with the rise of neo-liberal ideas as a core element in shifts in world orders. This development, in addition to other features of the new world order, led to the emergence of a new development discourse, as we discuss in the next section.

Shift in world order

The 1970s saw significant shifts in the core features of the prevailing world order including its hegemonic development discourse. As in the immediate period following World War II, this development did not occur in a vacuum. While several factors contributed to this development, our focus here is a discussion of role of ideas, dominant states and institutions, and changes in geopolitics. Shifts in the ideas underpinning the pre-existing world order played a major role in the making of a neo-liberal order. In the 1970s, a shift in the economic ideas at the core of the post-1945 world order was more and more noticeable as Keynesian economic thought and practices were increasingly portrayed as irrelevant strategies in addressing the global economic crisis that came to a head during this period and in promoting capitalist development in the South. Steadily, neo-liberal ideas became not only the hegemonic analytical lens utilized to explain the sources of global economic crisis, but also the new and accepted strategy in economic processes.

From a neo-liberal perspective, the extensive role of the state in the economy had generated the global economic crisis, which manifested in economic stagnation, budgetary deficits and high levels of unemployment. For example, in this line of thought, the power of the state in monetary and fiscal policy as advocated under the Keynesian-inspired Bretton Woods Agreement had significantly contributed to economic stagnation and limited the workings of financial capital. Further, the rise of labour policies protecting workers' rights and the establishment of social safety nets in the post-1945 era had resulted in unproductive expenditures. According to neo-liberal analysts, in the case of workers' rights, this development was a core source of the crisis of profits facing owners of capital in the 1970s. As the 1970s economic crisis deepened, it gave rise to a contentious debate on ways to address it. Colin Leys explains elements of this development as it unfolded in the USA and the UK:

> Both.... economies had experienced slow growth and declining international competitiveness in the 1960s. In both countries politics became polarised, between defenders of the post-war 'settlement' (the British term) or 'national bargain' (the US term)—in which the state played the role of both manager of the economy and provider of social services and social security—and those who feared that private capital risked losing its power and authority. One side of the New Right's successful campaign to 'roll back socialism' (or in the USA, 'liberalism') was to attack its domestic base in the labour movement through anti-union measures and higher unemployment, privatisation and reduced taxes on capital. The other side was to end controls over capital movements and reduce trade barriers, exposing the domestic workforce to competition from lower-paid workers in countries with weaker regulatory regimes—at the same time making it hard, if not impossible, for any future governments to reverse these changes. (2001: 12)

The deepening global economic crisis and the de-legitimization of the Keynesian framework paved the way for the return of the self-regulating doctrine, which had lost its hegemony following the economic chaos and social dislocations of the 1920s and 1930s. Notwithstanding its limitations as a strategy for freedom (Harvey, 2005)—despite the claims of its proponents on this score—by the late 1970s the doctrine of market-led development had emerged as the cornerstone of the new world order. For over three decades, this doctrine, inspired by classical liberal economic thought and advocated by scholars such as Milton Friedman and others, has reigned as the hegemonic idea as far as the role of the state in the economy and the modalities of the capitalist world system are concerned. The underlying idea of this doctrine is that the state's role in the economic sphere should be a limited one, since an expanded one results in the containment of freedom and distortions in the work-ings of the invisible hand of the market. For Friedman, for instance, 'competitive capitalism—the organization of the bulk of economic activ-ity through private enterprise operating in a free market' rather than state-led capitalism is the backbone of economic and political freedom (1988: 49). Following classical liberal thought on the state, Friedman calls for minimalist state forms whose duties are solely 'to protect our freedom both from the enemies outside our gates and from our fellow-citizens: to preserve law and order, to enforce private contracts [and] to foster competitive markets' (ibid.: 50).

From his perspective, before its contamination in the 1930s, the constitutive element of classical liberalism was the embrace of the self-regulating market as the best option for achieving freedom, economic development and progress. Following the Great Depression, however, as Friedman states,

> liberalism came to be associated with a very different emphasis, particularly in economic policy. It came to be associated with a readiness to rely primarily on the state rather than on private vol-untary arrangements to achieve objectives regarded as desirable. The catchwords became welfare and equality rather than freedom. . . . The twentieth-century liberal has come to favour a revival of the very policies of state intervention and paternalism against which classical liberalism fought (ibid.: 49).

For neo-liberal thinkers, then, the rise and consolidation of a capitalist world order underpinned by the self-regulating market doctrine since the 1970s is a momentous development in post-1945 economic theory and practice. From this perspective, such a development at a minimum means that liberalism has been rescued from the contaminating influ-ences of the reform liberal tendencies of thinkers such as John M. Keynes and, as will be highlighted shortly in the context of development dis-course, from the *dirigiste* Dogma (Lal, 1985) embedded in post-1945 development economic discourse.

While the return of the self-regulating market doctrine was a major factor leading to shifts in the world order, other developments were no less important. Thus, a second development that led to this develop-ment was the adoption of neo-liberal economic thought and practice by the dominant states in the world order. In this respect, as in the immediate post World War II period that saw shifts in the ideas framing the emerging world order such as Keynesianism and anti-communism, the dominant states greatly contributed to the rise of a world order characterized by neo-liberal ideas and shifts in development discourse. For example, with their rise to power at the height of the global capitalist accumulation crisis of the late 1970s and early 1980s, leaders influenced by neo-liberal thought, such as Margaret Thatcher in the UK, Ronald Reagan in the USA and Helmut Kohl in Germany, and the turn to the right in Canada with Brian Mulroney's conservative government in 1984 greatly facilitated this process. For these ruling elites, Thatcher's mantra that there was no alternative to global neo-liberal capitalism dominated by the market logic became the central truism of this new world order and its attendant development discourse. Further, the support of dominant states in the world system for the liberation of financial markets (Chapter 9), a core feature of the current world order, enabled the rise of a neo-liberal world order.

Beyond shifts in ideas underpinning the world order and the neo-liberal responses of dominant states to the economic crisis of the 1970s, institutions at the core of the capitalist world system have been instrumental in the rise and consolidation of the neo-liberal world order and its attendant development discourse. The extensive power of the institutional matrix of the global economy comprised of the World Bank, the IMF and WTO (GATT until 1994) underpins the working of the current world order (Bello and Mittal, 2002). As argued in Chapter 2, the power of these institutions stems from not only their material capabilities, but also their centrality in the production and circulation of knowledge pertaining to national and global political and economic processes. In the case of the World Bank, its pieces in publications such as the *World Bank Research News* have contributed greatly to the embedding of the core ideas of the current world order, especially as far as politico-economic processes in the South are concerned. Overall, institutions of global governance have greatly contributed to the production, dissemination and legitimatization of neo-liberal ideas, the effects of which have been acute in the South, given the peripheral positioning of most of its social formations in the capitalist world order as well as other social realities generated by the post-1945 modes of coloniality of power.

In addition to the above-noted developments, the *détente* between the East and West alliance that emerged in the 1970s and deepened in the 1980s, leading eventually to the end of Cold War geopolitics, provided an opening for the embedding of a neo-liberal world order and shifts in development discourse. While commitment to the socialist project continues to be invoked in Cuba and China, the end of the Cold War and the implementation of neo-liberal economic shock-therapy strategies in Russia and other parts of the former Soviet-led bloc de-legitimized socialism as a viable alternative to capitalism. With the end of the Cold

War, the trumpeting of the triumph of capitalism—and its (assumed) accompanying political practice of liberal democracy—over socialism was echoed loudly in academic and ruling elite circles. For instance, Francis Fukuyama (1992) wrote his often referenced text claiming that the world had entered a new epoch marked by the deepening of market capitalist logics and liberal democracy in all societies. For ruling elites such as George Bush Senior (1991) in the USA, the end of the Cold War in 1989 signalled the rise of a new world order characterized by the market doctrine and democracy. According to Bush, with the end of the Cold War era, 'the world has learned that free markets provide levels of prosperity, growth and happiness that centrally planned economies can never offer' and that 'prosperity encourages people to live as neighbours, not as predators, and supplies the soil in which democracy grows best' (ibid.).

Neo-liberal world order and development discourse

The developments discussed above that resulted in the emergence and consolidation of a new world order greatly contributed to shifts in the post-1945 development discourse. The new hegemonic development discourse—albeit sharing similar assumptions about the South with modernization discourse—has two interlinked components. On one hand, it calls for the promotion of market-led capitalist development and, from the late 1980s, for the establishment of multi-party democratic states. In contrast to the era of geopolitics of the Cold War and the hegemony of modernization theory, the TDHB is no longer interested in supporting 'friendly' developmental dictatorships. In its promotion of democracy in the South the TDHB contends that the development crisis facing the South is not solely the result of misguided economic development strategies, but rather a product of the authoritarian politics—a state of affairs it refers to as a 'crisis of governance' (World Bank, 1989: 60). For the World Bank, the solution to the developmental crises in the South is the establishment of democracy and practices of good governance, conceptualized as 'the creation, protection, and enforcement of property rights.... [and] the provision of sound macroeconomic policies that create a stable environment for market activity. Good governance also means the absence of corruption, which can subvert the goals of policy and undermine the legitimacy of the public institutions that support markets' (World Bank, 2002: 99). In its proclaimed project of promoting democracy and freedom in the South, the TDHB has utilized its structural power in the form of foreign aid, military presence, or threat, and covert and overt ideological forms of persuasion as powerful tools in the push for the establishment of minimalist multiparty democracy.[4] Although democracy promotion in the South is a constitutive element of the hegemonic development discourse that has emerged in the evolution of the neo-liberal world order, our focus here is on the self-regulating market doctrine as it has translated in this discourse.[5]

The neo-liberal inspired market-led development doctrine has been the hegemonic development discourse for over three decades. At its core, the neo-liberal development discourse makes several claims some of which we highlight here. First, in explaining the roots of economic crisis and stagnation that characterized most of the social formations in the South in the 1970s, they contend that this was a result of the extensive role of the state in the economy in the post-colonial period. Further, they say, this trend was especially evident in the dominant role that publicly owned enterprises played in all key sectors of the economy. From the neo-liberal perspective, these enterprises were inefficient and monopolistic and limited the growth and prosperity of private sector enterprises (Toye, 1993).[6] From this perspective, extensive bureaucratic bottlenecks characterizing the role of the state in the economy resulted in the suffocation of the entrepreneurial spirit and freedom, and created opportunities for corruption and rent-seeking activities. Second, neo-liberal thinkers challenge the claim that exploitation characterizes economic relations between the North and South (Bauer, 1984: 21–22). Overall, the consensus among neo-liberal thinkers is that local factors and not relations and practices of domination marking the world order are the source of economic stagnation and crisis in the South. Arguing along these lines and building on a report by the World Bank, NBER and Organization for Economic Cooperation and Development (OECD), Deepak Lal for instance contends that 'the obstacles to the growth of developing countries' are largely internal, not external and that 'economic agents in these countries have reacted to the distorting incentives created by protectionist regimes of trade control in the way that standard economic theory predicts; and that planners have often shown a lack of foresight, which would have swiftly bankrupted a private enterprise' (1985: 32).

Third, states' regulation of trade, financial and industrial sectors limited economic development. High tariffs and other national protective measures in the economic arena, argue proponents of neo-liberal development discourse, hindered the deepening of international free trade and foreign direct investment in the South. In the case of industrial development, the adoption of a nationally oriented industrial strategy of import substitution industrialization (ISI) by most states in the South had greatly contributed to their economic stagnation by the 1970s.

According to an influential study framed by neo-liberal economic thought from the OECD, 'ISI's bulky state administration created bottlenecks in the economy, further wasting resources through capacity underutilization, corruption, and sluggishness. The authors expressed the doubt common to all neo-classical theory that bureaucrats could gain access to the information needed to effectively administer the economy, and they disliked the fact that the controls used in ISI appeared to curb private initiative' (Rapley, 2002: 56). Overall, for 'counter-revolution' (Toye, 1993) thinkers in development economics, the misguided policies that characterized the approach of states in the South and the TDHB in the era of modernization development discourse have their origins in the emergence of the *Dirigiste* Dogma in development economics, an approach influenced by Keynesian thought and, in some cases, by neo-Marxist ideas (Lal, 1985: 5–7). As Lal argues, in the area of trade and industrialization for instance, this Dogma generated outdated ideas that contributed to economic stagnation in the South:

> [Although it] might have been expected to highlight the importance of international trade and investment in the development process, on the lines of the arguments developed by Adam Smith, it became, instead, the leading purveyor of an autarkic model of development. Theory and practice seemed to mutually reinforce each other, and many developing countries turned inwards during the 1950s and early 1960s in an attempt to foster a hothouse, import-substituting industrialisation behind protection walls, which were higher, more uneven (and hence arbitrary) in terms of the protection they afforded different commodities, and more comprehensive, than anything imagined by the mercantilists castigated by Adam Smith. (1985: 17)

Given the claims cited above, advocates of the neo-liberal development discourse contend that the way forward for the South is to roll back the role of the state in the economy and embrace market-led development. As they see it, the implementation of a self-regulating market regime of accumulation explains the rise of South Korea, Singapore and Taiwan out of economic stagnation and backwardness and other features of underdevelopment. In their promotion of market-led development, advocates of this discourse call for the implementation of a set of economic measures such as privatization of state-owned enterprises. According to neo-liberal development discourse, privatization would facilitate the emergence and expansion of the private sector, leading

to private sector-led development and the elimination of monopolistic economic structures, corruption and other inefficient economic
practices that characterized the era of state-led development. Other elements of neo-liberal development discourse include the removal of trade
barriers and the liberation of financial sectors through measures such
as devaluation of currency and the removal of state controls on the
operation of financial markets (Chapter 9).

Promotion of market reforms in the agricultural sector is another economic reform advocated by proponents of the neo-liberal development
project. Like other neo-liberal policies, their advocates claim that they
would create market incentives for farmers and eliminate unproductive
involvement in this sector by the state. According to neo-liberal development discourse, states in the South have adopted these economically
backward policies as part of their political strategy of concentrating
on appeasing urban constituents who are their main sources of political support. Such an approach to agrarian production has also created
openings for rent-seeking activities, corruption and stagnation of the
agricultural sector. In the context of the agricultural sector in Africa
and in other areas, Robert Bates (1981 and 1989) has been at the forefront of scholars elaborating this market and urban bias argument. From
a neo-liberal perspective, the core strategies in the agricultural sector
involve the privatization of agrarian public enterprises, the introduction of private traders and the removal of subsidies to farmers, and an
export-led growth economic strategy focusing on primary commodity
production—which is the comparative advantage that most social formations in the South possess. From this perspective, these strategies will
not only enable these countries to move beyond conditions of economic stagnation, but also finally dismantle the myth of nationally
focused ISI as a viable development strategy in their march to capitalist
modernity.

In the main, a call for the reconstitution of state forms along neo-
liberal lines in the South has been at the core of the TDHB's hegemonic
development discourse. In this regard, states are expected to institute
measures that ensure a friendly environment for capital and strategies, such as deregulation and privatization. Further, states have had
to demonstrate fiscal and monetary discipline, for failure to do so,
especially for most states in the South, leads to disciplinary measures
imposed by the TDHB. Essentially, in the neo-liberal epoch, the objectives of state policies and practices are to promote the deepening of
a commodification logic in the economy, social life and nature. This
trend is not new, as Karl Polanyi's work on the rise and dominance

of the self-regulating doctrine in previous historical moments illustrates (2001). With the return of this doctrine, what its proponents are promoting again under the slogans of freedom and democracy is the marketization of society—the resurrection of what Polanyi refers to as the expectation of 'liberal utopia' that marked the early part of the twentieth century leading to the Great Depression (2001: 266). While this social phenomenon is not new, it has taken a broader bent in the current neo-liberal age. As David Harvey posits:

> Commodification, privatization of hitherto public assets has been a signal feature of the neoliberal project. Its primary aim has been to open up new fields for capital accumulation in domains hitherto regarded off-limits to the calculus of profitability.... The intellectual property rights established through the so-called TRIPS agreement within the WTO defines genetic materials, seed plasmas, and all manner of other products as private property.... The commodification (through tourism) of cultural forms, histories, and intellectual creativity entails wholesale dispossessions (the music industry is notorious for the appropriation and exploitation of grassroots culture and creativity). (2005: 160–161)

In the promotion of the commodification logic as the *raison d'être* of economic practices in the South, the TDHB has played a significant role in the reconfiguration of the role of the state in social and political arenas. In these interlinked processes, the TDHB has utilized extensive surveillance strategies on states' practices. These strategies are aimed at punishing states seen to be deviating from the market doctrine and other economic and political features of the neo-liberal world order. In this endeavour, the TDHB uses the mechanism of conditionality to discipline states considered delinquent in instituting the neo-liberal project. A range of states including but not limited to Argentina, Malawi, Kenya, South Korea and Angola, have borne the brunt of this policy. On the whole, the surveillance of states' practices is a core feature of contemporary 'disciplinary neo-liberalism' which is,

> ... a concrete form of structural and behavioural power, combining the structural power of capital with 'capillary power' and 'panopticism' that is 'bureaucratized and institutionalized, and operates with different degrees of intensity across a range of 'public' and 'private' spheres, in various state and civil society complexes.... Disciplinary neo-liberalism is institutionalized at the macro-level of power in

the quasi-legal restructuring of state and international political forms.... This new constitutionalism underpins the workings of institutions of global governance and regional trading agreements such as NAFTA. (Gill, 2003: 130–132)

While in the last decade there have been numerous new reports claiming to represent a 'rethinking' of the core tenets of the neo-liberal development discourse (epitomized by phrases such as the 'post-Washington consensus') by the World Bank and other members of the TDHB, the core of their development strategies remains neo-liberal (see also Chapters 7 and 9). This is not surprising given that overall, the TDHB has generated a plethora of strategies and concepts claiming to be improvements over the previous or current development strategy at various historical moments in the post-1945 period. As Escobar argues, a close review of this period indicates that in a given juncture, 'new objects, new modes of operation are introduced, and a number of variables modified (for instance, in relation to strategies to combat hunger, knowledge about nutritional requirements, the types of crops given priority)', but the 'discursive' structure of hegemonic development discourses remains the same (1997: 89). In terms of the current discourse for example, some brief examples from Paul Cammack's detailed analysis of World Bank reports illustrates how, while the TDHB claims shifts in this discourse, its neo-liberal development logics are being reproduced:

The 1998/99 Report, *Knowledge for Development*, promoted procapitalist solutions to the 'problem of development,' proposing the Bank itself as a rapid-response task force capable of producing market solutions on demand, and revealing the networks it had put in place to extract from the poor themselves the local knowledge needed to boost exploitation and accumulation. The 1999/2000 Report, *Entering the 21st Century*, mounted an ideological offensive to persuade the world's population that there was no alternative to the new international capitalist regime, presenting 'globalisation' as a remote and unstoppable force driving states and peoples willy-nilly into the world market, and Bank policy as ideologically neutral, pragmatic and benevolent. The 2000/2001 Report, *Attacking Poverty*, then offered globalizing capitalism as the only means by which poverty could be addressed. (2005: 163)

To sum up, the preceding sections have discussed the rise of two hegemonic development discourses in the context of shifting world orders in the post-1945 period. The discussion has attempted to indicate the close link between shifts in world orders and the emergence and nature of the constitutive elements of hegemonic development discourses. Such an approach to the study of development discourses demonstrates their deep embedding in global politico-economic processes and to shifts in the projects of the TDHB. The approach thus challenges the abstraction of these discourses from the constitutive elements of a prevailing world order and their representation as neutral scientific ideas geared solely to facilitating the transition of the South to capitalist modernity along the lines of social formations in the North. Before moving on to the next chapter that highlights the analytical poverty of hegemonic development perspectives in the study of political and economic processes in the South, we highlight some of their core effects.

Hegemonic development discourses: theory as coloniality and other effects

While hegemonic development discourses discussed in the preceding sections emerged during different historical conjunctures and emphasize different politico-economic strategies, they nonetheless share similar underlying assumptions about economic, cultural and political processes in the South. In the discussion that follows, then, we endeavour to offer a critique of the core assumptions of these discourses and where necessary to highlight in specific terms the effects and assumptions of either modernization or neo-liberal development discourse. Additional implications of these discourses and the contemporary development discourse of human security will be discussed in Chapters 4 and 7 respectively. The underlying premise here is that the two development discourses that are the focus of this chapter have had significant effects on politico-economic processes in the South. Among other effects, they have enabled the reconstitution of coloniality of power in the post-1945 period. We begin with a discussion of the ways in which these discourses have facilitated the reconstitution of coloniality of power for the age of development. In the final section we highlight their other effects.

Since their emergence, hegemonic development discourses have enabled the reconstitution of coloniality of power in two fundamental ways: their reproduction of the racial classification of humanity and linear view of history. Racial classification of humanity was of course the underbelly of colonial ideas and practices. Thus, while sharing evolutionist assumptions like those promoted by scholars such as Auguste Comte and the nineteenth European doctrine of development and its underlying 'theory of trusteeship' (Cowen and Shenton, 1995: 34), racial thinking was a core element of whatever development doctrine emerged in the colonies. In the colonial classification of humanity and spaces, civilized and developed Europe portrayed itself as the trustee that could be trusted to lead 'heathen', 'savage' and 'child-like' societies outside Europe towards progress through development. From that perspective, colonial politico-economic projects were socially constructed as moral duties and as emancipatory projects for the unciv-ilized non-European Other or, in the eyes of the capitalist Cecil Rhodes, as 'philanthropy' with a 5 per cent rate of return (quoted Kothari, 2005: 50) for colonial capital. Echoing Europe's racialist ideology and practice coded in a civilizing-developing frame, Paul Leroy-Beaulieu (1874) states: 'colonialization is one of the highest functions of soci-eties that have reached an advanced stage of civilization.... The merit of a colonizing people is to place the young society it has brought forth in the most suitable conditions for the development of its nat-ural faculties; to smooth its path without hampering its initiative; to give it the means and tools that are necessary or useful for its growth' (quoted in Rist, 2004: 54). Overall, contrary to claims by intellectual and policy defenders of colonialism (Ferguson, 2003), development as an idea and practice emerged in the colonies as an externally imposed and exploitative project; the latter abstracted from structural and other forms of power that underpinned the expanding capitalist order.

Intellectual theorizing and state practices dividing humanity between civilized Europe and uncivilized non-Europe was the 'common sense' (Gramsci 1971) of European ruling elites and leading intellectuals between the fifteenth and nineteenth centuries. Such theorizing had political, cultural and economic effects. In terms of colonial state pol-icy, it provided openings for public and private colonial functionaries to represent local cultural, political and economic geographies as defective and thus in need of urgent tutelage by civilized and developed Europe. In such a colonial move, for instance, Harry Johnston, the first colo-nial governor of contemporary Malawi, had no qualms representing local political-cultural-economic geographies in crude racialized terms in efforts to legitimize Britain's colonial project. As Crush highlights, in less than three years of British colonialism, Johnston was celebrat-ing colonialism's civilizing and developmental effects: 'an increasing number of natives are able to read and write, and, above all, are trained to respect and to value a settled and civilized government... A planter gallops past on horseback, or a missionary trots in on a fat white donkey from a visit to an outlying station' (1995: 1.). Thus, in this colonial representational system 'the civilized, ordered, white, male, English landscape erases its unordered, savage, chaotic, dangerous, African predecessor' and in the process sets 'loose the redemptive powers of development' (ibid.: 1–2).

Post-1945 development discourses have reproduced the colonial racial classification of humanity through coded binary tropes, for example, traditional–modern, developing–developed, tribes–nations, backward–advanced and, in the contemporary era, as Chapter 7 will indicate governable–ungovernable spaces. These tropes underpinning development discourse carry out the work of overt racial thinking that marked ideologies such as the civilizing mission and the White man's burden that characterized the colonial classification of humanity. Thus, post-1945 hegemonic development discourses need to be situated within the larger history of Euro-American coloniality of power in the South, including its racial classification of humanity. We suggest that the classification of societies under racially coded tropes such as traditional–modern and so forth in hegemonic development discourses has de-legitimatized the humanity of people in the South by representing them as the inferior Other. The covert, overt and structural power embodied in these discourses have enabled them to reproduce the colonial cultural-economic coded racial classification of humanity and in the process they have de-legitimatized the humanity of people in the South. This de-legitimatization of the humanity of non-European peoples has ensured the continuation of the psychological violence that began with the overt racial ideologies and politico-economic practices of colonial states and other colonial actors, a form of violence and its de-legitimatizing effects that Frantz Fanon (2004; 2008) has powerfully articulated.[7] Essentially, the evolution of the world politico-economic system has 'robbed' non-European peoples of their 'share' of humanity (Fanon, 2008: 90). For Fanon, in the 'white world' people of colour face 'difficulties in elaborating [their] body schema' for the image of their bodies 'is solely negating', as it is an image 'in the third person. All around the body reigns an atmosphere of certain uncertainty' (ibid.: 90). In the case of the African continent, the de-legitimatization of African humanity through development discourse reproduces Hegel's views on the continent. For him, Africa was outside human historical development (Thiong'o and Sahle, 2004) and thus its people could only be civilized through slavery and other practices of coloniality of power.

Beyond facilitating the reconstitution of coloniality of power through their reproduction of the colonial classification of humanity, hegemonic development discourses have carried out this task in other ways. Theoretically parsimonious and neutral sounding as their linear view of history—embodied for instance in Rostow's stages of growth schema—may appear, underlying it are assumptions about the South that have facilitated the reconstitution of coloniality of power. In terms of enabling this process, these discourses' linear view of history has contributed to it in three significant ways. First, it has enabled the reproduction of the colonial linear conceptualization of historical processes. From their emergence in the immediate post-1945 period to the current conjuncture, an assumption that all societies follow the same politico-economic and cultural development path as that treaded by Europe and former European settler colonies such as the USA and Canada has marked these discourses. In the era of formal colonialism, such a view of history provided the intellectual basis for the legitimatization of colonial cultural, political and economic projects.

The reproduction of the colonial linear view of history in the post-1945 period through hegemonic development discourses signals the covert power of these hegemonic discourses as representational systems. This power has resulted in the consolidation of the representation of the historical trajectory of the North as the universal model awaiting the South. This Euro-centric representational system has perpetuated the colonial representation of non-European peoples as 'people without history' (Wolf, 1982)—people whose entrance into human history can only be enabled by reproducing the experience of people of European descent, who naturally have history. Like the colonial representation of the South, then, hegemonic development discourses have dispossessed the people of the South of their own past and future history. Thus, these discourses are intrinsic to colonial ways of knowing and politico-economic practices. Overall, like colonizing discourses they construct—and with powerful politico-cultural-economic effects—the South in ahistorical terms for as Crush contends:

> Not only are the objects of development stripped of their history, but they are then reinserted into implicit (and explicit) typologies which define a priori what they are, where they've been and where, with development as guide they can go. Perhaps the best known of these formal typologies to students of development is Rostow's 'stages of growth model.' But the basic trope—that Europe shows the rest of

the world the image of its future – is of much broader and deeper purchase. (1995: 9)

A second way in which development discourses' linear view of history has facilitated the reconstitution of coloniality of power in the post-1945 era is their normalization of the political, cultural and economic developments and practices that contributed to Europe's and North America's processes of capitalism. This approach dispossesses the world of a historical understanding of the cultural, political and economic processes that have shaped social change not only in the North but also in the South. The linear representation of the politico-economic trajectory to capitalist modernity of social formations in the North neglects the violence, the myriad local and external forms of 'accumulation by dispossession' (Harvey, 2005) and other forms of dispossession that characterized this development. For Harvey the multiple processes of accumulation by dispossession, which under-pins historical and contemporary capitalism, include, but are not limited to,

> commodification and privatization of land and the forceful expulsion of peasant populations; the conversion of various forms of property rights (common, collective, state, etc.) into exclusive private property rights; the suppression of rights to the commons; the commodifica-tion of labour power and the suppression of alternative (indigenous) forms of production and consumption; colonial, neo-colonial, and imperial processes of appropriation of assets (including) natural resources; the monetization of exchange and taxation, particularly of land; the slave trade; and usury, the national debt, and ulti-mately the credit system as radical means of primitive accumulation. (Ibid.: 145)

The ahistorical approach to social change embodied in development discourse facilitates the reproduction of the enclosed European narra-tive describing the processes leading to capitalist modernity: a de-linked Europe that managed to pull itself up by its boot straps and march to political and economic capitalist modernity at no expense to or with no contributions (material or otherwise) from other societies, and at no social or political cost to marginalized social forces in var-ious European social formations. Yet in Europe, dispossessions of all sorts, as Polanyi's work demonstrates in the case of England during the high noon of the enclosure movement, and strong-arm strategies by the state and owners of capital aimed at creating a labour market were the norm.[8] Overall, covert and overt disciplinary tactics of power deployed by European states in the processes leading to capitalist modernity facilitated their practices of dispossession. As Escobar argues,

> People did not go into the factories gladly and of their own accord; an entire regime of discipline and normalization was necessary. Besides the expulsion of peasants and serfs from the land and the creation of a proletarian class, the modern economy necessitated a profound restructuring of bodies, individuals, and social norms.... The result of this process—Homo oeconomicus—was a normalized subject that was produced under certain physical and cultural conditions. (1995a: 60; see also Harvey, 1990; Foucault, 2003)

In European colonies, a range of practices that resulted in the economic dispossession of local communities were the hallmark of this form of rule. In Africa, commodification of land for cash crop production, inhuman wages for workers (because Africans under colonial racial classification of humanity were not considered human), extraction of raw materials to fuel and deepen industrial capitalism in Europe and many other practices of accumulation by dispossession characterized European colonialism (Rodney, 1972).[9] In Asia, inter-European and USA competition saw the implementation of economic strategies to service the needs of colonial imperatives at the expense of the human security of local communities. As in the European colonial states in Africa, in Dutch-ruled Indonesia the colonial authority ensured that Indonesians involved in cash crop production met only its own economic needs (Bagchi, 1982: 70). In the case of coffee production, the colonial state not only attempted to 'restrict its cultivation' by Indonesians 'as they had done with the valuable spices', but they also 'paid absurdly low prices for the coffee they "bought" as forced deliveries' (ibid.: 71). Even in partially colonized social formations such as China (Chapter 6), under the treaty trading port system the colonial pattern of accumulation by dispossession became the norm. During the wars that characterized colonial competition for the control of China, the country in a sense had to pay for its conquest and colonialism through the monetary compensations that it had to pay various colonial interests at the end of each defeat. For instance, with the signing of the Treaty of Nanjing that gave British interests the right to pursue economic activities in Canton, Amoy, Foochchow-foo, Ningpo and Shanghai, China had 'to pay $6 million for opium, confiscated by imperial commissioner Lin Zexu in Canton $3 million for debts owned to foreign merchants by the Cohong, and another $12 million' to Britain for its expenditure during the war (Cartier, 2001: 114).

Third, hegemonic development discourses' linear view of history further facilitates the coloniality of power by naturalizing the unequal power relations that have underpinned the capitalist world system in the post-1945 period. As argued in Chapters 1 and 2, unequal power—structural, political and ideological—relations has marked the rise of a capitalist world system, with the social formations in the North being at this system's apex, and those of the South—while constitutive of it—taking historically situated forms of peripheral positions. This tendency to naturalize politico-economic arrangements has significant effects. For example, it provides legitimacy to hegemonic development discourses' representation of 'backward' internal dynamics as being the sole drivers of politico-economic processes in the South—that is, a South de-linked from contradictions, tensions and other political, economic and ideological developments generated by the capitalist world system and core elements of its conjunctural world orders. Yet, the power asymmetry underpinning this world system has significant effects on these processes. For instance, for advocates of the neo-liberal development discourse, the South should focus on its comparative advantage in primary commodity production for its economic projects. Such a claim ignores the restrictive policies by states in the North for market access for primary commodities from South. It neglects for instance, the barriers set by the WTO trading regime, multinational corporations and states in the North on primary commodities from the South and thus depoliticizes global power inequalities and facilitates the reproduction of this historical phenomenon for these neo-liberal times.

Under the neo-liberal informed WTO framework—mainly the 1994 Agreement on Agriculture—member countries are expected to reduce subsidies to their agricultural sectors. Since then, while states in the South have been pressured by the TDHB through its use of neo-liberal disciplinary tools such as the cancellation or delay in the delivery of loans to adhere to this agreement, the industrialized North has in the main ignored it. For the most part states in the North have during this period not only ignored this agreement, but also in most cases increased their levels of subsidies to the agrarian sector. According to one study, for instance, 'net public support to agriculture for OECD countries has as a whole rose to 40 percent of the value of total farm receipts in 1999.

In 2000, subsidies accounted for 39 percent of the total value of E.U. production and 22 percent of the value of U.S. production' (Hoekman and Anderson, cited in Gibbon and Ponte, 2005: 55). This practice and others marking the evolution of the WTO trading regime, has had significant effects. For example, because of the North's neglect 'to honor the spirit' of the 1994 WTO Agreement on Agriculture, social formations in the South 'have been unable to expand their share of global agricultural trade. On the contrary, as a result of subsidized exports, the combined share of the European Union and United States in world agricultural exports rose slightly from 49.8 percent in 1980 to 51.8 percent in 2001' (Gibbon and Ponte, 2005: 56). The documentary film *Life and Debt* (Black, 2001) that illustrates Jamaica's experience with the neo-liberal agrarian doctrine well captures this doctrine's social, cultural and political consequences, as does *Black Gold* (Francis and Francis, 2006), which highlights the every day experiences of Ethiopian coffee producers' in the age of neo-liberal globalization. Even with its significant effects on social and other processes in the South, the neo-liberal development discourse of the WTO and other members of the TDHB remains. In the main and contrary to the rhetoric of the neo-liberal doctrine that trade liberalization leads to rise in exports and thus development, this has not been the case for the majority of social formations in the global South. According to Peter Gibbon and Stefano Ponte, under WTO international trading regime, for instance, African countries have seen a decline in exports and whatever gains they have made in the manufacturing sector remain in the lower end—mainly processing of primary commodities—of value chains that characterize the international trading circuit. In the case of exports they state, 'Africa's export trade over the last half-century has been characterized by a low rate of growth. After 1980, this rate has been low even in relation to the continent's general level of economic development' (2005: 44).

In addition to their enabling the reconstitution of coloniality of power, hegemonic development discourses have had other significant effects on politico-economic processes in the South, some of which we briefly highlight. First, in the political arena, the constitutive elements of modernization theory coupled with anti-communist ideology of the TDHB, for instance, dovetailed well with political projects initiated by some ruling elites aimed at containing democratic space during the epoch of the geopolitics of the Cold War. Essentially, the anti-democratic nature of modernization development discourse provided local and global legitimacy to civilian and military authoritarian state practices in various parts of the South, enabling the emergence of 'bio-politics' in places such as Chile, South Korea, Argentina, Kenya, Malawi, Indonesia and many other places. Overall, in the conjuncture of the hegemony of modernization discourse and the legitimacy provided by the TDHB, several states in the South practiced 'a bio-politics concerned with the detailed administration of life' and were characterized by a form of 'sovereign power that' routinely exercised its 'right to death' (Dean, 1999: 138). In his discussion of the concept of bio-politics, Michel Foucault's entry point is an examination of the emergence of sovereign doctrine and sovereign power in the making of state forms associated with politico-economic and cultural modernity. According to him, with the rise of sovereign doctrine and power, the modalities of human life become a core domain of state power (Foucault, 2003: 239–240). As he states, '[With] the acquisition of power over man insofar as man is a living being... the biological came under State control' and the sovereign acquired 'the right to life and death', which Foucault argues was the sovereign's 'right to kill' individual men and women (ibid.: 240). Overall, with the rise of bio-politics came the deepening of the state's power over people as both political and biological beings: 'biopolitics deals with the population, with the population as political problem, as a problem that is at once scientific and political, as a biological problem and as power's problem' (ibid.: 245). The rise and consolidation of bio-politics and an extensive use of the sovereign's right to kill during the era of General Park's regime following the military coup of 1961, for example, characterized South Korea's state-led project of rapid development through an aggressive export-industrialization strategy (see generally, Hart-Landsberg, 1993). The utilization of the sovereign's right to life and death in the name of development in Africa during the era of the geopolitics of the Cold War and the hegemony of modernization development discourse informs Joseph Ki-Zerbo's pertinent observation:

> A certain mystifying discourse soon spread all over Africa. 'Partisan divisions are over. Everyone should unite behind the leader in the struggle for economic development.' In short: 'Silence! We are developing!' And in the process we have lost both development and democracy: 'Silence! We are killing!' Both through the open violence of the Kalashnikovs and the deaf violence of structures. (Ki-Zerbo, 1991, cited in Escobar, 1997: 88)

In this epoch of, 'Silence! We are developing!' the sovereign's preferred methods of demonstrating his right to life and death in Malawi were detention without trial, long-term imprisonment, firebombs, 'disappearance' in the Shire River as 'food for crocodiles' (one of President Kamuzu Banda's favourite phrases) and 'accidentization'. In terms of the latter practice for instance, in 1983, Dick Matenje, the Secretary General of the ruling Malawi Congress Party together with Cabinet Ministers Aaron Gadama and John Sangala and an MP named David Chiwanga were killed in what the state claimed was a car accident. However, as Malawians were to learn in the 1990s, their deaths were another case of the sovereign exercising his right to life and death. According to the findings by the Commission of Inquiry mandated to investigate the matter in 1994, state's security forces killed these individuals at a secluded forest in Mwanza district:

> A team of policemen was assigned to each of the four gentlemen to carry out the killing.... According to the evidence of Mpagaja, when the four gentlemen were taken out of the vehicle, he took Mr. Sangala to the edge of the road, with the help of two others made him sit down, and while still hooded and handcuffed, struck him on the head with a mallet (hammer used in fixing tents). It is in the evidence that the three others were killed in similar manner. The killing of the four gentlemen was simultaneous. (Republic of Malawi, 1994: 23)

Second, hegemonic development discourses have had major effects on economic processes in the South. For instance and as previously discussed (see also Chapter 4), in the era of the hegemony of modernization development discourse and anti-communist ideas, the TDHB rewarded states in the South that were in the anti-communist camp with generous financial support. Among its numerous effects, this practice contributed to the debt overhang in the South (Klein, 2007; Bond, 2008). Third, these discourses have had significant effect on social relations such as gender and class. Overall, in the era of a neo-liberal world order and its attendant development discourse, dominant class power (Bond, 2001; Harvey, 2005; Sahle 2008) has been reproduced through the establishment of neo-liberal policies such as privatization, among others. In the case of gender power dynamics, while the current neo-liberal development discourse 'recommends a fundamental reordering of the mode of regulation and a new definition of the public good', it has been profoundly 'silent about the gendered underpinnings of this shift' (Broddie, 1994: 48). For instance, the implementation of neo-liberal policies in the social sector have resulted in increased health risks for women, especially those from marginalized social classes, because of increased health costs (Sahle, 2008: 84). While a gendered lens is absent in neo-liberal theorizing about economic processes, what is in fact occurring is that women in the South have become the 'shock-absorbers' (Broddie, 1994: 50) of the economic, political and cultural effects of the neo-liberal project. Overall, a silence on gender issues has marked the evolution of post-1945 hegemonic development discourse (Sahle, 2008). Further, whenever these discourses have incorporated the concept of gender, such as in the gender and development and gender mainstreaming discourses, they have subsumed it within a capitalist-patriarchal discursive formation, which has set structural and political limits to the emancipatory potential underpinning critical feminist philosophy and ethics. Such tendencies are embedded even in emancipatory-sounding development discourses such as the current one of human security that informs the MDGs (Chapter 7). Generally, these discourses are a core manner in which the making of a developmental patriarchal knowledge apparatus and practices has occurred in the post-1945 period.

Conclusion

This chapter has discussed the rise of two hegemonic discourses in the context of shifts in the ideas and politico-economic processes underpinning the post-1945 world order. The analysis has indicated the influence of the constitutive features of a given world order on the emergence and nature of these discourses. Departing from the characterization of these hegemonic development discourses as neutral and solely geared to facilitating the evolutionary transition of the South to capitalist modernity, the discussion has highlighted the role of these discourses in the entrenchment of coloniality of power among other effects. While this chapter's central concern has been to highlight the nature, rise and effects of hegemonic development discourses in the context of shifting world orders, we now turn to an examination of what we suggest are their significant limitations as analytical tools in the study of politico-economic processes in the South, with a specific reference to the role of the state in the economy in Malawi and South Korea.

4
State, World Order and Development: Malawi and South Korea

The main premise of this chapter is that hegemonic development perspectives are significantly limited as analytical tools for studying politico-economic processes such as the role of the state in the economy in the South. Our analysis departs from them by demonstrating that while states, for instance, in Malawi and South Korea are agents of capitalist development their agency does not exist in a vacuum. As we suggested in Chapters 1 and 2, a core claim of the theoretical traditions informing this project is that historical developments greatly influence political and economic processes in the South and elsewhere. Thus, a first departing point in our analysis is that, while ignored in hegemonic development perspectives, historical legacies are a central factor in any explanation of the role and capacity of the state in the economy. Principally, our historical approach aims to disrupt the Eurocentric tendency that permeates hegemonic development perspectives. Such a tendency tends to claim that in the case of state formation processes and practices in the South, they reflect early stages of European history. As Mahmood Mamdani (1996: 11–12) argues, such perspectives represent the politico-economic practices of states in Africa as being similar to those of earlier state forms in Europe:

> Overwhelmed by societal pressures... the state has turned into a 'weak Leviathan,' 'suspended above society.' Whether plain 'soft' or in 'decline' and 'decay,' this creature may be 'omnipresent' but is hardly 'omnipotent.' Then follows the theoretical conclusion: variously termed as the 'early modern authoritarian state,' the 'early modern absolutist state,' or 'the patrimonial autocratic state,' this form of state power is likened to its ancestors in seventeenth-century Europe... often underlined as a political feature of the transition to

capitalism... What happens if you take a historical process unfolding under concrete conditions... as a vantage point from which to make sense of subsequent social development? The outcome is a history by analogy rather than history as process. Analogy seeking turns into a substitute for theory formation.

Overall, what is presented as universal history in hegemonic development perspectives as far as state politico-economic practices in the South are concerned is Europe's experience. Such perspectives have major analytical limitations. For example, in their ahistorical and positivist vein, they ignore the historical fact that the political, material aims and capacities of European states were achieved through exploitation of other regions of the world especially in the epoch of formal colonialism. The assumption that states in the South, then, will follow the European trajectory ignores the myriad conditions and factors that resulted in the emergence of and evolution of states in Europe and the contributions of other regions to this process especially to the material base of these states. The ahistorical approach of proponents of hegemonic development perspectives leads them to propose the emergence of de-historicized developmental states as the way forward for the South. In the era of the hegemony of Third World modernization theory, authoritarian ideology and practice was considered a central feature of these developmental states, as Chapter 3 indicated. In the current era of neoliberal promotion of democracy, procedural democracy is the political practice advocated for these state forms. In the case of the democracy-development nexus, the stress in works situated in this perspective is on developmental capacity of the state and not its democratic foundations or practices, for as one analyst of developmental state forms argues, their core function is to ensure 'annual average gross national product per capita growth of at least 4% for 25 or 30 years' (Low, 2004: 11). In their bare bones, developmental states are said to be characterized by Weberian bureaucratic instrumental rationality but more importantly by their embrace of the market as the determinant of economic development. In particular, when describing state forms that they consider developmental in the South, scholars writing from the hegemonic development perspectives emphasize the emergence of a politically insulated technocratic bureaucratic elite whose sole focus is the rational allocation of resources (Chan, Clark and Lam, 1998: 2) in pursuit of capitalist development.

Beyond a historical approach to the study of the role of the state in the economy in a given conjuncture, our analysis departs from hegemonic development perspectives on this question in other ways. A second departing point in this respect is an argument that a state's material base influences the nature of its role in the economy. Further, our third claim is that ideas and geopolitical imperatives underpinning the prevailing world order are no less important in such a process. Generally, in contrast to hegemonic development perspectives we highlight not only the agency of the state in the economy but also the interplay of local and global conditions on this process. We build our arguments in two parts. In both parts one and two, and with a focus on Malawi and South Korea respectively during the conjuncture of hegemony of the modernization theory and geopolitics of the Cold War, we demonstrate that the role of the state in the economy does not occur in a historical, local and global vacuum. In this regard, our analysis demonstrates how historical developments, material base of the state and geopolitical interests and ideas of the prevailing world order influence the role of the state in the economy.

State and the economy: Malawi

At independence in 1964, the Malawian state inherited a weak material base characterized by agrarian production. This structural inheritance was a result of a historical process that had seen the country incorporated in the international division of labour as a producer of primary commodities and as a labour reserve for European mining interests in colonial Southern Africa. Further, the end of colonialism coincided with a world order underpinned by Third World modernization development, and the geopolitics of the Cold War. In an attempt to provide a more nuanced explanation of the role of the state in the economy following the end of British rule in Malawi, we weave these conditions into our discussion of this process. We begin with a discussion of British colonialism in Malawi with a main focus on the core feature of the material base of the state. This is followed by a discussion that highlights the agency of the state in the economy after British rule and how historical conditions and the politico-economic imperatives marking the prevailing world order set the parameters within which this agency operated.

Colonialism and its structural legacies

Britain colonized Nyasaland (Malawi) in 1891, marking the beginning of 73 years of colonial rule. Prior to 1891, an intense Anglo–Portuguese competition marked this region of contemporary Southern Africa. After 1891, the stage was set for the reordering of local politico-economic arrangements along Europe's nineteenth century model of colonial rule in Africa. According to Mamdani (1996), under this model whether colonial political arrangements were marked by direct or indirect rule, the result was the consolidation of power in a despotic state form.[1] In indirectly ruled Malawi, the colonial state introduced several measures aimed at the consolidation of power in a despotic state form dominated by a small European planter class. The dominant ones were the creation of a centralized and authoritarian state structure with Executive and Legislative Councils at its apex; and the establishment of new traditional political architecture, the latter in conjunction with other colonial practices played a major in role in the reconfiguration of customary power (ibid.). Within the first decade of British rule, colonial administrators had divided the country into 12 districts, each headed by a Revenue Collector, which formed an embryonic state apparatus with headquarters in Zomba in the southern part of the country (Johnston, 1897). With the creation of this administrative structure, power was concentrated in the office of the Commissioner (the title was changed to Governor in 1907) under various orders-in-council. Thus, while the Commissioner was answerable to the British government, locally his office had extensive powers. For example, the British Central Africa Order in Council, 1902, vested all rights of Crown lands and 'all mines and minerals being in, under, or upon any lands in the occupation of any native tribe' in the Commissioner (Murray, 1932: 102–103).

In the political arena, Lord Lugard's colonial doctrine of Native Authority facilitated the consolidation of power by colonial rulers and the emergence of 'traditional ruling elite' unaccountable to the local communities and dependent on the colonial state for its reproduction. Thus, the colonial invocation of the language of 'tradition' notwithstanding the sole aim of this strategy was to enable the creation of a political architecture subordinated to imperial interests. In Malawi, the Lugard's doctrine was implemented through various *Native Ordinances*. In 1910, for instance, the colonial state established the post of Village Headman, and the 1912 District Administration (Native) Ordinance saw the consolidation of village areas into administrative units run by a Principal Headman; the latter an appointee of the Governor (Murray, 1932: 131). While Malawian communities, like others in pre-colonial Africa, had a variety of political arrangements, in the colonial epoch the centralized political structure with a chief answerable to the colonial state came to represent their political structures.[2] Overall, in Malawi and elsewhere in Africa, colonialists considered every 'tribe' as having a powerful chief with unchecked power and this meant that 'if there did not exist a clearly demarcated tribe with a distinct central authority, one had to be created' (Mamdani, 1996: 79).

As elsewhere, European colonialism in Malawi involved the reordering not only of local political structures but also of the material foundations of local communities. While taxes and immigrant earnings formed important elements of the state's material base, its constitutive feature was agrarian production. The rise of colonial agrarian production began with the alienation of land by the Sir Harry Johnston, who was the first colonial Commissioner. Between the years 1892 and 1894, Johnston's administration carried out a process that aimed to organize the structure of land ownership in the colony (Johnston, 1897: 112–113). The determination of land ownership signified the beginning of a new era in economic production since it introduced the notion of private ownership of land in the country, thus laying the foundation for agricultural production along capitalist lines. Prior to the establishment of colonial rule, Europeans (planters, missionaries, traders and adventurers) had settled in the country. A unifying factor among these various segments of the European population was their acquisition of land belonging to local African communities.

With the establishment of colonial rule and land alienation, the stage was set for the incorporation of the country into the world capitalist system. While this process had already begun with the slave trade, under colonial rule as Nyasaland became involved in cash crop agrarian production mainly geared for international markets it became solidified. The incorporation of the country into the expanding capitalist system saw the rise of a monocultural economic structure as the core of the state's material base. According to one estimate, starting from a very low base in the late 1900s, the value of agrarian exports rose to a £ 100,000 by 1909 and £ 1 million by 1940 (Pike, 1968: 174). In the early phase of colonial rule, coffee was the dominant crop producing its highest yield— £ 2 million—in 1900 (Pollock, 1971: 305). However, coffee exports declined in the early 1900s for a variety of reasons, with the core one being the rise of the Brazilian coffee industry in the international coffee market. The search then began for lucrative new crops and the process resulted in the introduction of tobacco and cotton in the early 1900s (Rangeley, 1957: 66). Although these two crops had been grown previously, they figured more prominently in the colonial economy after the collapse of the world coffee trade. Of these two crops, cotton production was the more strongly encouraged since Britain, like other imperial powers, viewed it as an important source of revenue in the context of a global 'cotton famine' following the abolition of slavery in the USA.[3] In 1902,

British cotton manufacturers for instance experienced a severe financial crisis because of this development: 'in Lancashire...manufacturers, spinners, and operatives lost about 2,000,000 pounds sterling' (Pollock, 1971: 306). Consequently, Britain began encouraging cotton production in the colonies and, in efforts to facilitate this process, the British Cotton Growing Association emerged in 1902 (ibid.).

Efforts by the state to serve the interests of political forces closely allied to it at the expense of African peasant agrarian producers characterized the evolution of the colonial state's agrarian capital accumulation strategy. To achieve this aim, the colonial state's agrarian production strategy composed of two sub-sectors estate and peasant: dominated respectively by Europeans and Africans, with the colonial state's political and economic imperatives shaping the evolution of both. The estate sub-sector, while facing contradictory responses from the state at times, received support from the state since estate owners were key allies of the colonial state's cultural, political and economic projects. This support manifested itself in different ways. To begin with, colonial land alienation processes saw the local European plantation owners—and other European interests—obtain the best land, which was located in the fertile Shire Highlands in the Southern Region (Pachai, 1978). According to one estimate, at the end of the Johnston land alienation process, '15 percent of the land area in Malawi went to Europeans; this represented about 3 3/4 million acres out of a little more than 25 million acres...in the whole country. For the most part these concessions were held by large estates. About 72 per cent of the area granted belonged to eleven companies or estate holders [and] with the exclusion of the northern grant to the B.S.A Company, most of the land obtained represented the finest arable lands...about one-half of which...became alienated in the form of private estates' (ibid.: 83).

The colonial state's justification for the alienation of land for the estate sub-sector in favourable terms was that the latter would be the engine driving the country's development process, given the so-called backwardness of African agricultural methods. In addition to obtaining the best land in the country, unlike African agrarian producers, the estate owners faced no restrictions from the state as to which crops they could grow. The production of lucrative crops such as flue-cured tobacco and tea was restricted to the European estates (Pike, 1968: 197). Further, estate owners had access to cheap labour, from the African population residing on the estates and elsewhere. The methods used to obtain labour varied, but the main ones were *thangata* and tax rebate. Prior to colonialism, *thangata*, meaning the mutual exchange of labour, among other things, within one's community, was part of the African social and economic arrangements (Kandawire, 1979: 10). The colonial interpretation of *thangata* amounted to forced labour. Africans resisted colonial strategy of forced labour and other exploitative economic practices at various times during the colonial period, such as during the John Chilembwe uprising of 1915.[4]

In the peasant sub-sector, the state's main objective was to control this sector. For example, in 1908, the colonial state introduced a law governing peasant production of cotton, and later instituted marketing mechanisms for peasant producers as a means of controlling their earnings (Vail, 1983: 48). While cotton remained a major feature of state-regulated peasant production and a generator of revenue for the state, tobacco, grown in both the Southern and Central Regions, became another prominent crop in this sub-sector. African growers were restricted to low-earning types of tobacco such as dark-fired western leaf (Pike, 1968: 197). A sharecropping arrangement with the estate owners who would buy the produce and resell it was the first manner in which African production of tobacco emerged. The state allowed, Africans living on Crown Lands to produce tobacco, although in limited plots averaging two acres per grower (ibid.). As with the cotton industry, however, the involvement of Africans in tobacco production saw increased interference by the colonial state. In 1926 for example, the state passed one of the many tobacco ordinances that it issued in efforts to control African involvement in tobacco production. This ordinance stipulated, among other things, that African growers on Crown Land be registered with the newly created colonial body, the Native Tobacco Board, and that those residing on the estates had to register with the respective plantation owners (Rangeley, 1957: 83). By the 1930s, African tobacco production was fully under the control of the colonial state; its development was to face more crippling measures over subsequent decades. For example, in the early 1930s, the colonial state established a policy that reduced African tobacco production to approximately 3750 tons, and instituted another policy that limited the emergence of new growers (Vail, 1983: 63–64). With these measures, the colonial state aimed at limiting African participation in tobacco production at a time when European producers were facing significant economic problems because of the global economic crisis that began in the late 1920s that was marked by declining prices and collapse of international markets for agrarian commodities.

Another colonial strategy of controlling African engagement in the agrarian sector was having the marketing of their agrarian produce monopolized by state marketing boards, a process that further subordinated the peasant sub-sector to the estate sub-sector. The Native Tobacco Board was the first to be established in 1926, while a cotton board was set up in 1952—previously private traders sanctioned by the colonial state marketed cotton (Kettlewell, 1965: 248). In 1952 a marketing board for foodstuffs, specifically maize, peanuts and beans, was set up, and in 1956 all these boards were consolidated to create the Farmers Marketing Board (ibid.). This board controlled all aspects of peasant agrarian production and thus left no room for peasants to make decisions about the future development of their plots or prices for their produce. In establishing these boards, the colonial state claimed that they were more efficient and that they would stabilize prices for peasant producers. The colonial state, however, through the Farmers Marketing Board, set the prices and paid the peasants what it deemed *'reasonable prices'* (emphasis in the original) after taking in profits and covering the costs incurred by the marketing board (ibid.). It is important to note then that the roots of the much maligned postcolonial state's owned enterprises—Chapter 3—lay in the colonial project, yet given its ahistorical entry point, the TDHB's neo-liberal hegemonic development discourse neglects to highlight their historical origins.

The preceding discussion shows the heavy dependency on agrarian production by the colonial state for its political legitimization and capital accumulation strategy. Further, it demonstrates the ways in which at various turning points the politico-economic imperatives of the colonial state marginalized African involvement in the agrarian sector, which was the mainstay of the state's material base. Underlying this approach to African economic practices were paternalistic and racist attitudes, which encouraged the idea of Africans working for the European plantation owners, rather than engaging fully in the key sectors of the economy. As the then Nyasaland Governor claimed in a letter to the Colonial Secretary in 1926, 'the educative value to Natives who engage in this sort of work is great and for some time to come better results will on the whole be obtained from this work than by production by Natives working for themselves' (quoted in Vail, 1983: 62). Overall, one feature characterized the material base of the state inherited by the nationalist political elite when Nyasaland became independent on 6 July , 1964. After a victorious election in 1963, the Malawi Congress Party (MCP), under the leadership of Dr Hastings Kamuzu Banda, took over the reins of state power. The nationalist political elite inherited a state whose economic base was a nascent form of peripheral capitalism heavily dependent on agricultural production. Industrial and commercial development was limited throughout the colonial period, and the agrarian sector formed the material base of the state: in comparative terms, the agricultural and manufacturing sectors accounted for 44.9 and 4.5 per cent respectively of Malawi's GDP (Nyasaland Government, 1962: 16). We turn to a discussion of developments following British rule with a focus on the role of the state in the economy.

State and the economy after colonial rule: history, agency and structure

During the period under review, the structural legacies of colonialism, leading among them a weak economic structure, facilitated the reproduction of Malawi's peripheral position in the capitalist world economy and consolidated the structural dependency of the state on financial flows from the TDHB, and local and international private financial agents; a development that contributed to high levels of debt that continue to characterize Malawi's economy. Compared to countries such as Senegal, Tanzania and Kenya, the Malawian state's structural dependency is acute. In the 1970s, for example, the following were the approximate levels of overseas development assistance in these countries: Kenya, 20 per cent, Senegal 30 per cent, Tanzania 20 per cent and Malawi 40 per cent (Lele, 1991: 19). Malawi's high dependency on financial flows from the TDHB, meant that the Malawian state was more vulnerable to shifts in hegemonic development discourses, and other features of the world order, which informed the development policies favoured by the TDHB.

As for the TDHB's involvement in the country during the period under review, beyond providing loans, it offered the state local and international legitimacy for its politico-economic projects. In the political arena for instance, authoritarian practices by the state were the norm. While authoritarian tendencies of the state were evident as early as 1964, these tendencies deepened with the 1966 adoption of a new constitution. The latter expanded the power of the President and the ruling party, while at the same time limiting the powers of the judiciary, the parliament and the public service sector, and failed to make provisions for the protection of basic human rights (The Republic of Malawi Constitution, 1966). Yet, during this period, there was no outcry or sanction from the TDHB on the deepening despotism of the state and the nature of the state's material practices. In the main, Malawi's steady economic growth in the 1960s and 1970s resulted in it being considered by TDHB as one of Africa's success stories and an example of a developmental dictatorship state. The TDHB's silence on the

Malawian state's authoritarianism reflected its general pre-1980 hegemonic development discourse, discussed in Chapter 3, which saw steady
economic growth and anti-Communism as signs of a peripheral country
on the right developmental path, and authoritarianism as benevolent.

While during this period the TDHB played a significant role in
Malawi's politico-economic processes, this does not mean that the state
did not have agency in its material and political practices. As the discussion will indicate, during this conjuncture, which was underpinned
by a world order characterized by geopolitics of the Cold War and a
hegemonic modernization development discourse, the Malawian state
instituted new measures in the key sectors of the economy. Further, it
embraced capitalist and anti-Communist ideas. President Banda's commitment to these ideas was declared time and time again in various
speeches during this period. For instance, in 1968 he stated, 'on the subject of different systems of government and economics—communism,
socialism and capitalism—I am glad that you have decided that whatever our neighbours may do or may want to do or say, the only
practical system of government and economics is that which passes for
capitalism' (Banda, 1968: 2). To achieve its agrarian based capitalism,
the state introduced key strategies in the agrarian sector. Nonetheless,
it also introduced measures geared to the expansion of its material
base by instituting strategies in the industrial and commercial sectors. In the agrarian sector, the state introduced measures geared to
increasing agrarian production. Rising agricultural productivity was its
core theme beginning as early as 1961, when the MCP won a majority in that year's general elections. The state's first development plan
(1962–1965) declared: 'production in agriculture must increase at a phe-
nomenal rate.... This is what the Government sets out to do in the
present plan' (Nyasaland Government, 1962 46). The state's hopes for
steady economic growth were realized due to local and global politico-
economic conditions. Malawi's annual GDP grew by 4.6 per cent per
annum between 1954 and 1963, by 6.8 per cent between 1964 and
1972 and by 6.4 per cent between 1973 and 1978 (Ghai and Radwan,
1983: 73–74). This development provided legitimacy to authoritarian
ruling elites' relentless refrain, contained in almost every issue of the
Hansard, that Malawi had developed 'beyond recognition' (Hansard,
1993: 1201).

The state's strategies in the agrarian sector were very much influenced by the legacy of colonialism. For example, it reproduced the
colonial pattern of having two agrarian sub-sectors, estate and the peasant sub-sectors with the state mediating their evolution. Like its colonial

predecessor, the state considered the subordination of peasant production to the estate sub-sector as the way forward in the economy. In this
regard, it offered extensive support to this sub-sector at the expense of
peasant producers. For instance, between 1972 and 1981, 76 per cent
of investments and loans by the state owned agrarian public enterprise,
Agricultural Development and Marketing Corporation (ADMARC)—the
equivalent of the colonial state's Farmers Marketing Board—went to
the estate sub-sector (Christiansen and Kydd, 1986: 9). Further, peasant agrarian producers were required to sell their produce to ADMARC
(Kydd, 1984: 333). By monopolizing the extraction of agrarian surplus
from peasants ADMARC accumulated significant profits. For instance, it
generated an estimated K 140 million in profits during the 1970s with
a large proportion of these profits being channelled into investments in
other sectors, including the estate sub-sector (Christiansen , 1984-: 447
and 468). A major reason for ADMARC's profits was the fact that the
institution paid smallholder producers prices well below international
prices, while the estate sub-sector was allowed to secure the Malawi
kwacha equivalent of international prices for its crops (ibid.: 446).

In addition, while peasants participated in the production of cash
crops, their produce was not highly lucrative. This was not an accident, but the result of a deliberate state policy which as in the colonial
moment barred them from growing lucrative crops such as flue-cured
and burley tobacco. The legal basis of this practice during the period
under review was the 1965 Land Act and the other land acts (discussed shortly), all of which expanded the state's control of land in
the customary land category. While the state's agrarian policies resulted
in the exploitation of the peasantry, it is important to note that this
sub-sector was not monolithic. For example, the size of land owned
by smallholder producers varied considerably (Government of Malawi,
1987: 22), a factor that contributed to social class differentiation among
them. Further, the state's 1967 introduction of the category of 'progressive' farmer—commonly referred to in Malawi as *Achikumbe* (equivalent
to the colonial concept of 'master' farmer)—led to further differentiation in this sub-sector (Thomas, 1975: 38–39) for progressive farmers
received 'extension services, credit, infrastructure, storage and marketing facilities, health, housing and rural water, as well as other benefits
through the promotion of irrigation and land improvement' (Ghai and
Radwan, 1983: 94).

Although colonial practices influenced the state's approach to the
agrarian sector, it nonetheless demonstrated its agency in this sector and
others by instituting new measures in the economy. One key measure

that would have significant social and political effects was the reconfiguration of the legal structure governing all aspects of land: ownership, use and disposal. While taking specific forms informed by historical developments, like elsewhere, law and in general, the legal apparatus emerged as a constitutive tool for the state's capitalist development strategies. As with other elements of the state's politico-economic agenda, changes to the legal structure governing all aspects of land were facilitated by the nature of the balance of political forces. During the period under review, pro-authoritarian nationalist elites dominated the country's political space. This was especially the case following the 1964 cabinet crisis because elites that Banda and social forces closely linked to him considered sympathetic to socialism or critical of Banda's increasingly autocratic practices left for exile, and those who stayed where marginalized in the politico-economic arena.[5] Recalling these historical conditions, Vera Chirwa states 'one could no longer express their ideas about our country's development around Dr. Banda since he increasingly made us feel that he owned the country and made us feel as if we had contributed nothing to our country. It was a difficult period but we did not know how difficult it would become following the cabinet crisis. But you know we created him in some way by giving him too much political room when he returned from the UK in 1958 and we did not check his misuse of power early on' (2006).[6] At any rate, in addition to the balance of social forces, given the authoritarian ideological and practices of the state, and the global context of modernization discourse that supported authoritarian state forms, the state easily achieved its agenda of reconfiguring the legal framework pertaining to the land sector without overt political challenge from local social forces and the TDHB.

Changes to the legal framework governing land were achieved through the state's introduction of several legislative acts in the 1960s and 1970s. The 1965 Land Act was the first of these acts. Under this act, three categories of land emerged: customary that is 'all land which is held, occupied or used under customary law'; private land 'all land, which is owned, held on claim, or which is registered as private land under the Registered Land Act'; and public land 'all land which is occupied, used or acquired by the Government' (Government of Malawi, 1965). During this period, small scale producers had access to both customary and public lands—in the latter mainly for those considered as 'progressive' farmers in government-run large-scale agricultural projects that were established with the financial support of the TDHB. The World Bank, for instance, played a key role in the establishment of these projects. Between 1965 and 1988 the Malawian state, in consultation with the TDHB established 12 large-scale agricultural projects to which the World Bank contributed US$ 118 million—two-thirds of its total lending to the country (Lele and Jain, 1991: 130). Britain was also involved in funding these large-scale agricultural projects and the expansion of the estate sub-sector during the period under review. Through the Commonwealth Development Corporation (CDC), Britain was, for instance, involved in the establishment of Vizara Estates Rubber, Karuzi Tea Company and the Kawalazi Estate, which produced tea, macadamia nuts and coffee. Further, it extended the Malawian state three loans to establish the Dwangwa Sugar Corporation, an irrigated estate covering 5200 hectares in the central region. It was also involved in the financing of the Kasungu Flue-Cured Tobacco Authority (Howell, 1991: 443–444).

Beyond the categorization of land, the 1965 Land Act expanded the power of the state in land matters claiming that this was necessary for economic development. Introducing this land act in Parliament, for instance, President Banda claimed: 'land being the most important asset in our economic life, it follows that we have to use it properly.... We can't spend all that 6,000,000 pounds which the World Bank is going to lend us and then let the people use it just anyhow' (Banda, 1965: 653–661). Consequently, the 1965 Land Act, like the others that were to follow—the Customary Land (Development) Act 1967a, the Registered Land Act 1967b, the Local Land Boards Act 1967c and the Malawi Land (Amendment) Act 1967d—expanded the powers of both the state and future presidents and social forces closely linked to the state in land matters. For instance, the 1965 Land Act expanded the power of the Minister of Agriculture and Natural Resources for it gave the Minister the power to 'make and execute grants, leases or other dispositions of public or customary land for any such estates, interests or terms, and for such purposes and on such terms and conditions, as he may think fit' and furthermore officials appointed by the Minister to administer this act could not be legally challenged (Government of Malawi, 1965).

Further, the power of the President in the public and customary land—which was the land category accessible to the majority of Malawians since the colonial era—was expanded with the introduction of these acts. Under the new legal framework governing land, all public land was vested in perpetuity in the President; and all customary land was 'declared to be the lawful and undoubted property of the people of Malawi and...vested in perpetuity in the President' (ibid.). Further, the Malawi Land (Amendment) Act 1967d (Government of Malawi, 1967) stipulated that customary land could be converted into private land, making it open to acquisition by local and foreign owners of capital. While foreign capital—the majority of tea and tobacco estates were owned by multinational corporations such as the Lonrho Group, Bookers (Malawi) Ltd, British-American Tobacco and the Imperial Tobacco Company—played a major role in the estate sub-sector; from the late 1960s, local capital increasingly became involved in it. For instance, research at the Malawi National Archives indicates that President Banda's Press Holdings (latter Press Corporation Limited, hereafter Press) through its subsidiary firm, Press Farming Limited acquired at least 27 large agricultural estates in the Central Region.[7]

The foregoing approaches to the agrarian sector led to the rise of a capitalist economic structure which, like in the colonial era, was dominated by estate agrarian production for export. A reconfigured legal framework and financial backing by the state and the TDHB supported the concentration of lucrative crop production in this sub-sector accounting for its large contribution to the country's export basket. The estate sector share of exports rose from 25.9 per cent to 66.1 in 1964 and 1979 respectively (Pryor, 1990: 86). Increased production in tobacco estates greatly contributed to this development. For example, Press emerged as Malawi's major actor in the production and processing of high earning flue-cured and burley tobacco, and by 1977 the company's contribution to Malawi's total earnings for burley tobacco alone accounted for 26 per cent (Press Corporation Limited, 1995: 13). Beyond the support of the state and the TDHB, external developments such as Southern Rhodesia's unilateral declaration of independence in 1965, contributed to the rise of tobacco production in Malawi because of international economic sanctions on Rhodesia, which included a ban on tobacco exports (Phiri, 1998). Malawi tobacco estate owners benefited greatly from this development which occurred during a favourable conjuncture in international prices for tobacco. To put the rise of the tobacco industry in historical perspective, its share of total exports rose from 37 per cent in 1964–1965 to 54 per cent in 1977–1978 (Ghai and Radwan, 1983: 75).

Because of historical structural legacies, the state's capitalist economic project concentrated on agricultural production. Nevertheless, like other states in the South during this period, the state instituted an industrial strategy underpinned by ISI ideas that aimed at expanding local industrial production. At independence and in the immediate postcolonial period, the commercial and industrial sectors, like the estate sub-sector, were controlled by multinational corporations such as the Lonrho Group, Bookers (Malawi) Limited and David Whitehead Malawi Limited (Dequin, 1969). In efforts to broaden the base of its capitalist development strategy, the state encouraged foreign capital's involvement in this process by creating a favourable investment climate. For example, with regard to investment incentives, the state provided 'exclusive protection [to prospective firms]: i.e., when such protection is granted, no other enterprise is granted licences to manufacture products deemed to be competitive with those manufactured by the protected firm' (Government of Malawi, 1970: 22). The state also prided itself on offering a political framework that was not available elsewhere in Africa:

> The twin threats of nationalization and communist activity, which have appeared in other African countries, are non-existent. Where the Government wishes to participate in a commercial venture, it may do so through the Malawi Development Corporation. As for communist activity, the Republic of Malawi maintains diplomatic relations with no communist government, while there is a complete absence of communism both within the Trade Unions and elsewhere in the country. (Ibid.: 23.)

A core aspect of the state's economic strategy in the industrial and commercial sectors was the establishment of joint ventures between local—private and public—and multinational corporations. In this respect, Malawi Development Corporation (MDC), ADMARC and Press formed joint ventures with foreign capital, and became heavily involved in these sectors in addition to others. For instance, in 1968 the state, through MDC, entered a joint business venture with Bookers Limited in order to benefit from the latter's already established manufacturing, shipping and commercial businesses (Banda, 1969: 19; see also MDC, 1979). Further, the previously mentioned rise of tobacco production led to the growth of tobacco processing industries (Laslett, 1984: 398). By the 1980s, (see Table 4.1) Malawi's industrial and commercial sectors were dominated by ADMARC, MDC and Press, in collaboration with foreign capital. This development gave these enterprises and their foreign partners control of a large proportion of Malawi's economic activities (MDC, 1979; Christiansen, 1984; Press Corporation Ltd, 1995). On the whole, these corporations played a key role in the expansion of Malawi's industrial sector, which in 1964 contributed 8 per cent of the GDP, a contribution that rose to 12 per cent by the beginning of the 1980s (Kaluwa, 1992: 204).

Overall, while Malawi saw increased levels of industrial and commercial activity, industrial development during this period was limited and mostly directed to the domestic market, although agro-processing industries such as sugar, tea and tobacco were export-oriented (ibid.: 218–219). Although contributing to Malawi's economic growth, the rise

Table 4.1 MDC–Press–ADMARC Interlocking Company Ownership, 1979

Company	MDC equity(%)	Press Holdings (%)	ADMARC(%)	Other (% and name)
The Portland Cement Company (1974) Limited	41.6		50.0	8.4 The Development Finance Company of Malawi (Definco)
Commercial Bank of Malawi Limited*	20.0	40.0	10.0	30.0 Bank of America
Malawi Distilleries Limited	40.8	20.0		39.2 International Distilleries and Vintners Limited
Carlsberg Malawi Brewery Limited	27.0	24.0		49.0 United Breweries of Denmark
Agrimal (Malawi) Limited	40.0	40.0		20.0 Massey Ferguson
David Whitehead and Sons (Malawi) Limited	29.0	20.0		51.0 David Whitehead and Sons Technical is a subsidiary of Lonrho
The Import and Export Company of Malawi Limited	51.0	49.0		

Source: Data compiled from Malawi Development Corporation, Annual Report 1979, pp. 7–18.

of these sectors did not transform the state's material base. Hence, the legacies of colonialism that saw the agricultural sector emerge as the backbone of the country's economy set significant structural limits as far as the transformation of the material base of the state is concerned. In the main, the state's pattern in the industrial sector during the period under review displayed features similar to those of others in the South: a mixture of the import–substitution–industrialization model and export-led development marked by 'lack of capital, competition from imperial firms, "liberal" economic policies promoted by states controlled by agro-export sectors, small internal markets, stiff competition in international markets' (Petras, 1978: 90). To conclude here, although Malawi experienced steady increased levels of economic growth because of high prices and stability of the international market for primary commodities, the state's initiatives in the key sectors of the economy did not transform the country's economic structure. Further, while the state demonstrated its agency, historical structural legacies and the geopolitics of the Cold War influenced the nature of its role in the economy. We now turn to a discussion of the state and the economy in South Korea.

State and the economy: South Korea

As we previously mentioned, hegemonic development perspectives present the South Korean state as the premier example of a developmental state, and thus one that other states in the South should emulate. Even President Barack Obama has promoted this view when he compared South Korea and Kenya's economic developments (Baker and Donadio, 2009). Scholars tend to argue that South Korea's rapid economic growth—prior to the crisis of the 1970s and the financial market crash of 1997—were mainly because of market strategies. For Deepak Lal, South Korea's economic trajectory is an example of what social formations in the South could experience if they instituted sound economic policies emphasizing 'free trade, care for microeconomic efficiency and the absence of government controls' (cited in Toye, 1993: 94). Moving beyond the ahistorical and reductionist approach marking hegemonic development perspectives such as Lal's, we argue that historical developments and geopolitical imperatives of the prevailing world order, and state's politico-economic projects shaped the role of the South Korean state in the economy. Thus, like in the Malawian's case, our discussion does not abstract the agency of the state from historical, structural and conjunctural factors.

Establishment of Japanese colonialism

The emergence of contemporary South Korea has its roots in historical developments that occurred during the era of Japanese colonialism and World War II. In the 1880s, the Korean peninsula was a major theatre of geopolitical competition among various powers, particularly the United States, China, Russia and Japan, as they vied with each other for economic and political advantage in the region. In the case of China and Japan, the competition for control of Korea deepened in the late 1880s and subsided only with the defeat of China in the Sino–Japanese War of 1885. Following this event, Russia and Japan tried to out-manoeuvre each other in their endeavour to conquer and control Korea, an intense competition that led to the onset of the Russo–Japanese war in 1904, which resulted in Russia's defeat in 1905. This development had significant implications for Korea and Japan. With the signing of the Treaty of Portsmouth, Japan 'acquired the Russian possessions in southern Manchuria' and thus acquired a wide opening to dominate the Korean peninsula (Wade, 1978: 7–8).

In 1910, Japan annexed Korea, a development that marked the beginning of over three decades of colonial rule and ended the 500-year Yi dynasty rule. In the economic arena, an agrarian bureaucratic apparatus that was heavily involved in the extraction of surplus from agrarian producers underpinned Yi dynastic rule. Koreans resisted Japanese colonialism for most of the first decade, but the ruthless responses by the colonial state to the March 1919 anti-colonial movement—which saw members of this movement go underground and some into exile until the 1940s—contained dissent. Like European colonialism, Japanese colonial rule imposed oppressive political, cultural and economic structures. Mirroring their European counterparts, the Japanese colonial administration brutalized the local population. On the cultural front, for instance, the colonial state insisted on the adoption of Japanese as the language of instruction in the schools and communication at home and limited the teaching of the Korean language to the first three years of elementary education (ibid.:13). The colonial state also forced Koreans to adopt Japanese names; for example, General Park Chung Hee, the post-1961 military dictator, had the Japanese name Okamoto Minoru. Further, Koreans were required to demonstrate their loyalty to the Japanese emperor and to engage in the colonizing society's religious practices (Hart-Landsberg, 1993: 13). The colonial state brutalized Koreans who resisted Japanese rule in various ways, including imprisonment, forced exile and execution, throughout most of the colonial period, especially during the first decade as the colonial state was pushing to consolidate its power (Peattie, 1984).[8]

Japan established a state apparatus in Korea during the first decade of colonialism. In this process, the Japanese Meiji revolution acted as the reference point. While authoritarianism and the centralization of power was a central element of the Japanese state during the Meiji period, the colonial state greatly expanded this political ideology and practice in Korea. At the apex of the colonial authoritarian state structure was the Government-General, who in the first decade was a military official with the most extensive power in Korea's economic, cultural and political arenas. Military officials, who dominated the upper echelons of the colonial state apparatus, aided the Government-General in his duties (Kohli, 1999: 103). To achieve its politico-economic objectives, the Japanese colonial state established an extensive security and surveillance system. As part of this process, within the first decade of colonial rule, the state established an extensive police network resulting in the creation of 13 provincial police centres, 250 stations at both the county and municipal levels and 2599 police sub-stations situated in Korea's 2504 townships. By 1926, the requirements of such intensive policing had pushed the number of police officers up to 18,463 (Chen, 1984: 223–224). As a means of ensuring control at a high level of colonial authority, the state vested policing power in the hands of the provincial governors and not local police officers (ibid.: 222–223). In addition to securing order for Japan's colonial interests, the state used its extensive security apparatus as an avenue for state propaganda and ideological control. During the war period in the late 1930s, for example, the police force was mandated to organize and reward Koreans who participated in 'current [political and military] situation discussion groups (*jikyoku zadankai*)' which were established to help contain dissent and tame Koreans who entertained 'dangerous thought' in the eyes of the state (ibid.: 223).

In addition to establishing an expansive security system, the colonial state deepened the pre-existing bureaucratic apparatus. Modelled along the modernizing logic of the Meiji bureaucracy and building on the legacy of Korean Yi bureaucratic dynasty, the colonial state established an extensive bureaucratic apparatus staffed by Japanese military and civilian officials in addition to Koreans. In comparative terms, the number of these officials was large:

> Comparing the French administrative presence in Vietnam with that of the Japanese in Korea underscores this point. France ruled Vietnam, which in 1937 had a population of 17 million people, with approximately 3,000 French administrators, 11,000 regular French troops, and about 38,000 Vietnamese who served either in the administration or the militia. The Japanese, in contrast, ruled approximately 21 million Koreans with a colonial administration employing 246,000 Japanese and an additional 63,000 Koreans. Nearly 42 percent of all Japanese in Korea in 1937 were in government service. (Hart-Landsberg, 1993: 106)

Colonialism, economy and legacies

The establishment of an authoritarian bureaucratic state facilitated not only the political aims of the colonial state but also its economic project. In Japan during the Meiji restoration period, the state played the central role in the economy and other matters. During this period, it was the state 'that conceived modernization as a goal and industrialization as a means, that gave birth to the new economy in haste and pushed it unrelentingly as an ambitious mother her child prodigy' (Landes, 1965: 182). Although as in other colonial contexts, Japanese colonialism in Korea enhanced its industrial growth, and served its other economic and political needs; this process left important legacies that would shape later developments. Two economic sectors—agriculture and industry— witnessed major transformations during the colonial period. As in Malawi, the colonial state's involvement in the agrarian sector began with a massive land survey, which took place in Korea immediately following annexation in 1910. The survey resulted in the classification of all the land in the country and with that accomplished the introduction of a land tax to expand the colonial state's material base (Myers and Saburo, 1984: 428–429). With the introduction of the land tax, the Japanese colonial state acquired a new and stable source of revenue as it had done at home following the Meiji agricultural reforms. According to one estimate, in colonial Korea in the period between 1910 and 1918 the land tax rose from ¥ 6.6 to ¥ 9.8 million (ibid.).

The surveying and establishment of colonial property rights shifted the power balance in the land sector. Japanese colonial authority and capitalists were the main beneficiaries of the land classification process.

As in British ruled Malawi, the most valuable and productive land was acquired by colonial interests. Japanese interests, for instance, owned over half of the best farmland in the highly productive areas of the South and, because of this pattern of land ownership, they accumulated enormous land rents ranging between 40 and 60 per cent annually and their production of rice accounted for 60 per cent of colonial rice exports to Japan (Ho, 1984: 373–374). This dominance of Japanese interests in the agrarian sector awarded them great social and political power, which, like the British planter class in Malawi, they could use to bargain with the state. Further, this social reality 'provided Japanese landowners tremendous economic and political leverage over individual Korean.... peasants, and they undoubtedly used this leverage to maximize their rent and to gain a larger share of agricultural income than would otherwise have been the case' (ibid.: 373). Nonetheless, as part of the Japanese political strategy of creating a local collaborating class and as a strategy of divide and rule, members of the traditional landlord oligarchy were given rights to their land on condition that they develop it along the lines of the economic projects promoted by the colonial state. During the Yi Dynasty, these landlords (*yangban*)—a social class with many privileges; exempted from paying taxes, forced labour and farm labour, in addition to other privileges such as extracting land rents from the peasants—were at the apex of the agrarian land power structure (Myers and Saburo, 1984: 423). Overall, the colonial land classification process weakened, but did not eliminate their power. Further, the reconfiguration of land ownership led to increased tenancy, approximately 75 per cent in the rural areas, and increased social dislocation for the majority of peasants (Chen, 1984: 230). Korean peasants, however, resisted the colonial state's land classification project and agrarian policy, a development that resulted in increased conflict between the peasants and indigenous and colonial landed interests, but the militarization of Korean society severely limited the political agency of the peasants in this struggle (ibid.).

The aim of colonial reconfiguration of land ownership was to open the door for the state to push its agrarian strategy in order to provide Japan with raw materials for its industrialization process and to achieve food security for the Japanese population. Thus, cotton and rice production was promoted relentlessly by the colonial state until resistance emerged in the 1930s from Japanese rice farmers who felt increasingly threatened by the importation of rice from Korea (Ho, 1984: 363). In terms of production, between 1932 and 1936, colonial interests at the expense of local consumption exported over half of the rice produced in

Korea to Japan (Chen, 1984: 231). Cotton production was also pushed to meet Japan's industrial needs and the state coerced Korean farmers into abandoning food production to grow more cotton (ibid.). The reconfiguration of land ownership further led to the extraction of minerals such as gold, silver and coal, a practice that contributed greatly to Japan's capital accumulation process (Hart-Landsberg, 1993: 105).

While the focus of the colonial state in the first two decades was the reconfiguring of the agricultural sector, a significant change in its economic strategies in Korea emerged in the late 1920s and deepened in the 1930s. From this period on, the colonial state launched industrial and commercial projects in Korea. Developments in Japan, in this case the onset of a new industrialization phase, which led public and private capital interests to intensify their search for markets and raw material, and investment opportunities generated the turn to industrialization in colonial Korea. To this end, Korea and Japan's newly conquered island of Manchuria became central sites for the achievement of Japan's industrial needs. The colonial industrial strategy in Korea followed the Japanese pattern of having large family-owned conglomerates—*Zaibatsu*—dominating the industrial sector. In Korea, these conglomerates, largely Japanese owned, played a key role in the establishment of an industrial base in the country. Korean owners of capital, while marginalized by the colonial state, also participated in various ways in this process. The leading indigenous owners of capital during this period emerged from members of the pre-colonial ruling strata, who the colonial state in its reordering of the local political structure had appointed as 'peers' in 1910. As the 1910 Imperial Ordinance stated, '[t]he blood relatives of Prince Yi, other than those accorded the status of princes of the Blood, men of high birth, and those who had rendered great services to the state, to the number of 76 in all, were created peers... among whom were 6 Marquises, 3 Counts, 22 Viscounts and 45 Barons' (McNamara, 1990: 45). From this peerage cohort emerged several Korean leading owners of capital, such as 'Marquis Pak Yong-hyo of Kyongsong Spinning and Viscount Min Yong-hwi of the Hanil Bank' (ibid.).

The colonial economic strategy saw rapid industrialization in Korea. Between 1925 and 1936, 'the total production of commodities rose from 17.7 percent in 1925, to 31.3 percent in 1936, and to 39 percent in 1939. Within the manufacturing sector itself, the share of heavy and chemical industries rose from 16.5 percent in 1930 to 47 percent in 1939' (Hart-Landsberg, 1993: 106). At the same time, the colonial state promoted the emergence of the commercial sector and controlled its evolution through the state-supported peninsular-wide chambers of commerce, with the Chosen Chamber of Commerce and Industry acting as the arch-administrator of these chambers (McNamara, 1990: 46). As per state stipulation, membership in branches of the Chamber of Commerce was mandatory and although power imbalances permeated the modalities of these chambers, changes in laws governing their operations in 1915 resulted in Korean involvement (ibid.). This push for rapid and extensive promotion of both light and heavy industries in a colonial context differentiates Japanese colonialism from European colonial projects in places such as Malawi and elsewhere.[9] Granted the major beneficiaries were Japanese interests, but as Bruce Cummings argues, 'Japan is the only colonial power to have located various heavy industries—steel, chemicals, hydro-electric power—in its colonies, a remarkable fact when considered comparatively. They were built during the second grand phase of the Japanese industrialization process' (1984: 487). Industrialization was also accompanied by extensive infrastructural projects which resulted in the establishment of 'an extensive network of railways in the colony, so that by 1945 Korea had the most developed rail system in Asia outside of Japan.... [A]long with the development of roads and ports, this infrastructure put Korea substantially ahead of other developing countries in 1945' (ibid.).

In the evolution of its economic projects, the colonial state established a state–capital alliance, with the state taking the lead. Throughout the colonial period, Japanese firms such as the Oriental Development Company (ODC) were heavily involved in the evolution of Korea's colonial capitalist development. The ODC, for example, was involved in the agricultural, financial and industrial sectors. By 1942, this firm's extensive economic activities in Korea included 'an authorized capital of 100 million yen and 62.5 million yen paid-in, and an annual budget of 512.5 million yen' (McNamara, 1990: 41). In the case of the financial sector, the colonial state reconfigured the banking sector to ensure its control and to make it easier for the banks to provide credit to capitalist interests. The Bank of Chŏsen, in which the colonial state through the Government-General was the major shareholder, was the central pillar in the provision of credit in all sectors of the economy (ibid.: 41). In industrial and agricultural sectors, credit and other financial support were in large measure provided by the Chŏsen Industrial Bank, in which the state and the Japanese Imperial Household had significant shares. Within a decade of its establishment in 1918, the Bank had deepened its operations in Korea with extensive involvement in all the key sectors of economy. According to Dennis McNamara:

[The Bank] invested directly in infrastructure development on the peninsula, especially in transportation, and in various projects coinciding with the wider economic plans of the state. Such projects were usually undertaken in cooperation with other state-supported institutions such as the Bank of Chosen, the ODC, the Chŏsen Savings Bank, and Chosen Trust.... [F]inancial help for agricultural development, particularly for irrigation and land reclamation projects, represented a major area of Industrial Bank activity. Subsidies and low-interest loans for extensive land reclamation provided lucrative opportunities for larger firms with sufficient capital and technology to undertake the risky projects, but few Korean firms participated until the third decade of colonial rule when the Samyang Company added considerable acreage through projects supported by the bank subsidies. (Ibid.: 42)

By the 1940s, colonial state-led capitalist development had generated changes that would influence postcolonial political and economic processes. In terms of class formation, the colonial agricultural strategy saw increased tenancy and loss of livelihood for a large number of Koreans, especially the peasantry. This development, coupled with the industrialization push of the 1930s, saw most Koreans forced to seek means of livelihood in the emerging industrial centres, a process that led to the emergence of an urban working class (Cummings, 1984: 489). In sheer numbers, 'in 1931, there were only 106,781 factory workers and 35,895 mine workers employed in Korea. By 1937 ... those numbers had grown to 207,000 and 162,000 respectively. Finally, in 1944, approximately 600,000 Koreans were employed in factories and 350,000 in mines' (Hart-Landsberg, 1993: 107). As for the emergence of a Korean capitalist class, given the dominance of Japan's economic interests, its formation was constrained, nonetheless, as McNamara's (1990) study of business enterprises in Korea during the colonial period shows, a nascent capitalist class did emerge.[10] Unlike Malawi's experience with British colonial rule, on the eve of independence Korea had a diversified economy with an industrial base underpinned by both light and heavy industries. In addition, the country was incorporated into a 'Japan-centered regional' (Kim, 2006: 66) economic system and in turn the world system, not only as a producer of primary commodities but also a supplier of industrial commodities. While not being the sole determinant of politico-economic developments after Japanese colonialism, these structural legacies would greatly influence developments after this period.

Emergence of South Korea, state and economy: historical conjuncture, 1940s–1950s

Global political developments in the 1940s brought other changes to Korea. While Korean resistance to colonial rule continued—albeit covertly—even after the brutal containment of anti-colonial forces following the March 1919 movement, Japan's surrender during World War II opened a window of opportunity for anti-colonial social forces. Between the years 1945 and 1947, a powerful political movement whose origins lay in leftist anti-colonial resistance practices of earlier periods emerged as a powerful political force. This movement formed the Committee for the Preparation of Korean Independence in August 1945 and within a short period established branches throughout the country. By September, following a national congress, the movement emerged as the backbone of Korea's anticipated first postcolonial government by establishing the Korean People's Republic (KPR) (Hart-Landsberg, 1993: 119–120). Some of the core frames of the KPR were calls for national liberation and the establishment of a democratic state, empowerment of the workers through the nationalization of properties owned by Japanese and Korean capitalists and nationalization of the industrial and other key sectors of the economy (ibid.: 120–121). This political-economic agenda threatened the interests of local owners of capital and, in the context of Cold War geopolitics, members of the Western alliance, especially the USA, read it as a declaration of commitment to the establishment of a Communist society. As the competition between the Eastern and Western geopolitical blocs escalated following the collapse of Japanese resistance, the USA put a proposal to the Soviet Union to have Korea divided on the thirty-eighth parallel and these two parties agreed. This development laid the foundation for the official division of Korea in 1948.

The rise of the KPR and Korea's independence was short lived. The KPR political-economic project served neither the interests of the USA nor those of some elements of the propertied class in Korea. With the US military occupation of the southern part of Korea firmly established in 1945, the stage was set for the installing of political forces allied to American geopolitical interests. The military government nonetheless left the centralized and bureaucratic state apparatus established by the Japanese colonial authority intact and used the extensive police network to contain opposition forces (ibid.: 123–124). Thus, a concerted effort by the US government to dismantle the political base and legitimacy of leftist forces marked the period leading to the general elections of 1948.

The US objective of having a state allied to its geopolitical interests was achieved with the ascendancy to power of political forces allied to the anti-communist leader Syngman Rhee in the 1948 elections. This year also marked the official division of the country into two states, with the North emerging as the Democratic People's Republic and falling under the Soviet bloc, while the South became the Republic of Korea and firmly incorporated into the Western Cold War geopolitical-economic alliance.

The 1950s was a turbulent period for South Korea. To begin with, Rhee's regime, while supported by the USA, did not have legitimacy with the majority of Koreans and hence political instability was the norm during this period. Further, the onset of the Korean War saw massive social and economic dislocation in the country (Wade and Kim, 1978: 17). The War, however, resulted in the implementation of long-awaited land reform, which Rhee's regime and members of the landed gentry had previously opposed even though it had the support of the USA military government. As with the USA military government's original push for land reform in 1946, the land reform that occurred in 1952 was a result of fear of leftist forces rising again given the gains that the communist North was making in the war and the re-emergence of peoples' committees and the redistribution of land in some areas (Lie, 1998: 10–11). Nonetheless, this land reform marked an important political, economic and cultural development in South Korea. While the Japanese land survey identified land ownership and instituted a capitalist regime of property rights for some Koreans, the process did not fundamentally reconfigure the political economy of land among Koreans in the country. As mentioned earlier, this process led to increased tenancy and the retaining of *yangban* elites' social and economic power, albeit weakened. The 1952 land reform restricted ownership and thus significantly reduced the cultural and economic power of the landed gentry, especially in the rural areas. Changes emerging from these reforms were evident by the mid-1950s:

> One-third of farmland changed hands, which affected two-thirds of farming households. In 1944, the richest 3 percent of farming households owned 64 percent of all the farmland, by 1956, the top 6 percent owned only 18 percent. Tenancy dropped from 49 percent to 7 percent of all farming households.... Many peasants achieved their age-old dream of owning the land they tilled. (Ibid.: 11–12)

Economic reconstruction efforts began right after the end of the Korean War. The state through various institutions, mainly the Korean Reconstruction Bank (KRB) in addition to other local public, quasi-public and private financial sites, led the reconstruction project. Support from the KRB, for example, enabled the growth of the textile industry through extensive loans awarded to this sector. These loans accounted for 30 per cent of the Bank's total funding to the manufacturing sector in 1957, while commercial financial lending to the same sector amounted to US\$ 11 billion in the same year (McNamara, 1990: 129). As with the Japanese colonial state, then, relations between the state and owners of capital continued to be close, a factor that led to the rapid accumulation of capital by local owners of capital. In the 1950s, as would be the case in later decades, because of the geopolitical context of the Cold War, South Korea received significant amounts of foreign aid from the USA. From a total of US\$ 2.3 billion in foreign aid to the country, US aid amounted to 85 per cent (Lie, 1998: 29). The nascent capitalist class also benefited financially because of increased access to the US market. As part of its political project of containing Communism in East Asia, the USA lowered market access barriers for South Korean and Taiwanese goods following World War II (Shin, 1998: 17). Further, according to McNamara, US foreign aid through the International Cooperation Administration 'for plants and technology in manufacturing alone amounted to \$57.1 million between 1955 and 1959 [while]...supplies and aid for purchase of raw cotton amounted to \$138 million between 1953 and 1959' (1990: 130). The reconstruction effort however did not contribute to political gains for Rhee's regime, although the land reform instituted in 1952 did contain popular dissent, especially among peasants, and won the regime some measure of legitimacy. During this period, Rhee's regime autocracy deepened using avenues it inherited from the colonial legal framework and The 1948 National Security Law. Rhee's brutal authoritarian practices were legendary in the 1950s. For example, in addition to the execution of political leaders such as the Progressive Party's leader Cho Pongam, he pushed though a constitutional amendment so that he could run again following the end of his two terms in 1954 (Hart-Landsberg, 1993: 134).

State and South Korea's capitalist development 'miracle': General Park Chung Hee's conjuncture

Rhee's repressive tactics and the rigging of the 1960 elections brought about the end of his regime. The brutal actions of the state did not have their intended effects, as the student-led resistance movement of the early 1960s gained momentum, forcing Rhee out of office and, with the help of the USA, into exile in Hawaii (ibid.: 135). The student movement and leftist forces during this period demanded not only reunification with the North, but fundamental changes to the country's political-economic agenda. This trend and the perceived (especially by the military and the US government) inability of Chang Myon's regime to contain this movement, laid the basis for the 1961 military coup of Major General Park Chung Hee, whose regime, which lasted until 1979, is credited with ushering in South Korea's development 'miracle'. As highlighted previously, until the mid-1970s and increasingly after the 1997 financial crisis, hegemonic development perspectives portrayed the South Korean state as a model developmental authoritarian state, the kind advocated by a range of modernization theorists (Chapter 3). This focus on the state and authoritarianism, however, offers only partial insights into an understanding of South Korea's capitalist development trajectory prior to the rise of neo-liberal development discourse and other features of the current world order. As in the case of Malawi and elsewhere, the state was an important actor in the economic arena during the period under review. Yet, in economic terms, the results were different in the cases of Malawi and South Korea. Our contention here is that South Korea's so-called economic miracle was influenced by historical developments and the modalities of the prevailing world order, and thus not solely by the existence of a rational developmental bureaucracy, staffed by a politically insulated technocratic strata or, as claimed by the World Bank, by an adherence to 'market based outcomes' (World Bank, 1990: 299). We build this argument briefly by highlighting the influence of historical developments, the state and elements of the prevailing world order on South Korea's capitalist development trajectory during the era of General Park's authoritarian regime.

In basic hegemonic development terms, the 1960s and the early 1970s in South Korea are considered as characterized by rapid economic transformation along capitalist lines. According to some estimates, starting from a low base of 4 per cent GDP in the 1950s, by 1967 the figure had risen to 7.8 per cent (Chau, 2001: 118). As in Malawi and contrary to the World Bank analysis, the South Korean state played a central role in this process, but with different outcomes. While the material base of the state in Malawi remained a narrow agrarian and monocultural one, the South Korean state expanded its economic base to include by the 1970s a heavy industrial sector. Further, while Malawi experienced increased economic growth, the South Korean experience during the period under review yielded different results. What explains these differences? In the case of the South Korean state's material base, while the Korean War disrupted its economic base—and to protect its own economic interests, the USA was not keen on deepening the country's industrial sector—on the eve of General Hee's military takeover, the industrial base established by Japan remained. While taking cognizance of the fact that South Korea inherited mainly light industries, since heavy industrial development had been concentrated in the North during the era of Japanese colonialism, this inheritance provided the state strong starting structural conditions as it embarked on its capitalist economic strategies during the period under review. Thus, while the state, as will be highlighted here, demonstrated its agency in the economic arena, to ignore the historical legacy of the colonial state's industrialization process and other legacies, as well as the imprint of politico-economic imperatives of the prevailing world order as hegemonic development perspectives tend to do leads to limited insights.

In terms of capital accumulation strategies, an export-led industrialization project dominated the state's economic agenda. To achieve this goal, the state reconfigured its bureaucratic apparatus and created three institutional sites with a mandate of pushing economic development along capitalist lines: the Economic Planning Board (EPB), the Ministry of Trade and Industry, the Ministry of Finance and the President's Economic Secretariat. These institutions built on the legacy of the bureaucratic tradition that existed in the dynastic era, and which the Japanese colonial state deepened. Like other military and capitalist elites in South Korea, General Hee was an admirer of the Japanese modernist processes epitomized in the Meiji restoration project. He trained in Japanese military institutions in Manchukuo and in Tokyo, and was a lieutenant in the Japanese Imperial Air Force (Hart-Landsberg, 1993: 139). The Japanese experience greatly influenced his approach to economic development and the nature of the role of the state in economy. Like President Kamuzu Banda of Malawi, TDHB, and modernization theorists, General Hee also believed that an authoritarian state that could provide order and stability was central in the struggle for capitalist development in South Korea. In his view, the 1950s and early 1960s was a lost period in developmental terms, and the reason for this was the lack of political order and stability (1971: 105). For him, 'economic development in the capitalist manner requires not only an immense investment of money and materials, but also a stable political situation and competent administrators' (ibid.).

During the period under review, an authoritarian and coercive state with a bureaucratic apparatus underpinned by extensive power in the economy embarked on a path aimed at deepening South Korea's capitalist development. The state utilized the aforementioned reconfigured institutional pillars not only as sites for development policy formulation, but also as channels for extensive support for local owners of capital in their capital accumulation endeavours, and to control the involvement of foreign capital in the economic arena. The EPB, however, was at the apex of this institutional machinery for capitalist development. Under the new legal framework that emerged following the 1961 coup, the EPB was mandated to ensure the establishment of 'comprehensive plans for the development of the national economy and to manage and to regulate the execution of the development plans' (Economic Planning Board, 1982: 407). The central role of the EPB in South Korea's economy stemmed from its extensive power in, for instance, controlling credit and finance for economic activities and reviewing investment proposals of both local and foreign capital. The close links between the state and owners of capital continued during this period. In the case of local owners of capital—*Chaebol*, whose organizational structure is based on the previously mentioned Japanese family-owned *Zaibatsu*—the state supported their export-led economic activities by providing 'tax exemptions, allocation of credits at zero or negative interest rates, multiple exchange rates, direct cash payments, permission to retain foreign exchange earnings for private use and the privilege to import restricted commodities' (Chau, 2001: 126). From the perspective of the state, this approach would provide incentives for private capital to engage in productive economic activities in line with the state's project of export-led capitalist development. At the same time, the strategy was also a tool for disciplining individual capitalists who, at one point or another, the state considered enemies of its politico-economic strategies. In addition to receiving support from the bureaucratic machinery of the state mandated to push rapid economic development, local owners of capital received support from a range of quasi-state institutions. For example, the Korean Trade Promotion Corporation, the Korean Trade Association and the Korean Institute for Science and Technology, and owners of capital had opportunities to dialogue with General Park during the regularly held Monthly Export Promotion Conference, which he always attended (Ibid.).

During the period under review, two phases marked South Korea's export-led industrialization process. In the first phase, the state embarked on an expansion of the pre-existing light industrial sector, and by the late 1960s, the state began laying the foundation for the establishment of heavy industries. During both phases, the state's strategy was to protect the local industrial sector and local markets from foreign competition through the restriction of foreign commodities. This restrictive approach to foreign capital's involvement in the economy provided room for the rise and consolidation of local capital ownership, especially the large *Chaebols*. By the 1970s, most of the leading *Chaebols*—such as, Hyundai, Samsung, Daewoo and Lucky-Gold Star— which had increasingly diversified their economic activities—played a central role in the state-led industrialization project (Kim, 1997: 127–128). These conglomerates also benefited in direct and indirect ways through business ventures with their counterparts and contacts in Japan. The owner of Samsung, Lee Byung-chull, and the Lotte Group are some examples of this phenomenon (Lie, 1998: 61). Placed in a comparative context, between 1967 and 1971 foreign direct investment (FDI) in South Korea stood at 3.7 per cent, while during the same period FDI levels in Mexico, Brazil and Thailand amounted to 36.6, 33.8 and 26.1 per cent respectively (Hart-Landsberg, Ibid). It is important to note that South Korea's restrictive measures on foreign capital did mean that the state embraced the idea of autarky. As in China (Chapter 6), the main objective of this strategy was to tailor foreign capital's involvement in the economy to the state's economic aims. In line with its objective to expand—as discussed below—the country's industrial sector, for instance in the 1970s, the South Korean state allowed more room for foreign capital's involvement in the manufacturing sector as these figures from 1978 indicate:

The export/sales ratio of multinationals was especially high in targeted light manufacturing industries such as apparel (99.5 percent), textiles (72.2 percent), and electrics and electronics (65.4 percent). Multinational corporations were also major producers in targeted import-substitution industries such as petroleum (90.4 percent of local output), chemicals (44.2 percent), electrics and electronics (40.9 percent), and metal assembly and machinery (24 percent). (Ibid.)

While the focus on light industries had generated steady and high levels of economic growth in the 1960s, by the early 1970s the state shifted its industrial strategy towards the promotion of heavy industries. The state's heavy industrial policy covered the following industries: petrochemicals, industrial machinery, ship building, electrical and steel. Like in Malawi and as in other political-economic arenas, the South Korean state instituted a legal framework and other support mechanisms aimed at promoting its heavy industrial strategy. The state embodied the necessary legal stipulations in the 1967–1971 laws and in President Park's 1973 Decree. With the establishment of a Heavy and Chemical Industry

Planning Council, the state consolidated the ascendancy of its strategy. Industries identified as forming the core of the heavy industrial
strategy received extensive support from the state, especially through
the National Investment Fund, established solely for this purpose under
the National Investment Fund Act in 1973 (Chau, 2001: 131). Further,
the state sanctioned what it termed 'Policy Loans' to owners of capital
involved in the heavy industrial sector through the National Investment Fund on favourable terms, with figures amounting to 41 and
51 per cent of 'domestic credit' in 1975 and 1978 respectively (ibid.).
These conditions facilitated the reconfiguration of South Korea's industrial sector. Changes in the country's export basket reflect the impact
of this development. In 1961, exports comprised primary commodities and by 1971 the leading export products were 'clothing, plywood,
other manufactures including wigs and toys, electrical machinery, raw
silk and basic ores [and] by 1976 they were clothing, footwear, fab-
rics, electrical machinery, plywood and telecommunications equipment'
(Hart-Landsberg, 1993: 59).

Situating the state and South Korea's capitalist development

The preceding discussion of the state's economic strategies during the
period, considered as ushering in the South Korean economic miracle, while foregrounding the historical origins of this miracle, clearly
illustrates the agency of the postcolonial state in this process. However,
important as it was, the agency of the state was not the sole factor that
shaped South Korea's capitalist development. As we previously argued,
the manner in which a social formation is incorporated into the world
system and its position in the prevailing world order, while not determining in a mechanistic way the economic process of a given social
formation, nonetheless sets the 'limits of the possible' (Gill, 2008) and
influences this process in other ways. Returning to the nature of South
Korea's incorporation into the world system, at key turning points this
process differed from that of most countries in the South such as Malawi.
To begin with, the country's incorporation in the Japanese-dominated
regional economic system as an exporter of a range of commodities—
even though during the colonial period Japanese interests were the
main beneficiaries of this development—positioned the country advan-
tageously in the world system. Further, South Korea's incorporation into
the US-dominated security and economic architecture in the post-1945
world order greatly influenced the country's capitalist development
path. In addition to the previously mentioned market access to the

USA for its commodities, South Korea and other East Asian countries received extensive aid from the USA as part of the anti-communist containment strategy by the Western bloc. From 1960 to 1970, foreign aid contributed approximately 4 per cent to South Korea's economic growth (Shin, 1993: 145–146). Comparatively, between 1946 and 1978 US foreign aid to South Korea was US$ 6 billion, while its aid to the African and Latin American continents was US$ 6.89 billion and US$ 14.8 billion respectively (Hart-Landsberg, 1993: 145–146).

Being of importance to the achievement of America's security and economic interests opened another window of opportunity for South Korea to receive extensive financial flows during the Vietnam War. Exports of a range of commodities from the country to Vietnam increased during this period. For example, South Korea's earnings from exports of cement and fertilizers rose from US$ 1.5 million in 1967 to US$ 6.1 million in 1970 and in the case of fertilizers from US$ 1.2 million in 1968 to US$ 4.7 million during the same period (Lie, 1998: 64–65). Increased trade between the USA and South Korea, especially in the textile industry, also deepened because of the 'political goodwill' that the latter's involvement in the War as an ally generated in US political circles (US Department of State Bulletin, 1965: 274–278, cited in ibid.: 65). South Korean *Chaebols* such as Hyundai were also contracted by the USA for Vietnam's public infrastructural projects such as ports and roads, a development that gave these firms a chance to expand their economic operations and in the process accrue more economic surplus (Shin, 1998: 18–19). War activities generated over US$ 2 million, which, according to one estimate, accounted for 19 per cent of South Korea's 'foreign exchange earnings' between 1965 and 1973 (Hart-Landsberg, 1993: 148). In addition to public sources, the private banking sector in the USA and other member states of the Western alliance provided loans amounting to US$ 256 million to South Korea during the same period (ibid.).

The close links between South Korea and the hegemonic power of the prevailing world order thus provided the country with extensive financial flows and other forms of support that greatly contributed to the state's economic project. Beyond the financial and other forms of support from the USA, the normalization of the country's relations with Japan greatly benefitted the state's economic agenda. The process leading to the signing of the Normalization Treaty in 1965 was a result of US pressure on General Park's regime, although South Korean Diaspora social-political networks in Japan and the USA also played a role in this process (Lie, 1998). Following the signing of the Normalization Treaty, Japan provided the following levels of financial support to South Korea: US$ 200 million in the form of loans, '$300 million in grants.... [and]

$300 million in commercial credits' and in the years 1966–1967 '$90 million in grants and credits and over $100 million in private commercial banks' in addition to financial support for industrial infrastructural development (Hart-Landsberg, 1993: 145). Further, at the onset of its heavy industrialization strategy, the South Korean state received US$ 160 million from Japan in 1970 (ibid.). With the Normalization Treaty South Korea become deeply integrated into Japanese economic activities and came to depend heavily on the latter for technological transfer and support, an issue that would generate tensions between the two countries by the 1980s.

Conclusion

This chapter has highlighted the role of the state in the economic process in both Malawi and South Korea following the end of colonialism. While illuminating the political agency of these states, the analysis has illustrated the influencing role of historical legacies on this process. Further, the chapter has argued that the nature of the prevailing world order, especially its ideas and geopolitical imperatives played an important role in the evolution of capitalist development projects that the states were pushing in both countries. In addition, we have argued that the nature of each state's material base and their positioning in the world capitalist system set structural parameters of their economic projects in a given historical moment. Overall, the chapter concludes that while mediated by local conditions, global realities influence the nature of the role of the state in the economy and outcomes; issues that are ignored in hegemonic development approaches. Further, defending politico-economic practices of states in the South, such authoritarianism, and corruption, was not the objective here. Rather, our underlying contention was the tendency of hegemonic development discourses to present these practices as if they are biologically embedded among ruling elites in the South, not as a result of complex historical and contemporary developments, and also as practices not limited to Southern contexts. This chapter marks the end of the first part of the book. In different and complementary ways, the focus of the next five chapters is the question of transformation. We begin the discussion with an examination of debates in IR and IPE and global institution sites that are concerned with the question of rethinking global governance given the context of neo-liberal driven globalization and post-Cold War political landscape.

Part II

Neo-liberal and Securitizing World Order: Debating Transformation

5
Global Governance

Global institutions such as the World Bank and the IMF have played a central role in the evolution and consolidation of shifts in the post-1945 world order. As we argued in Chapters 2 and 3, these institutions have influenced key turning points in politico-economic processes in the South. Social movements such as those involved in the World Social Forum process (Chapter 8) increasingly contest the role of these institutions in the South and the world economy. Further, in the last two decades, there has been a growing debate in the fields of IR and IPE concerning the nature and modalities of contemporary global governance institutional complex. From the cosmopolitan tradition, theorists of cosmopolitan democracy consider the promotion of democracy at the global level as central to the reconfiguration of global governance arrangements along democratic lines. According to Anthony McGrew, in the context of contemporary globalization, 'the realization of substantive, as opposed to simply procedural, democracy—that is, a polity cultivating the active citizen as opposed to the passive voter—demands the extension of democracy beyond the nation-state to bring to account those global and transnational forces which presently escape effective democratic control' (1997: 232). For David Held (1995: 99) the political and economic developments that have emerged in the contemporary phase of globalization, call for the need to extend democratic political practices beyond the territorial boundary of nation-states. In this respect, he argues that 'there are disjunctures between the idea of the state as in principle capable of determining its own future, and the world economy, international organizations (IOs), regional and global institutions, international law and military alliances which operate to shape and constrain the options of individual nation-states' (ibid.).

In the case of the South, Held argues that the 'principle of conditionality' (ibid.: 110) whereby the IMF insists on a range of measures
such as limits to social spending, liberalization of financial markets
as conditions for the provision of loans, demonstrates the limitation
of a national-state-centric approach to understanding governance. In
this regard, he concludes that 'while de jure sovereignty may not be
directly infringed, the decision-making process' of global institutions
such as 'the IMF raises serious questions about the conditions under
which a political community is able to determine its own policies and
directions' (ibid.). Other scholars of global governance such as Craig
Murphy (2005: 90) contend that there is a need to re-think and take
seriously the nature of global governance institutional complex for 'ethical and moral' reasons given the political and economic realities of the
contemporary world. While the debate on ways to transform global governance in IR and IPE fields is wide ranging and highly contested, this
chapter's concern is to examine core elements of contemporary debates
situated within the liberal internationalist tradition—both institutional
and scholarly—given this tradition's significant influence on this debate
and its significant role in shaping the formulation and implementation
of policies that have major effects on the North-South power divide.

Transforming global governance: liberal internationalist tradition

In 1995, the UN established the Commission on Global Governance
(hereafter the Commission). The Commission comprised leading figures
from the world of national, global politics and civil society circles. The
Commission's mandate was to provide an analysis of the nature of
the post-Cold War global governance complex in addition to providing
a framework for its transformation. The creation of this Commission
marks one of the core efforts aimed at envisioning global governance
along liberal internationalist lines. According to liberal internationalists, the evolution of the modern world politico-economic order
has generated interdependency among societies, and institutions of
global governance have played a crucial role in facilitating cooperation among the diverse states that make up the contemporary world.
In essence, from this perspective, these institutions are central to the
evolution of world political and economic processes for they provide
stability and are sites of establishing norms and regimes to address
global issues. While institutions of global governance are a central pillar
of the world politico-economic structure, cultural, political and economic developments affect their ability to fulfill their functions in this

structure. Thus, major changes in these arenas in the current era call for the need to rethink the nature and capacity of the pre-existing global governance institutional complex. In this respect, liberal internationalists consider the contemporary epoch as characterized by significant politico-economic changes, which have generated instability and new issues in the arena of global governance. Consequently, they incorporate their vision of reconfiguring the global governance institutional complex in their explanations of these changes. Here we focus on economic and political changes that liberal internationalists highlight as being effects on global governance generated by neo-liberal globalization and the end of the Cold War. In addition, we highlight elements of their vision of transforming the current global governance institutional complex.

For liberal internationalists, the current phase of globalization has generated new economic realities that global governance institutions such as the International Monetary Fund cannot address on their own (Commission on Global Governance, 1995: 137). These realities are a result of economic globalization, a process that has led to deeper global economic interdependency. This interdependency is a result of a core feature of the current process of globalization, which has seen an expanded global reach and power of multinational corporations and the liberation of financial markets; the latter development has resulted in the freeing of capital to move across national borders. As the Commission notes, financial markets and multinational firms operate across spatial scales with limited control from national governments (ibid.: 136–137). The Commission also claims that new technologies and other developments in the era of a neo-liberal world order are contributing to the generation of wealth for all societies. However, it also contends that these developments have also opened up the world economy to instability and to disruption since 'no satisfactory [institutional] mechanism exists to anticipate or respond promptly' to shocks and others forms of instabilities that might emerge in the current era' (ibid.).

The end of the Cold War and the cultural, political and economic processes of globalization are developments that liberal internationalist scholars consider as generating instability and complexity for global governance. For James N. Rosenau (2002) fragmentation and political anxiety are central markers of the contemporary global politico-economic conjuncture. According to him and other analysts within this tradition, the era of bipolarity provided stability in the global system while this current period is marked not only by interconnectedness but also by fragmentation on many levels. In the context of fragmegration Rosenau argues,

...the interactions between worldwide forces pressing for fragmentation and those exerting pressure for integration, fragmegrative dynamics are pervaded with contradictions and tensions. They tug people and institutions at every level of community in opposite directions, often forcing choices favouring localizing or globalizing goals... This pervasiveness of fragmegrative dynamics is readily traceable in a wide variety of situations, from cultural sensitivities to inroads from abroad to fears of jobs lost through the demise of trade barriers, from linguistic distortions fostered by the Internet to environmental degradation generated by expanded productive facilities. (Ibid.: 71)

Global interconnectedness and fragmentation, argue liberal internationalists, make issues such as climate change, poverty, terrorism, drug trafficking, health pandemics, financial markets and other features of the global political economy transnational and, thus, a concern for institutions of global governance: hence the calls for the reconfiguration of these institutions so that they have the capacity to deal with these developments. This would relieve the profound sense of insecurity felt by citizens in various parts of the world because of their knowledge that 'events in any part of the world can have consequences for developments in every other part of the world [and] that the internet and other technologies have collapsed time and distance' (ibid.: 70). In the context of global interdependence, a strengthened global institutional complex will enable global cooperation and the containment of conflict in the modern Hobbesian world that has high potential for chaos and instability (Keohane, 2002a: 325). A way forward in this respect is the adoption of a 'networked minimalism' form of governance:

Networked—because globalization is best characterized as networked, rather than as a set of hierarchies. Minimal—because governance at the global level will only be acceptable.... if its intrusions into the autonomy of states and communities are clearly justified in terms of cooperative results. (Keohane and Nye, 2002a: 204)

The decline of state sovereignty and the capacity of states to address material, cultural, environmental and political issues is another development that liberal internationalists highlight in their call for the transformation of global governance. The localization and globalization tendencies that characterize the contemporary world are contributing to the extension of 'control [mechanisms] that extend beyond national boundaries while others... are leading to the diminution of national entitles and the formation or extension of local mechanisms. The combined effect of the simultaneity of these contradictory trends is that of lessening the capacities for governance located at the level of sovereign states and national societies' (Rosenau, 2005: 50). Overall, there is a consensus among liberal internationalists that while states continue to serve important functions, their capacity to fulfil their traditional functions is limited not only because of economic pressures generated by economic globalization but also by the reality of deepening interconnectedness that has led to the emergence of 'global neighbourhood' (Commission on Global Governance, 1995: 55). For the Commission, rapid globalization 'is currently outstripping the capacity of governments to provide the necessary framework of rules and co-operative arrangements to ensure stability and prevent abuses of monopoly and other market failures. National solutions to such failures within a globalized economy are severely limited' (ibid.: 137).

While states are experiencing a decline in their authority, the emergence of an activist bloc of states from the South calling for reforms in the global governance institutional complex is a development that is posing a challenge to the pre-existing system of global governance. According to liberal internationalists, in the early 1970s, a radical bloc of peripheral states embarked on a campaign calling for the establishment of a new international economic order. By the mid-1970s, their campaign disintegrated. In the last decade a new bloc of activist states from the periphery has emerged which is increasingly calling for the reconstitution of global governance arrangements especially as they pertain to the modalities of international trade. In 2003 for example, this bloc of states, vigorously contested the unequal nature of the WTO trading regime at the Ministerial meetings in Cancun. The collective protest of this bloc of states comprising Brazil, South Africa, Tanzania, Pakistan and many others—with the support of civil society groups—resulted in the collapse of the scheduled trade negotiations. While these states continue to generate tensions and instability for global governance, liberal internationalists contend that their aims are different from the bloc of the 1970s. Their demands are mainly fuelled by a desire for inclusion at the table of the contemporary global governance complex, which is led and controlled by the leading states and a diverse group of civil society drawn from the North (Keohane and Nye, 2002b: 224). As such, compared to the earlier bloc, this new bloc of activist states is not calling for fundamental restructuring of the world economic order.

The current phase of globalization has seen the rise of diverse sites of private political and economic authority. The emergence of these non-state sites of governance presents new realities in world politics and consequences for global governance. As Rosenau argues 'considered in a fragmegrative worldview, not only have states lost some of their earlier dominance of the governance system, but also the lessening of their ability to evoke compliance and govern effectively is in part due to the growing relevance and potential of control mechanisms sustained by transnational and subnational systems of rule' (1997: 173). These non-state sites of governance include non-governmental organizations (NGOs) that, in the era of rolling back the role of the state in the economy, are increasingly involved in the provision of public goods such as education, health and emergency relief efforts. As Craig Murphy argues:

> Today it is, more often than most of us realize, NGOs which run the refugee camps, provide disaster relief, design and carry out development projects, monitor and attempt to contain the international spread of disease, and try to clean up an ever more polluted environment. Moreover, most of them do so primarily with public funds from major donor governments and intergovernmental organizations, officially enamored of the efficiency of NGOs and the 'empowerment' that they foster, but also, many analysts suspect, because NGOs provide these necessary international public services on the cheap. (2005: 95).

In the era of neo-liberal global governance, the Commission considers NGOs as having the capacity to articulate 'genuine development needs' and map out development projects, and institute them in an efficient manner (1995: 35). Currently, developmental NGOs and private profit making firms are increasingly involved in development policy formation and projects at various levels. In the case of humanitarian aid delivery, Mark Duffield's work has extensively demonstrated the increased role of NGOs in this sector, in addition to their incorporation in the security architectures of dominant states in the world order.[1] Through their extensive networks, NGOs play a central role in the generation and dissemination of norms and expectations of the global governance institutional complex at this historical moment marked by uncertainty. Fundamentally, these networks facilitate the emergence of 'rule systems and control mechanisms' through their regular contact and in the process 'a form of recurrent behaviour that systematically links the efforts of controllers to the compliance of controllees through either formal or informal channels' (Rosenau, 2005: 46–47) in the world order. Transnational networks comprising both private and public entities then engage in diverse ways and in the process contribute to global governance (ibid.). For Keohane, various networks, some of which are inter-state while others are private, link diverse groups of transnational NGOs: this complex web of connections is part of the reality of contemporary global governance (2002b: 225).

Essentially, liberal internationalists envision the emergence of a global governance institutional complex underpinned by technocratic networks of experts at various spatial scales. As Keohane argues, as in the earlier phases of globalization, the success of the current one is dependent on the existence of institutions that can generate 'effective governance' marked by cooperation by interstate institutions and a range of actors drawn from private authority sites (2002a: 325). The expansion of global governance to include public and private institutions at regional, national and global levels will provide a more stable world order, as these institutions can respond in a coordinated manner to global issues such as conflict, environmental stress, terrorism and many others. Moreover, these institutional networks' embrace of universal 'neighbourhood values' (Commission on Global Governance, 1995) of justice and equity, liberty, respect for life, mutual respect, caring and integrity, will enable them to work closely in efforts to ensure stability and well-being for all in the new 'global neighbourhood' (ibid.). With the doctrine of public–private sector partnership and the dominance of the view that the private sector is more efficient and productive than the state, liberal internationalists view owners of private capital as crucial actors in global governance. As we highlight in Chapter 9, in the context of liberalized finance, the enormous structural and other forms of power that underpin transnational private capital, such as multinational corporations, give it a comparative edge when compared to states in the neo-liberal world order. Highlighting the central role of private capital in the emergent system of global governance the Commission states:

> The extensive movement in favour of market-driven approaches... has recast transnational corporations into mobilizers of capital, generators of technology, and legitimate international actors with a part to play in an emerging system of global governance. Many TNCs, now manufacture on several continents, buying and selling world... The change in the economy policy environment has

also helped many vigorous small entrepreneurs emerge, particularly in developing countries. This is another facet of the trend towards greater empowerment world-wide. (Commission on Global Governance, 1995: 26)

For liberal internationalists, when compared to national state apparatus, the reliance on expertise and technocratic knowledge of a multi-layered network of global governance will result in efficient responses to global issues, for the shared values of these expert networks will mitigate tensions and disagreements that tend to delay and cause inefficient responses to global issues. These public–private networks of global governance will enable the management and control of the world political landscape for, as Rosenau posits, 'systems of rule' like those that underpin global governance 'can be maintained...even in the absence of established legal or political authority' if conditions exist for 'the evolution of intersubjective consensus based on shared fates and common histories, the possession of information and knowledge, the pressure of active or mobilizable publics, and/or the use of careful planning, good timing, clever manipulation and hard bargaining can—either separately or in combination—foster control mechanisms that sustain governance without government' (2005: 47).

Liberal internationalism and transformation of global governance: implications

Contemporary debates within the liberal internationalist tradition raise crucial issues concerning the nature of global governance in the contemporary era. That neo-liberal economic, political and cultural globalization is generating a complex set of issues that cut across national boundaries is a key marker of the current world order. Thus, the liberal internationalist domestic-global lens challenges national-centric approaches to the study of the world political economy. Further, their focus on the central role of institutions of global governance in the world order is an important reminder of the centrality of these institutions in the rise and consolidation of a given world order. In addition, the liberal internationalist tradition's discussion of the rise of private authority (Strange, 1996) in the era of neo-liberal globalization highlights an important development. Further, this tradition's contention that nation-states are not the only moral agents or actors in the world order highlights the limitations of traditional approaches in IR and IPE, especially the realist perspective that considers states as the only actors in the modalities of a Hobbesian world polity including its governance. The preceding contributions notwithstanding, the liberal internationalist tradition debate pertaining to the reconfiguration of global governance institutional complex puts forward a vision of the transformation of this complex that is very limited on several counts, some of which we discuss here.

First, as it stands, the liberal internationalist vision ensures the reproduction of the status quo in as far as the global governance institutional complex is concerned rather than transformation. Its emphasis on the need for steering mechanisms of control and management of global issues aims for a vision of global governance that focuses on order, stability, compliancy and the manipulation of the citizens in addition to other undemocratic strategies. As previously highlighted, opposition to practices of global governance are considered unnecessary and a source of instability, anxiety and chaos.[2] The authoritarian, managerial and disciplinary ideology informing the liberal internationalist vision of reconfiguring global governance is striking. The underlying premise in support of such an approach to the transformation of global governance is the instability and fragmentation that liberal internationalists argue have emerged in the post-Cold War era and in the context of developments generated by the contemporary form of globalization. Thus, the fragmentation of the current world is one of the core factors that make it necessary to institute what Rosenau refers to as 'corrective steering mechanisms' (2002: 78). While acknowledging that fragmentation does not mean that all 'fragmegrative' tendencies are 'inherently negative or destructive, he contends that 'some fragmegrative situations are fragile, deleterious, violence-prone, and marked by publics who resent, reject or otherwise resist the intrusion of global values, policies, actors or institutions into their local affairs. It is these situations that pose problems for global governance [and] given the world scope of such situations, effective mechanisms of global governance seem eminently desirable' (ibid.).

Second, while the rhetoric of equality among global North and South states and non-state actors in the system of global governance peppers the liberal internationalist vision of transforming global governance, this tradition fails to acknowledge the power asymmetry that characterizes the North–South divide in terms of global governance. Given this tendency, this tradition sheds very limited light on our understanding of the dynamics of global governance, for it depoliticizes this process. As Ngaire Woods (2002) argues, the multilateralism framework that underpins the inter-state system of global governance is far from being one of equal partnership. In her view, 'the most powerful states in the world enjoy the luxury of being able to "shop around" for the arena in which they can best achieve their ends. Sometimes this means turning their back on the multilateralism ideology that is supposed to frame the workings of institutions of global governance by pursuing their goals through private-public alliances, regional, unilateral or mini-lateral means' (ibid.: 29). This practice is one of the many features of the contemporary system of global governance that has led countries in the South to contend that they are not only 'underrepresented' but also 'ill-served' in this system whose leading institutions 'act like "rich men's clubs" ' (ibid.: 30). The failure to consider the power imbalance that marks the pre-existing system of global governance in the liberal internationalist tradition stems from the liberal philosophy that informs its analysis including the transformation of governance at the global level. A core element of this philosophy is an assumption of equality among political actors in the world order. Such an approach ignores the asymmetry in structural and ideation power that characterize the world order including its governing institutions that neo-Gramscian scholars theorize (Cox, 1987; Gill, 2003).

Third, the role of institutions of global governance, historically and in the contemporary juncture, in the reproduction of an unequal capitalist world system does not feature in the depoliticized and ahistorical approach in liberal internationalists discussions of the pre-existing system of global governance and its transformation. As world system theorists and neo-Gramscian scholars remind us, a system of global governance has been a core element of the evolution and consolidation of the unequal world capitalist system. Arguing from a world system perspective Giovanni Arrighi, for example, states, a 'system-level governance on an increasing and eventually global scale has been a fundamental enabling condition of the enlarged reproduction of the modern world system' (2005: 58). For him 'the development of historical capitalism as a world system has thus been based on the formation of ever more powerful cosmopolitan-imperial (or corporate-national) blocs of governmental and business organizations endowed with the capacity to widen (or deepen) the functional and spatial scope of' this system (ibid.: 61). Consequently, enabling the expansion and workings of the world capitalist system marked by inequality has been a central feature of the global governance institutional complex at a given conjuncture, and in turn, the capitalist system forms the material base of this complex. Yet, liberal internationalists abstract this complex from its material foundation by presenting it as something that floats above the capitalist world system and merely facilitates global stability, interconnectedness, sharing of 'global neighborhood' norms, all unstructured or mediated by the modalities of this system. Further, this tradition's approach to global inequalities generated by this system renders its vision of transforming global governance limited. Generally, its tendency is to view institutional reforms as the main avenue through which to address global inequalities that practices of institutions of global governance and the capitalist system in general have generated. It considers measures such as the strengthening of existing institutions, and if need be, the creation of new international regimes to address issues of poverty and environmental stress as adequate in this regard. Thus, gradual institutional responses to global issues including inequality, without any fundamental reconfiguration of the current world capitalist order is considered as the best option in the liberal internationalist vision of a transformed global governance institutional complex. For scholars and policy makers working within this tradition, the liberal philosophical roots of their thinking on global governance leads to a 'belief in the possibility of ameliorative change facilitated by multilateral arrangements' (Keohane, 2002b: 58).

Fourth, as the discussion here has indicated, liberal internationalists envision the existence of an expert knowledge network as central to the emergence and success of a reconfigured global governance institutional complex. While taking cognizance of the need for global institutions that can respond to planetary issues, their emphases on the need for control mechanisms that facilitate the framing of issues, establishment of norms and consensus among members of global governance networks neglect the political and other effects of these networks. Yet, power dynamics that enable the reproduction of the historically unequal system of global governance, among other things, underpin the practices of these networks. This emphasis on expert and elite knowledge networks ensures the promotion of regimes of truth (Foucault, 1980) on a range of issues emitting from dominant sites of knowledge production in policy, civil society and in the academic circles at the expense of other forms of knowledge. As we highlighted in Chapter 2, power is knowledge, for those who hold it determine what counts as knowledge (Alvares, 1992). Liberal internationalists' reliance on expert knowledge networks naturalizes the political role of these networks since it presents them in neutral terms, as providers of scientific and impartial knowledge on global issues. In the process, they reinforce the dominant knowledge systems that grid the world order. Essentially, the liberal internationalist tradition's approach to the transformation of global governance is very much like the tradition regime theory in IR and IPE, which tends to 'focus on cooperation rather than power, and on 'getting the job done' rather than on the justice or legitimacy of the process' (Woods, 2002: 34).

Overall, the expert knowledge and network logic that dominates liberal internationalist debate on the transformation of global governance, especially its preoccupation with 'ever more expertise through the gathering of technical and sophisticated knowledge disguises the fact that the decision about whom to include as contributor of knowledge is already a political act' (Späth, 2005 38). Thus, this debate's vision of transforming global governance is a hegemonic move that promotes a moving but normalized picture of a transformed regime of global governance. This vision portrays the emergence of an undemocratic liberal vision of a selected few, which relies heavily on control mechanisms, compliance and elite cooperation strategies deployed by global networks of governance as representing the universal common good. Such a view is embodied in terms such as global neighbourhood values emphasized by the Commission. This hegemonic universalistic logic contributes to the consolidation of a global elite-consensus on global governance arrangements and practices in the guise of promoting transformative human values. Overall, this logic presents a narrow vision of global governance based on expert knowledge and elite consensus as universal and necessary in this chaotic, unstable, fragmenting and globalizing world, and, in the process facilitates the reproduction of the status quo rather than a fundamental transformation.

Fifth and finally, the liberal internationalist approach to contemporary global governance and its transformation ignores the impact of institutions of global governance on social relations such as gender power dynamics. As feminist studies (Whitworth, 1994; Rai and Waylen, 2008) focusing on institutions of global governance indicate, ideas and practices of these institutions are a major source of the marginalization of women in historically situated politico-cultural-economic places in the South. For instance, and as we argued in Chapters 2 and 3, these institutions are central sites in the international apparatus of hegemonic development knowledge production and dissemination. Hegemonic development discourses, while presented as neutral, have gendered foundations and effects. These discourses are a constitutive element in politico-economic processes such as ongoing neo-liberal capitalist projects that enable the reproduction of a gendered coloniality of power in the South. Yet, for liberal internationalists, their call for the transformation of institutions of global governance neglects the gendered nature of hegemonic development ideas and practices generated and disseminated by institutions of global governance.

In essence, what they are proposing as a way forward are not fundamental changes to the core function of these institutions but rather
the consolidation of their role in the deepening of gendered neo-liberal
disciplinary capitalism at this historical conjuncture. Even a leading
advocate of global governance along liberal internationalist lines has
highlighted the limitations of this philosophy as a tool for social
emancipation broadly defined:

> [liberalism] accommodates easily to dominant interests, seeking to
> use its institutional skills to improve situations rather than funda-
> mentally to restructure them. Liberalism is also relatively insensitive
> to exploitation resulting from gross asymmetries of wealth and
> power. Liberals may be inclined to downplay values such as equality
> when emphasis on such values would bring them into fundamental
> conflict with powerful elites on whose acquiescence their institu-
> tional reformism depends... To satisfied modern elites and middle
> classes, liberalism seems eminently reasonable, but it is not likely to
> be as appealing to the oppressed or disgruntled. (Keohane, 2002b: 58)

Conclusion

This chapter's central concern has been a discussion of debates concerning the nature and transformation of global governance with a focus on
debates within the traditionally powerful liberal internationalist school.
Our discussion has suggested that the liberal internationalist vision of
re-imaging global governance in the contemporary epoch offers a limited vision. Overall, their focus, among others, is on the need to create
transnational elite networks that enable the reproduction of the status quo in global governance. In addition, this tradition's neglect of
the power dynamics underpinning global governance and the world
capitalist system leads to a naturalized approach to the question of
transformation. Essentially, and as Michael G. Schechter (1999: 239)
argues, taken to its logical conclusion, the liberal internationalist vision
as represented for example in the report by the Commission on Global
Governance illustrates the 'limits of problem-solving theory' as articulated by Robert Cox (1986: 208), a theory which in the main 'takes
the world as it finds it, with the prevailing social and power relationships and the institutions into which they are organized, as the given
framework for action' and whose main objective is to enable existing 'relationships and institutions work smoothly by dealing effectively
with particular sources of trouble' (ibid.). Limited as the vision for transforming global governance promoted by liberal internationalists is, it

is important to pay attention to it, for this vision and its underlying liberal philosophy frames the ideologies and practices of leading global institutions such as the UN and its agencies and the World Bank. These institutions and their private counterparts embody overt, covert and structural elements of power articulated by Gill and Law, highlighted in Chapter 2, a political reality that gives them wide space to influence not only the workings of the world system including its governance but also politico-economic processes in the South. In Chapter 7, we illuminate the underlying power of these institutions by examining their—and other members of the TDHB—role in the rise of the current development discourse and modalities of world politics by discussing their ethically framed discourse of human security development discourse that informs their development projects such as the MDGs.

6
Russia, China, Africa and Multi-polarity

The rise of countries such as China, India and Brazil, and Russia's repositioning itself as a major actor in the world order post-Cold War, especially during President Vladimir Putin's era, has seen a renewed interest in the possible emergence of a multi-polar world. Scholarly sites (Armijo, 2007; Clegg, 2009) are not the only ones invoking such an idea. Ruling elites in China, Venezuela and Russia view the consolidation of what they consider as an emergent multi-polar world order as vital in the emergence of a balanced and just world order. Echoing this view, the President of Russia, Dmitry Medvedev, recently declared that, 'the world should be multi-polar. Unipolarity is unacceptable, domination is impermissible. We cannot accept a world order in which all decisions are taken by one country, even such a serious and authoritative country as the United States of America. This kind of world is unstable and fraught with conflict' (quoted in Weitz, 2009). As we highlight later, the notion of multi-polarization as the organizing principle in the world order peppers the foreign policy discourse of Chinese intellectual and ruling elites.

This chapter attempts to address two issues linked to the central concerns of this project. First, and focusing on Russia and China, it considers whether the rise of these two countries signals the emergence of a counter-veiling power structure committed to the transformation of the core features of the current neo-liberal world order. Second, whether the nature of these countries' engagement with social formations in the South represents a major transformation from that of the TDHB. In addressing the first question, we examine the nature of these countries' approach to the contemporary world order. With a focus on the nature of China's involvement in contemporary Africa, the chapter attempts to answer its second question, which is the extent to which China's engagement with social formations in Africa marks a transformative move from the coloniality of power that has underpinned the practices of TDHB. The chapter begins with a discussion of Russia's engagement with the neo-liberal world. We follow this with an examination of the same question as it pertains to China. The final part focuses on the nature of China's role in contemporary Africa.

Russia and the neo-liberal world

From the 1980s to this first decade of the twenty-first century, Russia has seen significant changes in the ideas underpinning its politico-economic processes and its approach to the dominant neo-liberal world order. During this period, Russia embarked on a neo-liberal trajectory both at the political and economic level and re-configured the nature of its engagement with the world order. These developments did not occur in a local and global politico-economic vacuum. For instance, at the global level, the neo-liberal world order that emerged in the 1970s had consolidated itself. This order was at its peak at the juncture in which the post-1945 Soviet Union's politico-economic system was unravelling. Developments that led to this unravelling, some of which we highlight shortly, were thus occurring in the context of a new world order underpinned, as Chapter 3 indicated, by neo-liberal political and economic ideas about democracy and self-regulating market. Locally, the 1980s saw political and economic developments that led to a new approach to the world order by Russia. By 1991, these developments had generated a significant 'general crisis of the State' (Gramsci, 1971: 210). This crisis resulted in a decline of legitimacy for the Soviet system, a development that provided an opening for shifts in politico-economic ideas and practices in Russia and Soviet satellite states.

Developments that led to a legitimacy crisis of the state and the enveloping Soviet system included economic crisis generated by contradictions of this system. As Simon Clarke (2007: 14) argues, from the early days of the Soviet Union system's industrial development, dependency on export of primary commodities in order to meet its imports was a core feature of this system. The importation of machinery and technology were particularly important given the Soviet Union's competition with the Western alliance in the development of military industrial architecture in the context of geopolitics of the Cold War (Castells, 1998: 67). This strategy resulted in its dependence on the export of natural resources to meet the cost of imports for this sector. In the 1970s for example the Union had to not only use its 'gold reserves' but also export a range of primary commodities that included 'rare metals, and diamonds, and, above all, oil and gas' in an effort to maintain some parity with the Western alliance military capabilities (ibid.). The Union's dependency meant that it was 'vulnerable' to shifts in prices for primary commodities in the capitalist world system at given juncture (Clarke, 2007: 14). To illustrate this point, for example, while the early part of the 1980s saw increased revenue for the state because of better terms of trade at the global level, when the tide turned by 1985 the Union entered a period of serious economic dislocation (ibid.: 15).

Beyond the economic dislocation generated by heavy dependency on the export of primary commodities, increasing industrial plant failures from the 1970s generated a crisis of supply of basic commodities (Kagarlitsky, 2002: 25). The crisis in the industrial production sector and its attendant social effects deepened in the early 1990s. Economic crisis in the military industrial sector and the introduction of neo-liberal policies resulted in the decline of the industrial sector and other key sectors of the economy, and these developments generated major social dislocations for the majority of Russians (Castells, 1998: 69–70). While the economic crisis and the social dislocations it generated laid a foundation for the legitimacy crisis of the state, political developments were no less important. Of importance were political developments emerging out of the evolution of President Mikhail Gorbachev's 'New Thinking' doctrine embedded in his *glasnost-perestroika* project. In articulating this project, Gorbachev claimed that it was drawing on socialist principles (1989: 8). *Glasnost* (openness) and *perestroika* (restructuring) represented ideas concerning the political and economic arena respectively. *Glasnost* informed political reforms were geared to encouraging public political discourse without fear of reprisal from the state apparatus. Reiterating the arrival of a new era in the public sphere, Gorbachev claimed, 'we want more openness about public affairs in every sphere of life. People should know what is good, and what is bad too, in order to multiply the good and to combat the bad' (Ibid.: 8).

In terms of the political arena, while the *glasnost* project opened spaces for participation in the political process, especially with the passing of the law on the press that led to the expansion of press freedom (Miller, 1993: 99–100), it did not lead to the deepening of the democratization process. However, the limited democratic space that emerged under *glasnost* conditions lead to a politico-cultural shift where the normative underpinning of democracy gained legitimacy as evidenced by the negative response by a range of social forces to the August 1991 coup whose organizers had hoped to contain Gorbachev's reformist agenda.

Further, *glasnost* created an opening for the embrace of Western liberalism by dominant political and intellectual elites; a social force, which as we will discuss shortly came to play a major role in the rise of the neoliberal project in the post-1991 period. From Gorbachev's perspective, *perestroika* was a revolution aimed at 'the demolition of all that is obsolete, stagnant [that] hinders fast progress' (ibid.). It is important to note that Gorbachev's commitment to instituting measures aimed at economic recovery were important at the national level given the sociopolitical instability that could ensue from a deepening economic crisis. Nonetheless, deepening economic crisis also had implications for Russia's continued status as a global super power (Malia, 1994: 412). Some of the economic reforms introduced during this period included liberalization of the export trade sector in an effort to encourage business owners 'to compete in world markets and to use the foreign exchange earned to acquire modern equipment' (Clarke, 2007: 15). Other economic reforms involved the liberation of the cooperative sector that allowed involvement of cooperatives in economic activities outside the centralized state planning system (Miller, 1993: 103).

By the end of the 1980s, Gorbachev's *perestroika* project faced major constraints and contradictions leading to the demise of his regime in 1991 and the ascendancy of neo-liberalism. The economic reforms introduced under the banner of *perestroika* had not reversed the economic decline. Nonetheless, like the political opening generated by *glasnost*, they generated legitimacy crisis for the centralized Soviet system. For example, the decentralization of economic activities as part of the *perestroika* saw the rise of 'isolationist mini-economies, a development that resulted in a situation whereby Presidential orders from the centre of the Soviet system "conflicted with local ones that were popular and made sense"' (ibid: 154–155). Thus, the introduction of the market incentives aimed at encouraging business to engage in economic activities outside the state centralized production system saw the state lose its historical control on the process of extracting economic surplus (Clarke, 2007: 16–18). This development resulted in the making of new economic elites for 'the surplus which had been appropriated by the state' was now being 'retained by enterprises and/or appropriated by the new financial and commercial intermediaries that arose to handle the emerging market relations' (ibid.: 16). This new elite—commonly referred to as 'the oligarchs' and in dominant Western circles as 'reformers'—would play a significant role in the reconfiguration of Russia's relations with the neoliberal world order in the 1990s and beyond. Consequently, while the market reforms introduced by Gorbachev's regime were limited, mainly aimed at the making of a mixed economy underpinned by socialist ideas, they nonetheless generated significant contradictions that deepened the legitimacy crisis of the Soviet system. Further, Gorbachev's hopes for financial support to address the economic crisis from the dominant states in the world system whose leaders had welcomed his reform agenda were not forthcoming. Leaders of these states insisted on Russia introducing neo-liberal economic strategies as a condition for extended financial support (Klein, 2007: 276). For Gorbachev the measures they were proposing for Russia's transition to neo-liberal capitalism were 'astonishing' (cited in ibid.: 277).

The rise of nationalist movements in general and demands by the republics linked to the Soviet Union in the 1980s for independence from the Center contributed to the legitimacy crisis of the centralized Soviet system. The *glasnost-perestroika* project had enabled the rise of these movements by encouraging involvement in the political process and loosening up of the centralized economic system. In fact, some of the nationalist movements, for instance the National Front in Estonia, contended that they were establishing their national forums in support of Gorbachev's *perestroika* agenda (Matlock, 2004: 148). Further, Gorbachev's proposed Unity Treaty that he was to sign on August 20, 1991 created hopes for autonomy in the republics. This impending development, however, generated a rift within Russia's political bloc, with one faction viewing the treaty as a surrender to the satellite republics. This faction's response was the staging of a coup on August 19, a political development that contributed to the dissolution of the Soviet Union and a deepening legitimacy crisis for Gorbachev regime.

The preceding economic and political developments in the Soviet Union, in the context of a neo-liberal world order and intensification of arms race under Presidents Jimmy Carter and Ronald Reagan, greatly contributed to the turning of a page in Russia's approach to the capitalist world order. The contradictions generated by Gorbachev's *glasnost-perestroika* project generated a shift in balance of local political forces and a new approach to the world order. While under Gorbachev's regime the stress was on a politico-economic reform project inspired by socialist ideas, by late 1991 Boris Yeltsin and others who were to emerge as the new ruling bloc advocated the adoption of neo-liberal economic ideas and engagement with other features of the neo-liberal world order as the way forward for Russia. The August coup and the dismantling of the Soviet Union at the end of 1991 marked the end of Gorbachev's reformist agenda and the ascendancy of a neo-liberal age in Russia.

Russia and the neo-liberal world order: neo-liberal ideas and practices

With the 1917 October revolution, socialist ideas as articulated by Lenin and other Russian political and intellectual voices emerged as the hegemonic philosophical foundations of the state. Following World War II, these ideas, Russia's rapid industrialization process under Stalin, institutional arrangements such as the Council for Mutual Economic Assistance (COMECON) and the Warsaw Pact saw the Soviet Union evolve as a counter-veiling power structure to the post-1945 liberal capitalist world order. As indicated earlier, by the 1990s, however, with shifts in local and global conditions Russia's approach to the prevailing world order and the ideas underpinning its political and economic pratices changed. Since then, neo-liberalism as a state idea and practice emerged as the dominant discourse. However, this is not to say that there are no other contending ideas on the national political economy and the world order: these do exist and promote different, although at times converging political, cultural and economic visions (Tsygankov, 2004). For instance, ideologies advocating national Communism exist and promote a distinct view of how to organize Russia's politico-economic processes and approach to the world order contending, in the case of the latter, that as a socialist civilization, the country's ideas and practices are in stark contrast with the capitalist world (ibid.: 51). However, even with the tensions and pressures generated by other ideologies and associated social forces, the state has sought and demonstrated a commitment to engage with the core features of the contemporary world order. This is evident especially in its adoption of the neo-liberal ideas framing this order and its openness to the practices of dominant institutions of global governance such as the World Bank, the IMF and WTO during the era of Presidents Yeltsin and Putin.

Signs of Russia's shift in its approach to the neo-liberal world order emerged clearly with Yeltsin's rise to power. Yeltsin and social forces closely linked to him—the 'reformers' in dominant policy and intellectual sites—had proposed the adoption of neo-liberal economic ideas prior to his ascendancy to the presidency. For example, in October 1991, Yeltsin declared his commitment to neo-liberalism before becoming President on 1 January, 1992. Yeltsin's regime introduced measures aimed at ushering in neo-liberal inspired shock-therapy economic policies (Reddaway and Glinski, 2001: 246–247). These policies included the core elements of the neo-liberal self-regulating doctrine discussed in Chapter 3, which calls for the privatization of state enterprises, liberalization of financial markets and other markets as part of getting prices right and rolling back the role of the state in the economy. From the beginning of the implementation of shock-therapy policies in the country, the ideas of the neo-liberal world order dovetailed very well with those of Yeltsin's ruling bloc. For example, from the perspective of Sergei Vasiliev—a close ally of the Deputy Prime Minister and neo-liberal advocate Yegor Gaidar—the state 'must limit its activity in the economic sphere to the maximum extent possible and let the market, money, and entrepreneurs work' (quoted in ibid.: 247). Further, the ruling bloc strongly advocated the rapid introduction of a radical neo-liberal project. As Yeltsin claimed while promoting the shock-therapy agenda in October 1991, 'a one-time changeover to market prices is a difficult and forced measure but a necessary one. For approximately six months, things will be worse for everyone, but then prices will fall, the consumer market will be filled with goods, and by the autumn of 1992 there will be economic stabilization and a gradual improvement in people's lives' (quoted in ibid.: 231).

Ruling elites promoted a shock-therapy project in Russia similar to one implemented in Chile following the military coup led by General Augusto Pinochet, as the definitive path to the rise of a capitalist market society (Klein, 2007: 278). From their perspective, such a project would ensure the dismantling of all traces of socialist production structures, ideologies and practices. In the Chile case, a radical neo-liberal project was spear headed by a coalition of capitalists keen on deepening their international involvement and at the level of state economic policy formation, by neo-liberal inspired economists commonly referred to as 'the Chicago boys' (Silva, 1996: 97–135). While the project included the standard neo-liberal economic policy prescription, observers of Chilean political economy considered it radical on several counts. As Silva explains

> First, the draconian nature of the stabilization measures and the speed and thoroughness of market liberalization were without parallel in the recent history of Chile or Latin America. Second, the policies were intended to set in motion a sweeping transformation of the Chilean economy. Neoliberalism in Chile was also radical in its insensitivity to adversely affected economic sectors. (Ibid.: 97)

Neo-liberal shock-therapy policies marked a new epoch in Russia's post-1945 politico-economic history. To begin with, there was no longer a consideration of the social effects of these policies by the state, which was a core element of the state's effort to promote socialism as an alternative to the dominant capitalist ideas that underpinned the post-1945 hegemonic world order. While social inequality was a feature of Russian society in the era of state socialism because of the contradictions of the Soviet system that saw the rise of economic and political elite, social protection mechanisms for instance in housing, health, pensions and employment were part of the state's ideology and practice. The neglect of mounting social dislocations generated by shock-therapy policies by the state because of its assumption that these policies would lead to market equilibrium and the market would resolve social problems, was a significant shift in the ideation foundation of the state. This indicates the state's commitment to construct Russia as an emerging capitalist market society along Western capitalist lines. A few examples of the social dislocations generated by the shock-therapy policies will suffice here. In their first year, shock-therapy policies resulted in rising prices for consumer goods at a rate of 1354 per cent (Reddaway and Glinski, 2001: 249). Rising hyper-inflationary conditions led to massive losses of personal savings (ibid.). Further, rural agrarian food production declined and in 1999 the Red Cross had to intervene with calls for food aid in an effort to contain starvation (ibid.: 251). As the shock therapy polices deepened,

> Diseases once thought to have been conquered, diphtheria and in some places cholera, again made an appearance. The numbers of people infected with scabies and lice increased sharply....A shift to compulsory medical insurance ushered in the collapse of the entire health care system. Ambulance services, hospitals and regional polyclinics were left completely without funds.... According to figures cited by chief sanitary inspector of Russia, Yevgeny Belyaev, for the first time since the end of the Second World War the majority of Russian citizens were chronically malnourished. The buying power of the population fell to the levels of the 1950s. The country had not known such shocks in peacetime since the era of Stalin's 'reconstruction' in the 1930s. (Kagarlitsky, 2002: 99)

Conversely, while the majority of Russians were experiencing human insecurities, social forces closely linked to the state were reaping the material benefits generated by neo-liberal policies. In the rapid paced liberalization process, plant managers and high ranking bureaucrats in the state apparatus became the 'beneficiaries of privatization, creating a kind of "managerial revolution" by turning their executive control of economic enterprises into legal ownership' (Lane, 2000: 184). Out of this process, a small group of Russians—commonly referred to as the oligarchs—came to monopolize key sectors of the economy. In the energy sector for example, Victor Chernomyrdin became a major shareholder in Gazprom a major corporation in the gas industry. His route to emerging as a key player in the neo-liberal economy was enabled by many years in the state's energy sector and his later appointment by Yeltsin as his Deputy Prime Minister in 1992 (Goldman, 2008: 60). He and other members of the oligarchs were to emerge as newly minted billionaires in a society that didn't have millionaires prior to the implementation of the shock-therapy policies (Klein, 2007: 291).

By 1998, the implementation of neo-liberal shock-therapy policies had not generated the rapid transition to market capitalism that the Russian state, the oligarchs and the TDHB had claimed would occur. Economic decline and instability continued. During 1998–1999, the country defaulted on its debt and leading banks closed their business and many Russians including historical figures such as Mikhail Gorbachev lost 'their savings' (Goldman, 2008: 92). However, between 1999 and 2000 the state revenues increased mainly because of, 'a steady rise in world oil prices, which toward the end of this period had reached US$ 32–34 per barrel' (Kagarlitsky, 2002: 274). Globally, China and India's increasing demands for oil fuelled the rise of oil prices (Goldman, 2008: 78–79). Further, Russia also benefitted from Europe's dependency on the country for its energy needs (ibid.: 81–82). Increased revenues for the state did not result in the dismantling of the neo-liberal project in the last years of Yeltsin's regime or following the ascendancy of his hand picked successor President Vladimir Putin in 2000. Thus, while Putin's regime became less dependent on financial flows from institutions of global governance because of windfalls from high global prices for oil, its economic policies remained neo-liberal: what occurred under his rule was the reconstitution of state power and the continuation of the neo-liberal project with a neo-authoritarian state as a guide.

When compared to his predecessor, Putin did not pretend to be involved in a democratization process nor be in need of constantly seeking the legitimacy of the dominant Western powers in the world system. Overall, Putin's regime—like that of his hand picked successor Dmitri Medvedev—while reasserting the authority of the state in the politico-economic arena with at times a neo-nationalist tone, built on the neo-liberal legacy established in the 1990s. In terms of privatization for example, this process continued albeit with the state pushing to acquire increased ownership in the energy and media sectors. In the key sectors of the economy, the role of the private sector in economic development as articulated in neo-liberal thought continued, albeit differently. For example, Putin's approach to the oligarchs was different when compared to that of Yeltsin in that his was characterized mainly by a reward-push strategy, rewarding oligarchs who supported or refrained from criticizing the regime's politico-economic policies and pushing out those whom it considered a threat to state power (Baker and Glasser, 2005). Further, he introduced the strategy of 'national champions' whereby the state became a major shareholder in the key sectors of the economy, for instance, its purchase in 2005 of '50 percent plus one share of Gazprom's stock' (Goldman, 2008: 101) the country's leading company in the energy sector (ibid.: 101). Putin's administration considered building Russia's economy along neo-liberal capitalist lines vital to the country's project of emerging as a major actor in his envisioned multi-polar world. From Putin's perspective, Russia could achieve these goals through its national champions, which he hoped would emerge as 'the most effective and competitive companies on both the domestic and world markets', (ibid.: 97) in additional to being vehicles for promoting Russia's politico-economic interests.

Russia and the neo-liberal world order

Beyond the adoption of neo-liberal ideas as the economic philosophy of the state, Russia has since the 1990s embarked on a new approach to its engagement with other features of the world order. From the beginning of its neo-liberal project, the state considered engagement with institutions of global governance as central to its commitment to deepening the country's integration into the capitalist world order. In 1992, the country became a member of the IMF (Reddaway and Glinski, 2001: 293). Further, in 1993, the country applied for membership to the GATT, and its application process continued with the emergence of the WTO. These developments indicate Russia's commitment to being involved in the modalities of institutions governing the capitalist world order, which it had shunned when it considered the Soviet Union system and its attendant institutional structures as a viable alternative to this order. In addition, as part of its new approach to the world order, when Yeltsin's regime decided to institute shock-therapy policies, it welcomed the input of the TDHB. For Yeltsin, his regime was to 'turn officially to the IMF, the World Bank, and the European Bank for Reconstruction and Development, and invite them to elaborate detailed plans for cooperation and participation in the economic reforms' (quoted in ibid.: 292). Yeltsin's neo-liberal project for Russia had been articulated in a 1991 report sponsored by the World Bank, the IMF, the OECD and the European Bank for Reconstruction and Development (ibid.: 178).

In 1992, the Russian state sent an economic memorandum to the IMF, a move considered by scholars of the country's political economy as an acknowledgement that 'the Western approach had prevailed in the Kremlin' (Nelson and Kuzes, 1995: 24 quoted in ibid.: 293). Over the years, the IMF has provided several loans and its advisors have played a central role in the evolution of neo-liberalism in the country and its policies have been in support of 'austerity, budget cuts, and deflation, with little regard for the social consequences' (ibid.: 293). Further, the formulation of neo-liberal polices in the era of Putin have been aimed at meeting the requirements of the TDHB's neo-liberal agenda and further incorporation into the world order by Russia's accession to WTO membership (Worth, 2004: 149). For example, the redefinition of the relationship between the state and the oligarchs by Putin's regime was aimed at not only 'breaking the monopolies that were allowed to flourish' during Yeltsin's rule, but also to enable 'institutional requirements to control inflation and secure greater foreign investment and exchange', developments that were indicated as being crucial by institutions such as the World Bank to the country's application for WTO membership (ibid.: 151).

In addition, in the post-1991 period Russia welcomed the involvement of organic intellectuals of the neo-liberal world order such as Jeffrey Sachs and others associated at one time or another with the Russia Project housed at Harvard's Institute for International Development (Klein, 2007). These intellectuals played a major role in the legitimization and evolution of neo-liberalism in Russia. For their part these intellectuals, institutions of global governance and dominant states have been key in contributing to Russia's deepening integration into the world order along neo-liberal lines. Even after Yeltsin's coup in 1993 that saw his regime's security apparatus storm and burn the parliament, leading figures in dominant sites in the world order continued to legitimatize his regime's shock-therapy policies. From the perspective of the then first deputy managing director of the IMF, Stanley Fisher, what was needed after the coup was not a re-thinking of the neo-liberal project, but rather 'moving as fast as possible on all fronts' on it (ibid.: 291). Along similar lines Lawrence Summers, a dominant figure in President's Bill Clinton's regime, claimed that a rapid push for core pillars of neo-liberal policies 'privatization, stabilization and liberalization' needed to occur (ibid.). Overall, in the case of the USA, its leading neo-liberal lights embarked on a 'crusade' (Cohen, 2000: 7) to make Russia a market society:

> In that spirit, legions of American political missionaries and evangelists, usually called 'advisers,' spread across Russia in the early and mid-1990s. Funded by the U.S government, ideological organizations, foundations, and education institutions, they encamped wherever the 'Russia we want' might be proselytized, from political movements, trade unions, media, and schools to Moscow offices of the Russian government itself. Among other missionary deeds, U.S citizens gave money to favored Russian politicians, instructed ministers, drafted legislation and presidential decrees, underwrote textbooks, and served at Yeltsin's reelection headquarters in 1996. (Ibid.)

Russia, anti-hegemonism and multi-polarity

Russia's openness after 1991 to engaging with key features of the world order is a major departure from the previous 40 years. Nonetheless, while Russia remains committed to deepening its involvement in the capitalist world order this does not mean it has given up its project of achieving super power status in what it considers as a much-needed multi-polar world order. However, the Russian state is not engaged in a project aimed at the establishment of a counter-veiling power structure that contrasts or challenges the hegemonic capitalist world order. While Russia's ruling elites continue to invoke the urgent need for a multi-polar world order, their political and economic ideas and practices indicate a commitment to a political project that enables the country to reposition itself in the contemporary neo-liberal world order as a dominant power and not a dismantling of this order. To be sure, their discourse of multi-polarity has effects: it for instance opens a political space for Russia to emerge as a major actor among the group of countries – Brazil, China and India-that are calling for a multi-polar world order. This does not however mean a disengagement with the core elements of the neo-liberal world order. Like China—discussed shortly—Russia continues to adhere to the neo-liberal development discourse and seeks engagement with other features of the world order.

In addition, since 1992 Russia has embarked on a pragmatic anti-hegemonism at the global level. Russia's pragmatic anti-hegemonism is evident in its approach to USA's hegemony in the world order.

While confrontation and outright opposition to America's hegemony in the post-World War II capitalist world order was the norm during the geopolitics of the Cold War, since 1991 pragmatic anti-hegemonism underpins Russia's handling of this phenomenon. Its view that America's hegemony in the world order is a threat to the world and an unfair arrangement of power in this order remains. Nonetheless, selective efforts aimed at containing what Russia considers, at a given juncture, as America's use of its hegemonic status to achieve politico-economic goals is a core feature of Russia's pragmatic anti-hegemonism. Take for example the ushering of the war in Iraq by the USA in 2003. Putin's regime opposed the war viewing it as another example of America's unilateralism in the post-Cold War unipolar world. In a interview following a visit to France—a country that also opposed the war— he declared the proposed war as a 'grave danger' and indicated that he would not hesitate to use his country's veto power in the UN's Security Council to ensure that the war did not start (Baker and Glasser, 2005: 225). Yet, once the coalition forces ushered their attacks in Iraq, he did not raise his voice against the war and continued in his charm offensive with President Bush (ibid.: 226–230). The initial opposition to the Iraq war by Russia is in contrast to its support of America's invasion of Afghanistan and securitized approach to the war on terror. Following the 9/11 terrorist attacks, Putin's regime emerged as a keen supporter of USA anti-terror wars. In the war in Afghanistan, Russia provided 'basing rights, over-flights rights, and accelerating arms deliveries to the Northern Alliance' (Lynch, 2004: 25).

Russia's turn to pragmatic anti-hegemonism and the nature of response to it by the USA and other members of the TDHB seems to serve Russia's politico-economic interests and those of the bloc. For the Russian state, its approach to the world order in the post-1991 period is driven by the idea that, for it to achieve its national and regional goals it has to avoid a non-strategic confrontation with America and other dominant actors in the world order (ibid.: 27). Its economic project, whose aims are the country's emergence as a major power in the world order, is highly dependent on dominant capitalist states in the world order providing Russia with 'a degree of price stability that would in turn stabilize [its] finances... and allow for longer-term economic planning and development' (ibid.). Conversely, Russia offers an alternative to the Western capitalist world's dependency on the Middle East for its energy needs (ibid.). To summarize here, while Russia has embarked on building relations with regional powers such as the European Union, China and anti-USA hegemony countries such as Venezuela, it has not embarked on a path geared to a renewal of the pre-1992 constant and deep antagonistic relationship with the USA and the rest of the capitalist world. Further, while Russia continues to invoke its commitment to the emergence of a multi-polar world order, the nature of its engagement with the core features of the current world indicates a commitment to the stability of the current neo-liberal capitalist world order rather than its transformation.

China and the neo-liberal world order: from socialism to neo-liberal modernization

The rise to power of the Communist Party in 1949 marked a new phase in the nature of China's engagement with the capitalist world order and the state's politico-economic strategies. Prior to this period, the country had a long history of contact with the capitalist world system before the contemporary one (Lippit, 1987; Naughton, 2007; Hevia, 2003). For example, foreign powers partially colonized China through a treaty port trading system, at the height of European and other foreign interests' competition for colonial possessions in Asia in the 1800s. Prior to this period, China had economic relations with the West that involved trade in commodities such as silk, tea, crafts and silver. The export of opium by Britain in efforts to address the trade imbalance, which had resulted in China importing more silver, led to a new age in the country's relations with the Western world. For British economic interests, opium trade would not only generate enormous profits but also address the trade imbalance with China. With an increase in opium trade in the nineteenth century—3200 chests in 1861, with one chest containing 110 pounds of opium, compared to 40 chests in 1840—the two objectives where achieved (Lippit, 1987: 44). China's struggle to contain the opium trade, which was generating economic and social problems, led to the Opium Wars with Britain resulting in China's defeat and the establishment of treaty ports controlled by foreign powers. For some Western leaders such as President Quincy Adams of the United States, Britain's aggression against China during the Opium crisis was 'a just...."Christian precept"... of open trade' (Kornberg and Faust, 2005: 12). Western powers, even prior to the Opium Wars, viewed China's insistence on restricting trade to limited areas along its coastline under the tribute framework a barrier to their doctrine of free trade (Cartier, 2001: 113).

Following the 1949 Communist revolution, though, China pushed a politico-economic project aimed at striving for a process of social change that contained its further integration into the world capitalist order as a dependent social formation. In efforts to limit the political, cultural and material consequences of dependency and to deepen its autonomy from the capitalist world order, the Chinese state instituted strategies aimed at expanding the country's material base. To begin with, the state instituted a major land reform in the hope of increasing agricultural production and reconfiguring the feudal land system that had historically marginalized a large segment of the peasantry (Gurley, 1976: 210). For the Chinese state, raising agricultural productivity was central to its industrialization project: 'large amounts of funds are needed to accomplish both national industrialization and the technical transformation of agriculture, and a considerable part of these funds has to be accumulated through agriculture' (Zedong, 1977: 182). From the 1950s until the marketization of the agrarian sector in the era of neo-liberalism, the state's strategy in this sector included the establishment of collective farming structures, first in the form of cooperatives and later into people's agricultural communes. In addition to agrarian reforms, the state pushed for an industrialization process in efforts to expand its material base and to contain external dependency. As part of this process, a significant portion of state expenditure went to the industry sector with the heavy industry accounting for over 80 per cent of this expenditure, resulting in the expansion of China's industrial base: 'between 1952 and 1978 industrial output grew at an average annual rate of 11.5%. Moreover, industry's share of total GDP climbed steadily over the same period from 18% to 44%, while agriculture's share declined from 51% to 28%' (Naughton, 2007: 56).

The aim of the state's project of expanding the country's industrial base, like its other politico-economic strategies, was to lay the foundation for the emergence of a socialist society marked not only by social equality but also by economic, political and cultural autonomy from dominant forces in the capital world order. In this regard, the state emphasized self-reliance. This underlying approach to economic matters, however, did not rule out China's involvement with the capitalist world order. The state's imperative though was that engagement in external economic activities was to serve the country's prevailing national interests as defined by the ruling elites. For instance, in the case of foreign trade, the state welcomed it as long as it contributed to 'domestic needs and fostered domestic economic development, but not so much that it became either the driving force of economic growth, or a channel for the further integration of the economy in world markets' (Aiguo, 2000: 84). For the state, self-reliance and selective engagement with the capitalist world order would ensure not only some measure of autonomy from this order, but also would enable the country to achieve its long held goal of catching up economically with the industrialized West, albeit along socialist lines. In its project of catching up with the West, the state proposed that the country would: 'take an unusual path and adopt advanced technology as much as possible in order to transform China into a powerful socialist country in a relatively, short time... to catch up with and surpass Great Britain in five years or a bit longer and to catch up with and surpass the US in 15 years or a bit longer' (The General Guidelines of Socialist Construction, quoted in ibid.: 84).

It is important to note that while the political agency of the Chinese state enabled it to carve a sphere of autonomy in its engagement with the world capitalist order, other conditions were no less important in this process. At the domestic level, for instance, the country had historically been dependent on its own internal resources for its economic development and those from its tributary states during China's practices of accumulation by dispossession in Asia. Further, even with the experience of partial colonial rule through the treaty port economic architecture, the country's 'long history of subsistence through a combination of agriculture and handicrafts' was not significantly reconfigured, a historical condition that provided the state with a foundation as it embarked on its self-reliant economic project in the post-1949 period (ibid.: 82). In addition, China's emergence as a nuclear power in 1964 and its later membership in the United Nations Security Council expanded its power and autonomy in the world political and economy system when compared to other countries in the South.

Even prior to the consolidation of the current neo-liberal world order, China's engagement with the world capitalist order started to shift in the early 1970s. The *détente* with the world capitalist hegemonic power in 1971, following President Richard Nixon's visit, opened up trade between the two countries even though the USA delayed official recognition of the People's Republic until 1979. In the context of the geopolitics of the Cold War, then, the *détente* between the two nuclear powers provided ruling elites in China with legitimacy at the global level and economic opportunities for the country. Thus, while domestic political and economic developments enabled China to have extensive room to manoeuvre in its engagement with the world capitalist order, 'the invitation'[1] to this order, albeit significantly limited, that was accorded to China following the 1971 shift in relations with the USA played a crucial role in its economic trajectory. For example, following President Nixon's visit, in 1971, economic relations with the capitalist world expanded and thus deepened the country's engagement with leading members of the world capitalist order. China for instance spent US\$ 4.3 billion on imports of industrial equipment from the West (Naughton, 2007: 77).

The shift in China's approach to the world capitalist order took a decisive turn in the late 1970s with the rise to power of a faction of the ruling elite calling for a reorientation in the country's economic arena. The rise of this faction was a result of an intense power struggle among the ruling elites from the mid-1970s and the immediate period following Mao Zedong's death in 1976 (ibid.). Deng Xiaoping, and other ruling elites committed to changing China's economic practices, began to consolidate their politico-economic vision from 1978 onwards. Since 1978, the Chinese state has instituted measures aimed at deepening the country's involvement in the capitalist world order as part of its push for modernization along neo-liberal market lines although with 'Chinese characteristics' as the country's ruling elites consistently claim. The Chinese state's new approach to the neo-liberal capitalist world order is embodied in a concept popularized by Deng Xiaoping, 'grabbing with two hands', which on the one hand stresses 'reform and opening (economic globalization) as necessary' for China's objective of economic modernization and the other hand ensuring the containment of 'ideological and cultural pollutants from abroad (cultural globalization)' (Kim, 2006: 279).

For the new modernizing elites, self-reliance, central planning and state political-cultural programs such as the 1966–1976 Cultural Revolution had led China to economic stagnation. From their perspective, economic modernization through the embrace of the market doctrine and the deepening of the country's engagement with other elements of the world order was crucial for their legitimacy at the local and international level. For them, rapid and consistent economic growth was vital 'for domestic stability and regime survival as well as for long-term national power and security' as they reconfigured the Maoist politico-economic landscape (Moore, 2005: 122). They also viewed economic modernization through the market as a key element in the country achieving its long-term goal of becoming a major power in the capitalist world order. Overall, the gradual opening of the economy to market forces without democratizing the political system was the way forward for these elites if the country was to modernize. The opening up of the country to foreign capital and implementation of market economic strategies began with the creation of the special export zones—renamed in 1980 as Special Economic Zones (SEZ)—in the Southern coastal region of the country. Under the open-door-policy these zones were given an economic blueprint that indicated a fundamental shift in the state's approach to the economy. For instance, the policy called for the encouragement of foreign capital investment in the country, and as an incentive, provided a 15 per cent corporate tax and offered other forms of tax relief for foreign capital such as 'exemption from income tax on the remittance of profits' (Wang, 2003: 124). Further, the policy called for an end to 'state mandatory economic plans' and instead 'letting market forces regulate production under the guidance of state plans' (ibid.: 124–125). The shift in the state's economic strategies was a contentious process marked by divisions within the Communist Party, especially following the 1989 Tiananmen square student led uprising with elements of the elites contending that introduction of market capitalism and the emergence of a new bourgeois class had contributed to the political crisis (ibid.: 128).

By 1992 the ruling elite faction pushing for the introduction of the market logic in economic production had consolidated its power and vision as the state openly endorsed the emergence of what it termed as a socialist market economy as its main objective during the Fourteenth Congress of the Communist Party. Since then, China's state-led economic modernization project has increasingly seen the deepening of a process that began in the late 1970s of dismantling socialist inspired economic practices that characterized the Mao era. In the agrarian sector, this process has seen the introduction of a contract system in place of collective farming, privatization and introduction of private markets (Vohra, 1994: 50). Like in other sectors, the state has played a central role in this process. As Robert Weil states:

> The current 'market reforms' did not emerge from some spontaneous and liberal economic process, nor even by simply removing earlier statist restraints on entrepreneurial initiative. Quite the contrary, 'markets' were imposed on the Chinese people by government fiat, notably in the forcible breaking up of the agricultural commune system which had been developed under the leadership of Mao Zedong, to be replaced with a system of individual family contracts, and in the equally rapid and forcible demolition of socialist forms of collective public welfare now being imposed on state-owned enterprises... Thus it is not primarily through the working of 'free markets' per se that the economy has, in the first instance, been radically transformed, but rather by the very use of that state power and Communist Party control which Western observers so often deplore. (1996: 13)

Overall, since its introduction close to three decades ago, the state's open-door- policy has seen the deepening of foreign capital investment in the country. In 2002 foreign direct investment represented more than 40 per cent of the country's GDP and multinational firms were increasingly attracted by China's vast market potential and some of them, such as General Motors were 'reporting far higher' profits in China than in their US market (Harvey, 2005: 135). Further, in 2003, China was the leading destination for foreign direct investment with US$ 41,081 in newly approved investment (Zhimin, 2007: 52). Thus, what began as a gradual experiment of opening the country to foreign capital has become a central feature of the state's economic strategy in the contemporary era, although the state continues to place limitations on the workings of foreign capital in efforts to contain it from overpowering the role of the state in the economy (Harvey, 2005: 123). Nonetheless, while the state influences the involvement of multinational and national corporations the latter are keen on deepening their involvement in China because of their insatiable need to control a piece of the vast market that the country presents (Zhimin, 2007: 58).

Like in Russia and elsewhere, the Chinese neo-liberal experiment has not been neutral. This experiment has for example resulted in the decline of the state's capacity and interest in providing public goods in sectors such as health and education (Nolan, 2004: 31). In line with the neo-liberal market doctrine, the state has introduced fees in the social sector under the rubric of public finance system reforms. These reforms have not only shifted the costs of social sector spending to local communities but also deepened inequalities. In the case of the education sector, the implementation of market reforms has seen 'growing disparities in per capita [education] expenditure across regions, both inter-provincial and intra-provincial' (World Bank, 2002: 101, quoted in Nolan, 2004: 32). Neo-liberal based reforms have also led to economic inequalities. For example, between 1998 and 2001 rural dwellers, who comprise 65 per cent of the country's population, faced economic stagnation (*The Economist*, 2002). These developments have led some analysts to contend that the so-called market socialism marks a restoration of the capitalist mode of production with attendant social and economic effects (Hart-Landsberg and Burkett, 2005). For other observers of China's political economy, however, the country's economic trajectory in the post-Mao era 'not only compensates for the loss of Cold War strategic importance', a period in which the Chinese state strategically placed its interests in either of the blocs, 'but [also] uplifts China's structural position in the international political economy' (Zhimin, 2007: 50).

China, institutions of the neo-liberal world order and anti-hegemonism

Beyond engaging with ideas underpinning the neo-liberal world order, China has also joined core institutions governing this order, another indication of the country's reconfiguration of its approach to it in the post-Mao period. For China, the stability of these institutions is central to its national interests at this conjuncture especially the achievement of its modernization project and legitimacy at the global level. In this respect, at the level of public political discourse, the language of engagement and acting according to and in harmony with the norms embedded in the institutional framework of the contemporary world order rather than trying to transform them, informs the approach of the Chinese state to institutions of global governance. For instance, in its approach to the United Nations and its agencies, China's approach is one of maintenance rather than transformation (Kim, 1999). In state documents the language of 'keeping in line with the international tract', being a responsible international actor, supporting multilateralism and 'behaving according to international norms' are but a few examples of this new approach to global institutions (Changhe, 2007: 68).[2] In the arena of national and global security, the Chinese state's emphasis is on the notion of 'cooperative security among states' (ibid.: 70). For the Chinese state, a global political environment characterized by multilateral cooperative arrangements at the regional and international level assures its modernization drive and objective of emerging as a major world power. While stressing the need for cooperative security, the Chinese state nevertheless continues to emphasize its right to protect its interest in Taiwan by using force if necessary, and further its overall objective is to expand its economic, political and military capabilities in pursuit of what some scholars refer to as its goal of achieving 'comprehensive national power' (Deng, 2005: 65).

China's concerted effort to join the WTO is another example indicating its commitment to deepening the country's integration into the capitalist world order and the adoption of the market logic as a central feature of its economic strategies. This effort, which took 15 years, illustrates the evolution of the Chinese state's view of the world capitalist order and its view of marketization of the economy. In the early period of its WTO negotiations, phrases such as 'planning as the key instrument, with market regulation as a supplement' and 'the state will regulate the market, while the market will guide businesses', and the commitment of the state to the creation of a 'commodity economy' dominated the Chinese state's position. Representations of the dominant states and institutions in the world order did not welcome this position. With the passing of a resolution to build a socialist market economy at the ruling party's fourteenth congress in 1992, which built on Deng Xiaoping's claims from his now famous tour in special economic zones that 'under socialist conditions, China could also build a market economy', an opening emerged for the negotiations to move forward (Yongming, 2007: 101).

More importantly, given the contentious history of trade between China and the USA and the politico-economic power of the latter in the world order, the signing of a market access bilateral agreement between the two countries close to the WTO's Ministerial meeting in Seattle provided a major boost for China's push to join the WTO (Barfield and Groombridge, 2003: 31). This development was important not only for the USA but also for China. Dominant states in the world order such as the USA considered the country 'too big and too potentially important to be allowed in on its own terms', mainly because of its commitment to secure access to overseas markets especially US ones (Breslin, 2007: 93). In addition, the country was worried about new stipulations emerging out of the Doha trade negotiations that would make entry to the WTO difficult (ibid.). In early 2001, the Ministry of Foreign Trade and Economic Cooperation reconfigured the country's legal and trade regulatory framework in line with WTO principles, a process that resulted in the dismantling of 573 laws, changes to 120 existing laws and the creation of 26 new laws (Yongming, 2007: 103). By the end of that year, China joined WTO, a development that illustrates the state's commitment to deepening its economic strategies in trade, investment and agricultural arenas along neo-liberal lines.

The Chinese state's adoption of multilateral practices marks a significant shift from its earlier emphasis on self-reliance and isolation in order to meet its national objectives. As Su Change argues, 'historically the Chinese state viewed multilateralism as a constraint.... Yet today China plays an active role in the multilateral security dialogue on the North Korea nuclear problem, and is promoting the establishment of the ASEAN+3 Free Trade Zone. The Shanghai Six is the first international organization that China has helped establish since 1840, and reflects the important role of multilateral diplomacy in current Chinese foreign relations' (2007: 71). For the Chinese state, practices of multilateralism and joining international institutions are important tools in its struggle for domestic and international legitimacy and its emergence as a global power. As Yong Deng states 'only when greater international legitimacy as a rising great power can China enjoy a lasting benign strategic environment wherein it is no longer suspected as the most likely revisionist power bent on violently restructuring the international arrangement... These features are eminently manifested in China's international strategy, which puts a premium on generally status-quo-oriented constructive activism' (2005: 62–63). Essentially, as one analyst has posited, China 'will never be a nation that is satisfied with only food and shelter' thus expanding its capacity on all fronts and emerging as a global power is the end goal of its current politico-economic project (Wang, 2006: 23).

Overall, the Chinese state considers the maintenance of the current world order as crucial to its attainment of its strategic national interests of economic modernization through market capitalism and rise as a global power. In this regard, China 'appears to be betting its future on its efforts within the current international political and economic system' for to achieve its modernization goals, including its commitment to 'catching with the West', access to Western capital, technology and markets is vital (ibid.: 22). Consequently, to achieve these goals, China can ill avoid antagonizing the dominant states in the world order especially the USA (Zhimin, 2007: 57). Further, because the Chinese state has so far achieved its politico-economic objectives within the modalities of current world order, its collaborative tendency to this order suits its agenda (ibid.). Thus, while Chinese ruling elites and organic intellectuals continue to invoke their commitment to multi-polarization, an aggressive counter-hegemonic attack on America's hegemony and other dominant states in the contemporary world order, in order to create a foundation for a multi-polar world order, is not on their agenda at the current juncture. Rather the Chinese state's anti-hegemonism discourse seems to be limited to the containment of America's 'unilateralism and power politics in the name of promoting democratization' (Deng, 2005: 65) and other US political projects. In this respect, the UN provides China with a political space 'to forge some international checks on the excessive use of American power' (Zhimin, 2007: 56).

To conclude, the foregoing analysis suggests that while anti-hegemonism remains an aspect of the Chinese state's ideology, the state is mainly committed to the stability of the core features of the current world order rather than their transformation. Given this approach to the world order, it is unlikely that China will emerge as a counter-veiling power structure to this order at this conjuncture. This does not, however, stop Chinese elites from claiming that China is committed to the emergence of a multi-polar world, in addition to being a champion of the politico-economic interests of social formations in Africa and other regions of the 'developing world'. This rhetoric and other phrases meant to signal South–South solidarity as the driving force of China's growing involvement in a range of forums in the South, for example, Association of Southeast Asian Nations, Sino-Arab Cooperation Forum, China-Caribbean Economic Forum and in economic sectors such as energy and agriculture, pepper China's foreign policy discourse as it pertains to the South. It is to a discussion of China's engagement in Africa that we turn next.

China and Africa: the political economy of accumulation by dispossession

Africa and China have long historical links but contemporary relations have their foundation in the 1950s (Taylor, 2006a). Since this period, China has consistently defined itself as the largest developing country. While referring to itself as part of the developing World, China nevertheless has historically considered itself as the leader of countries in this category. This sense of superiority has a long lineage in China's history dating back to the thesis of China as a 'middle kingdom' with a great world civilization and the rest of the world as populated by 'barbarians' with the West being 'the most powerful barbarian' (Aiguo, 2000: 18). At any rate, for the most part domestic priorities coupled with developments in Africa and the geopolitical context of the Cold War informed the nature of China's involvement in Africa in the post-1945 period until the 1980s. In its engagement in Africa and elsewhere, China outlined Five Principles as the guiding framework. These Principles, which stressed peaceful coexistence, mutual respect for each other's territories, non-aggression, non-interference in each other's internal affairs and equality and mutual benefit, were reiterated by Prime Minister Zhou Enlai at the 1955 Bandung conference which was attended by representatives of Asian and African independent states (Harris, 1985: 28). In specific terms, China's involvement in Africa during the first three decades of the 1949 Communist Revolution included, but was not limited to, support for liberation movements, revolutionary movements[3] and socialist inspired state politico-economic projects (Taylor, 2006a).

Since the 1980s, China has reconfigured its approach to social formations in Africa and other parts of the South. During this period, China's involvement in Africa has deepened, and this trend continues in the early part of the twenty-first century. A concerted effort by the Chinese state to establish politico-economic legitimacy with African states has enabled this development. In general, a soft power approach under-pins China's drive for legitimacy in the continent. For Joseph Nye, 'soft power rests on the ability' of a state to 'shape the preferences of the others' (2004: 5). Such an approach can enable a country to 'obtain the outcomes it wants in world politics because other countries—admiring its values, emulating its example, aspiring to its values, emulating its example...want to follow it' (ibid.). Of course, the use of a soft power approach does not rule out the use of hard power underpinned by coer-cive measures such as military and economic sanctions to influence the responses of other states. China has for instance, used its economic power as a stick in the evolution of its relations between African states and Taiwan. In 1997, for instance, China cut off diplomatic links and provision of development loans to Chad following the country's accep-tance of a US\$ 125 million loan and recognition of Taiwan (Alden, 2005: 155). Overall, the Chinese state's soft power strategy in Africa is aimed at gaining legitimacy; a development that enables the creation of favourable conditions for it to achieve its national interests. In its drive for political legitimacy in Africa, China has demonstrated its soft power approach in several ways. First, China is actively involved in the building of, and in some cases, the rehabilitation of large infrastructural projects in various parts of Africa. In Mozambique and Gabon, China is involved in the building of railways (ibid.: 151). China's involvement in infrastructural projects further includes the building of hospitals, dams and government offices (Taylor, 2006b: 951).

Second, the nature of China's approach to African states is facil-itating its objective of gaining political legitimacy in a range of African social formations. A crucial feature of the Chinese state's approach to African states is the insistence on its contemporary Five Principles— non-intervention, sovereign equality, reliable friend-ship, mutually beneficial development and international cooperation (China.org.cn, 2003b). For the Chinese state, the doctrine of sovereignty translates into providing development loans without political con-ditions except on the issue of the One China policy. China's non-intervention policy and insistence on respect for sovereignty resonates well with African states. At the level of practice, this doctrine trans-lates to China having extensive relations with states considered by the TDHB as being extreme violators of human rights and instiga-tors of the emergence of political landscapes marked by no respect for the rule of law, international law conventions and good gover-nance practices, such as contemporary Zimbabwe, Angola and Sudan. In the case of Zimbabwe, while leading members of the TDHB have imposed sanctions, China has maintained ties. As the country has increasingly become isolated at the international level, China's economic and political support has provided Robert Mugabe's regime with political capital to contest and disrupt the historical hegemony of the TDHB in the country especially its former colonial ruler Britain.

In the case of Angola, when the state faced demands to institute good governance measures from the IMF as a condition for funding, it opted to negotiate a loan package with China, which did not come with political conditionality (Taylor, 2006b: 947). The Kenyan state followed a similar pattern by signing economic agreements in oil and other sectors with China at a time when members of the TDHB—in this case the Netherlands, IMF and the World Bank respectively—were in the Spring of 2006 suspending or withdrawing funding from the country because of what they considered as lack of progress in dealing with corruption (BBC News, 2006c and Taylor, 2006b: 952). In Sudan, ruling elites have welcomed Chinese capital because of the Chinese state policy of non-interference in domestic affairs and its disdain for the human rights and democracy promotion agenda of the TDHB. According to He Wenping, director of the African Studies section at the Chinese Academy of Social Sciences in Beijing, 'We [China] don't believe that human rights should stand above sovereignty', a perspective that he contends China shares with African states (cited in Taylor, 2006b: 939). The Chinese state's policy of non-interference and its approach to human rights and democracy is aimed not only at solidifying its legitimacy in African countries, but also at ensuring that the latter work in concert with China in multilateral settings. In the case of human rights and democracy, for instance, since the Tiananmen Square pro-democracy movement, China has come to rely on African states to contain efforts to condemn its human rights and democracy record in international political circles such as the UN. African countries such as Sudan and Zimbabwe can also count on China to support them in these political arenas as far as issues of human rights and good governance are concerned.

Overall, in African ruling elite circles China's non-interference is welcomed mainly because of its lack of political conditionality, for as a Kenyan government official remarked: 'You never hear the Chinese saying that they will not finish a project because the government has not done enough to tackle corruption. If they are going to build a road, then it will be built' (*USA Today*, 2005, cited in Tull, 2006: 467). In essence, China's approach to African countries is in stark contrast with the practices of the TDHB, discussed in Chapter 3, whose hallmark is the use of disciplinary measures for countries that fail to implement its neoliberal polices. In contrast, the Chinese state insists that its relations with African countries will respect 'independent choices of political system and development road by African nations according to their realities' and supports African states in their efforts to 'safeguard national independence, sovereignty and territorial integrity' and their 'struggles for economic development' (China.org.cn December 10, 2003a). To be sure, African states are not passive actors in this process, for China's soft power approach has generated a new geopolitical conjuncture that provides these states some measure of autonomy in their responses to the TDHB and in pushing their politico-economic projects (Taylor, 2006; Tull 2006).

Overall, China constantly stresses its solidarity and growing links with African countries. These links have deepened especially on the economic front. Trade between China and Africa, for instance, stood at US$ 2 billion in 1999: by 2004 and 2005 it had risen to US$ 29.6 billion and US$ 39.7 billion respectively (Taylor, 2006b: 937). Chinese capital is also increasingly operating in various places in Africa as the Chinese state encourages public and private capital involvement in the oil industry and other sectors. In the case of private capital, the state has committed itself to providing loans on easy terms and has set aside a financial fund aimed at supporting Chinese firms investing in Africa. Along these lines, China's state-funded national Export and Import Bank of China (Exim Bank) and China Construction Bank (CCB) are heavily involved in deepening the activities of the country's private and public capital in Africa (Holslag, 2006: 150). In 2003 Chinese firms representing a US$ 1.5 billion investment had businesses in Africa, and this trend will only increase once China's proposed free trade zone is established in the Southern African region (Tull, 2006: 464). To consolidate growing links between China and Africa, various institutional arrangements such as the Chinese African Chamber of Commerce and the Forum on China-Africa Cooperation (FOCAC) have emerged. The FOCAC was established in 2002 and it has emerged as a focal point for China–Africa states' bureaucratic and ruling elites, representatives of global and regional institutions and owners of capital interested in modalities of the growing links between Africa social formations and China. The Chinese state portrays the creation of these links and its growing economic activities in Africa in egalitarian terms and as being beneficial to African countries. Various African ruling elites also echo this view. For instance, in the case of the FOCAC, Seyoum Mesfin, Ethiopia's Foreign Minister contends that 'it is not a talk shop' since, from its inauguration, China has extended debt relief to various African countries and offered preferential tariff arrangements for some African countries (Xinhua News Agency, 2003).

China's soft power approach and the Sino-African elite consensus on the country's growing involvement in the continent fails not only to illuminate the power asymmetry between the two parties, but also the national interests underpinning China's growing engagement in Africa. Like its approach to the contemporary world order, a political strategy aimed at facilitating the achievement of its politico-economic strategic interests underpins China's soft approach in Africa. To be sure, the historical and contemporary exploitative and destructive practices of the TDHB in Africa continue. Nonetheless, China's and Africa's ruling elites' representation of the country's deepening economic involvement as a win-win situation and more egalitarian compared to the political and economic practices of the TDHB, is full of political rhetoric and myopia. Largely, the Chinese state's modernization project and its drive to emerge as a global power are at the core of its involvement in Africa and other places in the South and political spaces such as global multilateral institutions. It is in this context that, China's deepening involvement in Africa needs to be analyzed and understood. Further, in terms of military, structural and political power, China's pre-existing and growing power, and the autonomy that this social reality accords the Chinese state in its relations with African states, questions the 'equal partnership' thesis that dominates the official Sino-African elite view on the country's practices in the continent.

Departing from the Sino-African elite win-win consensus, our premise is that while China's soft power approach is to some extent enabling African states to disrupt the hegemony of the TDHB in the continent, the country's practices have major effects. In contemporary Africa, China's modernization drive has resulted in economic practices akin to those of the colonial conjuncture. These practices, some of which we highlight shortly, bring to mind the politico-economic objectives of European ruling classes at the 1884 Berlin Conference that led to the carving up of the African continent among European powers. At the conference, King Leopold of Belgium declared that he was determined to have a 'piece of this magnificent African cake' (Davidson, 1984b). The process of having a piece of Africa's magnificent cake, which resulted in the plundering of the continent's resources and laying the foundation for weak economic structures, was in the European imperial discourse constructed as a civilizing mission that would introduce Africans to the civilizing ethos of commerce and Christianity. Ruling elites in China do not construct their engagement in Africa in such terms, although China does consider itself as a leading civilization and a model of development that African countries should emulate, rather they present it as a win-win situation; a strategy that yields mutual benefit for all involved.

In fact, Chinese ruling elites and their counter-parts in Africa view the suggestion that China's role in Africa represents a new form of imperialism as misguided. According to President Hu Jintao, 'Africa has rich resources and market potentials, whereas China has available effective practices and practical know-how it has gained in the course of modernization' and hence a strategic partnership between China and Africa will be mutually beneficial (BBC News, 2006b). For sure, a simplistic analogy of the Chinese state's involvement in Africa to European imperialism might be problematic given the different historical conjunctures, the multi-faceted nature and violence which characterized imperial rule, and the consent provided to China by contemporary African ruling elites. Nonetheless, while the Five Principles continue to be invoked by the Chinese state, especially the concept of 'mutual benefit', its pattern of economic engagement has the markings of imperial processes of accumulation by dispossession (Harvey, 2003 and Chapter 3).

China's practice of accumulation by dispossession is evident in its various economic activities in contemporary Africa. Take for instance, the debt relief packages that China has offered some African countries. While China's debt relief has accorded the country political legitimacy with African states and, in the case of the latter, room to manoeuvre in their responses to the TDHB, the practice is contributing to the reproduction of the national debt trap, a structural reality that places constraints on the economic capacity of African states. Further, these loans cover various sectors including the military industry. While China has not been the only major power supplying arms to African countries, through the period 1996–2003 its share of arm supplies accounted for 14 per cent of the arms trade in the continent, while Russia was the leading supplier during this period (Eisenman, 2007: 48). For China, supporting the expansion of the military industry in Africa serves several purposes including that of protecting the interests of its capital (ibid.: 49). Increasing Africa's debt trap and China's other practices of accumulation by dispossession have significant implications for African countries, as our brief examples of China's drive to secure markets, natural resources and public infrastructural projects will indicate.

Like European powers in the era of their industrial revolutions, rapid economic growth and deepening industrialization has resulted in the overproduction of commodities in China. This development has resulted in the search for new markets all over the world by Chinese economic interests. As one commentator has declared, in the contemporary era 'the words Made in China are as universal as money: the nation sews more clothes and stitches more shoes and assembles more toys for the world's children than any other...China has also become the world's largest maker of consumer electronics' and so forth (Fishman, 2005: 1). In Africa, Chinese commodities dominate the market place, as a glance at figures relating to Chinese exports to West African countries indicates. In Nigeria for instance, in 2003 China's exports grew from US$ 1.76 billion to US$ 2.28 billion in 2004, (Tull, 2006: 464). Chinese exports to Ethiopia amounted to 93 per cent of the trade between the two countries (Eisenman, 2007: 40). While African's trade with China has increased, economic relations between China and the continent are occurring on unequal terms. China's commodities going to African countries range from cheap low-end consumer goods to high-end manufactured goods, such as machinery, textiles and apparel, accounting for 87 per cent of the country's exports to the continent (Broadman, 2007: 83). Conversely, the backbone of the African export basket to China is primary commodities.

A process of de-industrialization is one core result of the flooding of African markets with Chinese commodities during this conjuncture. Given China's level of industrial development and capacity to produce commodities cheaply, African countries find themselves at a severe disadvantage. In Dar es Salaam, Tanzania, for instance, the country's only manufacturer of flip flops, OK Plast, has had to cut jobs from 3000 to 1000 because of the flooding of the Tanzanian market with cheap flip flops from China (BBC News, 2006d). This has negative effects not only on the local manufacturing sector, which for historical reasons was small to begin with, but also on state revenue. As a general manager of OK Plast factory contends, in Tanzania the 'end of line stock from Chinese factories is "dumped" here, sold for less than the cost of materials, dodging customs and import duties' (ibid.). This trend is occurring even in countries with stronger industrial and economic capacity such as South Africa, with the country's leading steel firm Iscor (now Mittal Steel), for instance, raising alarm bells of the potential threat by Chinese capital to the steel industry (Alden, 2005: 157). Manufacturing sectors in African countries are not the only ones facing crisis because of increasing imports from China. Chinese retail traders with the support of the state are increasingly taking hold in countries such as Angola, South Africa, Malawi, Tanzania, Uganda, Nigeria, Kenya and many others. This development is generating tensions in various parts of Africa where local traders face tremendous obstacles given the abundant availability of cheap commodities offered by Chinese traders. In Uganda, for instance, the Kampala City Traders Association has contested what they consider as unfair trade practices by Chinese traders (ibid.: 161–171). China's unequal trading pattern with African countries, in the context of a neo-liberal world order promoting the opening up of domestic markets not only shrinks the already limited space for local traders and manufacturers given the years of neo-liberal policies and the nature of the international division of labour but also constrains the industrialization processes in African countries.

In addition to the search for markets, securing and ensuring that it has reliable access to African natural resources is at the centre of China's economic strategy in Africa. Nowhere is this more evident than in China's strategy in the oil sector. China is increasingly dependent on external sources for oil since becoming a net-importer in 1993. The country's demand for oil is rising at a rapid pace and analysts project that that this trend will continue into the next decade. In 2004 for instance, oil consumption increased by 16 per cent from its 2003 level, and by 2010 it is estimated that China will be dependent on external sources for 45 per cent of its oil consumption (Taylor, 2006b: 943). For China, deepening its involvement through ownership, among other strategies, limits its dependency on the modalities of the international markets for oil (ibid.: 942). To be sure, historical and contemporary politico-economic conditions affect how China's strategy in the oil sector translates in each African country. Nonetheless, the growing involvement of China in the oil industry in Africa is not in question. In the oil sector, China is actively involved in leading oil producing countries such as Nigeria, Sudan, Angola and Libya among others with the aim of ensuring its immediate and long-term demands for oil. To this end, its approach involves not only securing access to oil but creating strategic long-term bilateral relations with African states. China's strategy in the oil sector dovetails well with its soft power approach and facilitates China's extensive involvement in all areas of the oil commodity chain: exploration, extraction, processing and shipping oil to its shores (Eisenman, 2007: 38).

Increasingly Chinese capital controls a large share of the oil sectors in various African countries. In Sudan, China's National Petroleum Corporation controls 40 per cent—the highest stake in shares—of the country's oil sector, and according to analysts, its involvement in the sector is bound to increase as more oil generating sites come into operation with the resolution of political conflicts in country (ibid.: 39). Further, Chinese capital is heavily involved in Angola especially following Sinopec's acquisition of 40 per cent of a significant site for the country's oil industry: the oil block 18 (Taylor, 2006b: 945). China's involvement goes beyond seeking control of shares in the oil sector. Keeping an eye to its future economic and political needs, China has signed oil deals that will increase its control of the evolution of the oil industry in a range of African countries. In 2006, China committed itself to acquiring two oil blocs one in the Niger Delta and another in an off-shore oil field in Nigeria, in addition to becoming a dominant owner of an oil refinery in Kaduna that produces 110,000 barrels of oil per day (BBC News, 2006a). Eastern and Horn of Africa countries such as Kenya and Ethiopia have signed deals with Chinese interests ranging from an offshore exploration deal with CNOOC in Kenya and exploration drilling with Zhongyuan Petroleum Company in the Gambella basin in Ethiopia (Taylor, 2006b: 945). By securing these strategic oil deals, China is ensuring that its modernization project and the demands it generates, especially in the energy sector, and the social energy demands of dominant class forces that have emerged during the modernization epoch are met.

To sustain its current economic growth and demands of the new industrializing society, China is also, through its soft power approach, ensuring access to a range of other primary commodities found in Africa such as copper and timber. In terms of copper, China leads in global consumption and relies heavily on exports of copper from the Democratic Republic of Congo and Zambia (Eisenman, 2007: 40). China's concerted involvement in Zimbabwe is driven by the extensive range of minerals available in the country: from the global status of the country having the second largest deposits of platinum to having other minerals such as uranium, copper, coal, gold and so forth (ibid.). China has already secured its access to Zimbabwe's coal deposits through agreements between its National Aero-Technology Import and Export Corporation and North Industries Corporation and the Zimbabwe state (ibid.). China's search for natural resources will continue to rise in the near future. According to some estimates, the country's imports of copper will rise by 10 per cent and by 2010 imports for iron ore, copper and aluminium will stand at 57, 70 and 80 per cent respectively (Holslag, 2006: 141).

China's drive for oil and other minerals has significant implications for economic processes in Africa, among other matters. To begin with, the drive to have controlling stakes in the oil sector, limits the room to manoeuvre for African social formations in mapping out the evolution of this sector, even while taking into consideration the lack of economic transparency in countries such as Angola and Nigeria, among others. China's monopolistic tendency in the oil sector is very similar to economic practices during the imperial age and those of multinational corporations in Africa, and thus challenges the continuous refrain of equal partnership and mutual benefit that permeates Sino-African elite discourse. Further, China's concentration on extracting surplus of non-renewable resources such as oil, coal and natural gas increases the vulnerability of already weak local economic structures given the international division of labour. A decline in oil and mineral production in African countries, for example, would result in a significant decline in trade between the continent and China. In the main, the increased trade between African countries and China stems mainly from the latter's high levels of trade with oil producing and mineral rich countries such as Angola and South Africa that accounted for 27.4 per cent and 20.6 per cent respectively of Sino-Africa trade in 2005 (IMF, cited in Taylor, 2006b: 938). Further, the environmental effects generated by the extraction of non-renewable resources have effects on the human security of local communities, as the cases of oil rich Nigeria's Niger Delta and mineral rich Sierra Leone indicate. While claiming to have instituted sound environmental measures at home and being committed to implementing them in its practices in Africa, China's environmental record indicates a different story. While China's contemporary economic strategy has led to rapid economic growth and the expansion of the Chinese political and structural power in the world order, this process is occurring at the expense of the health of its workers and the environment (Kahn, 2003).

In addition to its search to secure access to oil and various minerals, China is also engaged in the agrarian sector in various part of Africa. As in other sectors, China's involvement in agriculture production is aimed at providing access to raw materials to fuel the country's modernization agenda and the Chinese state's objective of meeting the needs of its citizens to ensure domestic legitimacy and political stability. In the case of agriculture, China has a double-edged strategy aimed at ensuring food security and expanding its power in the global trading chain of agricultural commodities. Rapid industrialization and urbanization is resulting in the decline of food production in China. In 1994 it was estimated that the country's grain production area had 'dropped from 90.8 million hectares...to an estimated 85.7 million' between 1990 and 1994, and the trend was expected to continue with the deepening of the modernizing project (Brown, 2001: 24). The Chinese state has responded to this by supporting private and public capital involvement in the agricultural sector in African countries. In Tanzania, Zambia and Zimbabwe Chinese interests have signed leasing agreements on agricultural land (Alden, 2005: 149). Ensuring food security is important to the Chinese ruling elites, for a food crisis in the context of ongoing peasant resistance and demands by other social forces could generate political instability, a development that from the state's perspective would derail or put into question its top-down driven economic project. Investment in agro-industries is another feature of China's strategy in Africa. For China, a key strategy is to utilize investment opportunities created by initiatives such as the African Growth and Opportunity Act (AGOA). In the case of AGOA, China aims to secure market access offered to African countries under this framework and further to evade restrictions imposed on China, for instance, in the textile sector by the WTO (Tull, 2006: 471).

As previously mentioned, China is involved in a range of infrastructural projects in African countries. Like other sectors, these projects have material and social effects. On the economic front, Chinese capital has come to dominate large public work projects through its public enterprises such as China Roads and Bridges. In Rwanda this enterprise has been the dominant force in all the major road construction projects and has now opened offices in the country and in Burundi in order to deepen its interests in the region (Holslag, 2006: 159). China is also actively involved in public work projects in Ethiopia, Tanzania, Nigeria, Angola, Democratic Republic of Congo and many other African countries. China's involvement in public work comes through various avenues such as outbidding other contenders but also through tied aid. In Angola for example, the previously mentioned loan agreement that the country signed with China's Exim Bank in efforts to escape IMF's conditionality was offered on condition that a significant number of contracts in the construction industry would go to Chinese interests (Taylor, 2006b: 947).

Beyond dominating the contemporary public work landscape in various parts of Africa, China's labour practices in this arena are having effects on local livelihoods. While the involvement of China in large public work projects has created jobs, local workers are not the beneficiaries of this development in places such as Ethiopia where Chinese capital has contracts to construct a major highway and a dam on the Tekeze River. In both projects, Chinese capital has brought workers from China (Eisenman, 2007: 47). This practice is evident in China's other public work projects in Angola, Uganda, Rwanda and other countries. The trend will continue since Chinese loan agreements pertaining to public work projects have clauses insisting on substantive use of Chinese workers in these projects (Holslag, 2006: 162). In the case of Sudan, where China has won a bid worth US$ 650 million to construct the Merowe Dam on the Nile River, the ratio for workers will be 80 and 20 per cent Chinese and Sudanese respectively (Goldstein et al, 2006:

85). In Uganda, Gabon, Tanzania, Nigeria, Lesotho, Zambia and other countries, the use of Chinese workers, from professionals to manual labourers, is generating tensions and resentment from local communities and it has led to violence in Zambia and Lesotho (Alden, 2005: 157). Resentment to the practices of Chinese capital is evident in Uganda as the following commentary from a local newspaper indicates:

> Residents and local leaders of Jinja district, especially in the Municipality, are very discontented from the lack of benefits to the local community from the huge $70 million (Shs 70bn) Owen Falls Dam civil work being done by the Chinese company Sichuan International Engineering and Technical Corporation (SIETCO). They mainly complained that the project has not employed significant numbers of people from the area; has not consumed [local] food, and other goods and services. (*The Monitor* quoted in Holslag, 2006: 163)

To sum up this section, while South–South economic cooperation is a theme that has been emphasized by China and others states in the South since the 1955 Bandung conference, China's practices in contemporary Africa in substance represent processes of accumulation by dispossession rather than mutual benefit. In fact, when China perceives a threat to its economic practices, it does not hesitate to indicate its commitment to protecting its interests. For example, when trade unions in South Africa demanded that the state institute measures to protect the textile industry, the Chinese state response was, 'any move by the South African government to restrict textile imports from China would violate the WTO free trade agreement' (Tull, 2006: 473). In large measure, China's drive to secure natural resources and markets facilitates the reproduction of African social formations as producers of primary commodities in the capitalist world economy, a development that has major structural and political implications. It is important to note that even though African countries are key producers of primary commodities, given the international division of labour that underpins the world system, they do not have a monopoly on natural resources. Thus, important as these resources are, other countries including China depend on other regions such as Latin America, the Caribbean, Asia and even core countries such as Canada and the USA for primary commodities, especially in the agrarian sector. African countries, then, face major competition from other parts of the world system and given the restrictive trading architecture instituted by states in the North and the unequal approach to agrarian subsidies, their options in terms of international trading patterns are narrow. These economic and political conditions make the possibility of these countries breaking through the structural constraints of the contemporary world economic structure limited.

Conclusion

This chapter has highlighted developments in Russia and China in the era of a neo-liberal world order. The chapter has suggested that while both countries claim to be committed to the emergence of a multi-polar world order, at this historical conjuncture deepening engagement with this order seems to be their practice rather than a concerted effort to transform its core features. Further, while anti-hegemonism is a core aspect of the ideology of both states, pragmatism marks their contestation with the USA, which they consider as the hegemon of the post-1945 world order. Overall, our conclusion is that while continuing China and Russia discourse of multi-polarity opens a discursive and political space to challenge hegemonic practices at the global level, there is need to interrogator this discourse. For instance, what ideas and practices underlie this discourse? The assumption of this discourse as espoused by the current President of Russia is that a multi-polar world order is just by its nature. The position taken here is that such an approach is reductionist for it neglects to take cognizance of power dynamics. In the main, there is need to ask who looses and who benefits from the multi-polar world order envisioned by ruling elites in China, Russia and elsewhere. As their proposals stand and their practices indicate, power dynamics are at their centre of politico-economic projects and one cannot assume that they will evaporate in their proposed multi-polar world order. As the nature of China's involvement in contemporary Africa indicates, power dynamics are at the centre of the country's relations with the continent, even though China is at the forefront of pushing a discourse on multi-polarity. Further, portraying themselves as just political actors when compared to the TDHB because of their claims of multi-polarity and solidarity with the South masks the national interest and imperial foundations of their politico-economic projects, as examples of practices of accumulation by dispossession by China in contemporary Africa have indicated.

7
Human Security, Neo-liberalism and Securitization of Development

The last decade or so has seen the rise of the concept of human security in studies of world politics and development. The rise of this perspective, however, has not occurred in an intellectual or politico-economic vacuum. During this period, scholars in the fields of IR and IPE have been interrogating the concept of security in efforts to broaden it. Further, this period has seen growing resistance, to human insecurities generated by the neo-liberal project (Chapter 8) and other features of the current world order such as increasing securitizing practices by states in various parts of the world. On the political level, the end of Cold War geopolitics opened an opportunity for the rethinking of security in broader terms. These developments, then, have resulted in calls to broaden the notion of security to include issues such as economic, gender, development, environmental, political and global security. For instance, in IDS, human security has emerged as the new development discourse underpinning policies of institutions of global governance such as the UN and the World Bank, and other members of the TDHB. In this chapter, while we highlight some of the intellectual and political origins of the notion of human security, our objective is not to review the growing literature[1] on the concept, rather it is to interrogate this concept as it pertains to a core concern of this book: the emergence and evolution of hegemonic development ideas and their effects on politico-economic processes.

The underlying premise of this chapter is that, while the TDHB increasingly invokes the concept of human security and calls for its mainstreaming in its development strategies, the potential of this development to transform contemporary development ideas and practices is extremely limited. To begin with, powerful as the normative underpinning of the human security development perspective is, the latter does not fundamentally dislodge the contemporary hegemonic development discourse promoted by the TDHB and their ideological allies in the South. Thus, while the bloc's adoption of the language of human security might open a space for a range of actors involved in the transnational development industry—such as NGOs—to push what they consider as a progressive development agenda, the rise of this discourse in the development strategies of the TDHB legitimizes the prevailing hegemonic development discourse rather than transforms it. Further, in even more overt ways, the securitization of development and security in the new global geography of the war on terror contradicts and limits the human security development agenda that THDB invokes. The chapter has three parts and begins by highlighting various perspectives focusing on rethinking security in IR and IPE and from institutional sites concerned with development. The last two parts focuses on an examination of the possibilities and contradictions of human security inspired development discourse of Millennium Development Goals (MDGs) given, first, the context of neo-liberalism and second, securitization of development.

Rethinking security

In the traditional realist conceptualization of security in IR and IPE, the state remains the referent object in discussions of security. The assumption that the state is the only political actor that can provide security in a given territorial political community informs such an approach to security. Further, realists tend to conceptualize national and international political space in Hobbessian terms. According to Thomas Hobbes, in the state of nature individuals face constant threats perpetuated by internal and external forces. This social reality leads them to seek the emergence of sovereign authority that will ensure their security from internal and external threats.[2] From a realist perspective, the social contract underpinning the modern state enables citizens to have security as they pursue their self-interests. In this realist Hobbessian worldview, states are insecure for they cannot control activities of other states given that the international system lacks a sovereign authority that ensures their security. Given this scenario, the expansion of a state's military capabilities is central in strengthening its capacity to respond to internal and external threats. From a realist perspective, because of the anarchic nature of the world polity, the security dilemma governs the dynamics of inter-state relations, hence the need to focus on the security of the state in discussions of security (see generally, Waltz, 1979).

The traditional conceptualization of security is increasingly challenged from various perspectives, three of which we highlight here. From the Copenhagen school, scholars such as Barry Buzan, Ole Wæver and Jappe De Wilde have called for the re-conceptualization of security beyond the state.[3] What the school calls for is a consideration of the interaction between the various sectors and referent objects in analysing security. As Buzan et al. state, 'relations of coercion do not exist apart from relations of exchange, authority, identity, or environment' and thus, while 'sectors might identify distinctive patterns...they remain inseparable parts of complex wholes' (1998: 8). From their multi-sectorial perspective, then, while in the case of military threat, the state is usually the main referent object, such threat could be linked to issues of environmental and economic security (ibid.: 21–23). In addition and departing from the realist perspective, the Copenhagen school argues that a close examination of the nature and practices of states indicate that the latter can be a source of social threat (Buzan, 1983: 24). Buzan acknowledges that there are differences in state forms specifically between the John Lockean version of minimalist state and the maximal states that in the Marxist interpretative tradition would have their own interests, and between weak and strong states. Nonetheless, he argues that regardless of the nature of a state form, the extensive sources of power available to states can be sources of threats. States can be a source of social threats to citizens in direct and indirect ways. In the economic sphere, for example, state economic projects can lead to insecurity for individuals through practices that result in loss of job, income or property (Buzan et al., 1998). Further, the judicial and legal framework and practices of a state can also lead to insecurity for citizens if there is 'inadequate or excessive policing and prosecution practices' (Buzan, 1983: 25). In addition 'miscarried or deficient justice can have an immense impact on the life of the individual concerned, and cases of both types are an inevitable cost of any attempt to balance effective law enforcement with protection of broad civil liberties' (ibid.).

As the preceding insights from the Copenhagen school indicate, the realist approach, which naturalizes the role of state, leads to an assumption that the state is a benevolent provider of security. This is a limited view of the state, for it neglects the coercive foundation of state forms and the numerous ways in which states can be sources of threats. When one considers the political, economic and social threats generated by states in various historical junctures in Germany, Spain, Chile, China, Argentina, USA, South Africa, Indonesia, Canada and many other countries, the limitations of the realist approach are illuminated. In the contemporary era, the state practice of extraordinary rendition is an example of how state practices can be a source of human insecurity. This practice entails individuals being 'arrested in an airport, abducted in a foreign country, detained at a border crossing and then bundled off to jail cells in foreign countries were torture is the norm and where the rule of law quite simply does not apply' (Neve, 2007: 121–122). While the USA has been at the forefront of this practice, Alex Neve contends that in the post-9/11 geopolitical order, this has become a common practice in a range of countries (ibid: 121). During this period, for example, USA security agents at John F. Kennedy airport arrested a Canadian citizen, Maher Arar, in 2002. He was then detained in the US, Jordan and lastly in Syria. As the Commission of Inquiry (CI) established to investigate the 'actions of Canadian officials in Relation to Maher Arar' (http://epc.lac-bac.gc.ca) states: 'the RMCP (Royal Canadian Mounted Police) requested that American authorities place lookouts for Mr Arar and his wife, Monia Mazigh, in US Customs Treasury Enforcement Communications System (TECS). In the request, to which no caveats were attached, the RCMP described Mr Arar and Dr Mazingh as Islamic Extremist individuals suspected of being linked to the Al Qaeda terrorist movement' (ibid.). Yet, in 2006, the CI's Commissioner, Dennis O'Connor, declared 'I am able to say categorically that there is no evidence to indicate that Mr Arar has committed any offence or that his activities constitute a threat to the security of Canada' (ibid.). While the Canadian state issued an apology to Arar in 2007 following the findings of the CI, the fact remains that, for more than a year, his basic rights were not secured by the state, and the actions of the latter contributed directly to his experiences of human insecurity especially through torture. Describing his torture in a Syrian jail, Arar states: 'the beating started that day and was very intense for a week...I could hear other prisoners being tortured, and screaming and screaming...At the end of each day, they would always say, "Tomorrow will be harder for you" ' (Neve, 2007: 118).

The critical security studies (CSS) perspective forms another tradition in the post-Cold War field of security studies. Scholars associated with CSS consider sources of threats as myriad including the state (Booth, 2005: 3). Thus, from their perspective states are not neutral actors in the security domain. For scholars such as Ken Booth the individual is the 'ultimate referent' (Booth, 1991) object in debates concerning broadening the concept of security. In addition, this perspective links security to human emancipation especially in the work of scholars such as Richard Wyn Jones (1999), Booth (1991) and Steve Smith (1991; 2005). For Booth, a focus on state security ignores the myriads of threats facing humanity that could emerge from environmental stress, state political practices, terrorism and many other things (Booth, 1991: 321). In this respect he contends that 'it is illogical to place states at the centre of our thinking about security because even those which are producers of security...represent means and not ends' (ibid.: 320). Re-thinking security beyond the state can lead to political projects that may engender emancipation and thus enhance human security, for 'security and emancipation are two sides of the same coin' and in this line of argument it is emancipation that leads to security rather than 'power and order' (ibid.: 319).

From a critical feminist perspective, the realist tradition's representation of security, states, and world orders in gender-neutral terms ignores the gendered nature and effects of these structures of power. In the case of state security, the realist approach ignores the masculine foundation of, for example, the military industrial-complexes (Enloe, 1990, 1993 and 2007; Whitworth, 2005: 90–102). For feminist scholars, a theory of security and international politics that does not take seriously the gendered nature of states, military apparatus and pre-existing world order is extremely limited and contributes to the normalization of militarized masculine norms and security practices that historically and in the contemporary era have contributed to insecurity for the majority of women. Fundamentally, a critical feminist approach to security brings to attention the 'extent to which gender hierarchies themselves are a source of domination and thus an obstacle to a truly comprehensive definition of security' (Tickner, 1992: 53), a social reality that is ignored in the realist naturalized representation of security. Further, moving beyond state-centric approaches to security is crucial, for 'the achievement of peace, economic justice, and ecological sustainability is inseparable from overcoming social relations of domination and subordination' since comprehensive security entails 'not only the absence of war but also the elimination of unjust social relations' (1992: 128). In re-thinking security, a feminist lens is crucial because it moves beyond narrow approaches to security not just in the realist tradition but also other perspectives on security that neglect the ways in which militarism and war contribute to gendered human insecurity. Thus, while welcoming recent efforts aimed at broadening the definition of security, critical feminist scholars contend that without a gendered analytic, this development will not transform security studies (Truong et al., 2007).

While scholars working with the realist framework such as Stephen Walt (1991) and Laurence Freedman (1998) criticize attempts to broaden the concept of security, the new approaches have generated new lenses through which to consider it. Scholars in this area, now pursue issues that have traditionally been considered outside the purview of security studies in IR and IPE, such as environmental degradation, development, and gender, economic, and political marginalization as central questions. The re-thinking of the concept of security in the post-Cold War period has thus influenced broader intellectual and policy debates, especially in the area of international development. The individual as a referent object on the security question has increasingly emerged as a central feature in this arena, giving rise to a human security-centred perspective in the development blueprints emerging from institutions of global governance and other members of the TDHB. As in scholarly circles, then, debates calling for a re-thinking of the concept of security have emerged in development policy circles such as UN agencies and the World Bank. In the context of the UN, the 1994 United Nations Development Programme's (UNDP) report marked the ushering in of the concept of human security. The UN Commission on Human Security's (CHS) 2003 report, *Human Security Now*, consolidated the usage of the notion in development policies of the TDHB.

The UNDP 1994 report considered the geopolitics of the Cold War era as characterized by emphasis on state security as states in both the North and South mainly concentrated on expanding their security (UNDP, 1994: 22). The central focus on state security meant that 'legitimate concerns of ordinary people who sought security in their lives' were off the agenda (ibid.). The end of this historical juncture then provided a window of opportunity to rethink security in broad terms focusing on 'human life and dignity' rather than weapons and the security of the state (ibid.). In promoting a human security development discourse, the report claimed that 'how people live and breathe in a society, how freely they exercise their many choices, how much access they have to market and social opportunities and whether they live in conflict or in peace' (ibid.: 22–23) were some of the core developments from such as a perspective. Further, achieving human security from a UNDP's perspective meant individuals could live under conditions marked by 'freedom from fear and freedom from want' (ibid.: 24). The UNDP report identified several issues as being central to any project geared to the achievement of human security: economic, food, health, environmental, personal, community and political security. Taking an approach to security similar to the Copenhagen school's multi-sectorial perspective, the report viewed all these spheres of human security as interdependent, for insecurity in one can lead to insecurity in another.

In 2000, the establishment of the CHS—which issued its final report in 2003—was one of the developments following the Millennium Summit that argued forcefully for the idea of human security to be the foundation in international development and other global issues. The CHS viewed expanding security beyond its traditional state-centrism as crucial in a global context characterized by interconnectedness and the 'proliferation of menace' to human security in the twenty-first century (2003: 2). For the CHS, the emergence of an interdependent world meant acceptance of 'shared sovereignty' by states, for no society was unsusceptible to social threats emerging from acts of unilateralism and human insecurities generated by other societies. Given these conditions, the CHS considered the human security perspective as providing a 'comprehensive' approach to global issues such as development and security (ibid.: 4). Like the earlier UNDP report, the CHS perspective on human security proposed a people-centred approach to security; a development that reverses the historical tendency by states to use national resources to expand their security and other statist interests (ibid.: 6) at the expense of the human security of citizens. Further, the era in which scholars and policy makers considered states as the only actors providing security at the national and international level was long over. For the CHS—echoing a liberal internationalist perspective outlined in Chapter 5—in the contemporary era of globalization, institutions at the regional and international levels and a range of groups in civil society were key actors in the national and international security complex. It also claimed that empowering 'the people' was central to the achievement of human security, a goal that could be realized through the 'protection strategies' being provided by states, international institutions, the private sector and NGOs (ibid.). From the CHS's perspective, empowerment enables individuals to achieve human security for it helps the 'development of its vision of their potential' and that of their communities (ibid.: 11).

The CHS put forward several recommendations to advance the achievement of its vision of human security. These included, but were not limited to the extension of universal primary education as a tool for empowerment (ibid.: 140) in addition to the promotion of a global trading system and market-led development geared for the benefit of the poor, since for the CHS market strategies and trade are the two pillars of economic development, and thus they continue to be central to any project aimed at addressing the needs of the poor (ibid.: 137). Overall, the interest on broadening the concept of security in academic and international development circles has contributed to the rise of the concept of human security as a dominant theme in the development discourse of TDHB. Does the current adoption of a human security discourse then represent a fundamental turn in the TDHB's development discourse? Further, what is the viability of its human security development projects such as the Millennium Development Goals? It is to a discussion of these issues that we turn for the reminder of the chapter.

Promoting human security in the South: Millennium Development Goals[4]

The development discourse of the TDHB is increasingly including the underlying features of the human security ideas embedded in the UNDP report, the CHS and from scholarly debates calling for the broadening of the concept of security. This is especially the case in the TDHB development discourse of the MDGs. As the extract below indicates, the normative underpinnings of debates concerned with the broadening of the concept of security largely influence the MDGs:

Goal 1: Eradicate extreme poverty and hunger
Goal 2: Achieve Universal primary education
Goal 3: Promote gender equality and empower women
Goal 4: Reduce child mortality
Goal 5: Improve maternal health
Goal 7: Ensure environmental sustainability
Goal 8: Develop a Global Partnership for Development

The normative thrust of the human security discourse that underpins the MDGs framework may provide a window of opportunity for social forces in the South to push for initiatives geared to addressing human security issues such as poverty and unequal social relations. In the case of struggles for gender equality, as in the era of the UN decade for women (Jain, 2005), it may represent a political opportunity structure for women's organizations and movements in their struggles for gender equality. In general then, and as Wendy Harcourt argues, the MDGs framework provides an opening for civil society groups to push 'the idea of global solidarity and social justice into the international intergovernmental arena; one that can be seen as a strategic entry point into critical international debates on poverty that pivot around North–South solidarity and engendered sustainable development' (2004: 7). While acknowledging that the MDGs may provide a political opportunity structure for social struggles, we consider it as a limited frame for the achieving of substantive human security. Our contention is that the rise of a human security development framework in the development discourse and strategies of the TDHB represent old wine in new bottles. As a discussion of the MDGs framework will indicate, emancipatory as it sounds, the approach of the TDHB to human security remains overly simplistic, technocratic and ahistorical. Overall, it ignores the structuring power of the neo-liberal context in which its human security inspired MDGs are being implemented. We begin with a discussion of the limitations of the MDGs as a strategy for promoting human security with a focus on some of its core goals: gender inequality and the empowerment of women, poverty eradication, environmental sustainability and global partnership for development.

Gender equality and empowering women

A close reading of the MDGs framework indicates a reductionist and a depoliticized approach to human security and development. Take for example its second and third goal whose objective is to address gender inequality. In the MDGs development discourse, ensuring gender parity in elementary and secondary education is the pathway to equality between women and men. While there is a consensus that education can be a tool for liberation, education processes do not occur in a social, political and economic vacuum. Similar to the overall human security agenda of the TDHB, the assumption in the MDGs framework is that access to education will expand the range of choices for women. What this approach neglects is the fact that individual choices do not occur in an abstracted context. Thus, while education can be a tool for the emancipation of women, local patriarchal ideologies and practices from the state apparatus and foundations of hegemonic development discourses or from other sites of power have structuring and ideological effects on the choices women make at a given juncture.

Thus, the political-economic contexts in which education processes occur do influence the transformative potential of education. In the current conjuncture, the neo-liberal development project has had significant effects in the education sector. Since its ascendancy, the project has seen states limit their spending in the education sector, especially at the secondary and tertiary levels, in addition to introducing school fees. In Africa, institutions of global governance especially the World Bank and the IMF have been key actors in the decline of public institutions at the tertiary level and the trend towards the commodification of education. As various scholars have argued, this development and other elements of the neo-liberal development model have had gendered effects on education such as the deepening of the historical disparity between girls' and boys' school enrolment (Tsikata and

Kerr, 2000; Sahle, 2008). Yet, the TDHB ignores its role in the implementation of practices and developments that have contributed to gender disparity in education at the same time that its rhetoric of achieving human security through education has heightened. In addition, tensions and contradictions characterize the MDGs goal of achieving gender parity in elementary and secondary education as an avenue for gender equality. After achieving their primary education certificates, where will the graduates go given the crisis facing institutions of higher learning in various parts of the South because of the marketization of the education sector and the economy? While enrolment of girls may increase with the implementation of MDGs, it will result in a massive number of young women with only the bare minimum level of education and, thus, with a limited capacity to exercise the much-evoked individual choice in the TDHB's human security development agenda given ongoing neo-liberal inspired economic processes in most parts of the South.

Essentially, reductionism is the dominant thread in the MDGs framework and it is quite evident in its approach to gender equality. As has been highlighted, achieving education parity between girls and boys in the lower levels of education is the policy development considered to lead to the achievement of gender equality. MDGs' focus on education as the sole tool for liberation for women echoes classical liberal philosophy that considered education to be the tool for liberating women from their 'natural' irrationality and emotional tendencies. With education, accordingly, women, like men, would make decisions about their lives based on reason (Wollstonecraft and Poston 1975; Jaggar, 1983). Overall, the MDGs development discourse is silent on other measures that could facilitate the achievement of reproductive, political and economic rights for women, a development that could greatly contribute to human security for most women. This silence is startling given the centrality of these rights to securing security for women in their specific historical contexts. For most analysts of the MDGs framework, the exclusion of these rights and the limited approach to gender equality in this framework indicates the traditional political lens that envelops the TDHB approaches to human security. This framework's neglect of reproduction and sexual rights, for instance, signals the influence of the views of 'the US government and other countries negative approach to women's health and rights' in the framing of the MDGs (Harcourt, 2004: 37). Arguing along similar lines, Samir Amin states, given MDGs' limited approach to gender equality 'the neoconservative Christian fundamentalists of the United States, Poland and elsewhere, the Muslims of Saudi

Arabia, Pakistan and other countries, and the fundamentalist Hindus agree on eliminating any reference to the rights of women and the family' (2006: 3).

Poverty

Poverty reduction forms another human security inspired goal of the MDGs development discourse. The first target involves reducing by half the number of people 'whose income is less than one dollar a day' by 2015 and the percentage of people 'who suffer from hunger' (http://www.un.org/millenniumgoals/). This begs the question of what happens to the other half facing insecurity because of poverty and hunger. Who determines which half facing insecurity generated by these social threats will be addressed? What happens to the lives of people that are outside the MDGs 2000–2015 interregnum? Is the market or the downsized state going to take care of their human security needs or are they disposable? Given the concept of human security's normative foundation, these issues cry out for answers. However, as with the other goals, the MDGs approach to issues of hunger and poverty is technocratic. Yet, historically and in the contemporary era, the existence of these social threats to human security and commitment to address them lies in the realm of politics. Hunger and poverty are not natural states; they are results of power relations both locally and internationally. The capital accumulation strategies that ruling elites in the South institute and the TDHB supports at a given juncture tend to have significant implications for human security ethical concerns such as the eradication of poverty and hunger. Further, the social protections mechanisms that states institute are not neutral: political and power dynamics characterize them. In addition to the MDGs framework's reductionist and technical approach to issues of hunger and poverty, it ignores the local and global politico-economic contexts of its human security agenda. The mapping of the MDGs neglects the profound ways in which the neo-liberal development discourse and other features of the current world order set structural and political limits to the eradication of poverty and hunger. While additional blueprints keep emerging, the core approach to development remains neo-liberal. Thus, in the case of poverty reduction, even if extra funding to address this social threat were available, other neo-liberal policies will end up cancelling out whatever gains might emerge with such a development. Thus, while, on the one hand, the TDHB claims to promote human security, its dominant development discourse has generated and continues to generate human insecurity.

Neo-liberal development discourse's stress on export-led growth, for instance, has major implications for the achievement of human security-inspired MDGs. In terms of the eradication of poverty and hunger, the emphasis on cash crop production has increased food insecurity in various countries in the South. In recent decades, these countries have had to focus on exporting primary commodities not only to meet their economic goals but also to generate earnings to meet their debt obligations to institutions of global governance and other members of the TDHB, and private financial institutions. This echoes a return to the era of imperialism when local food production systems were de-centred to enable the production of cash crop commodities to meet the tastes of new industrializing societies in Europe at the costs of securing human security for local people (Rodney, 1972; McMichael, 2003). In the era of state-led development and global Keynesian economics, food security was defined as a national public good, but under the neo-liberal framework, it is now conceptualized as a private commodity (McMichael, 2003), whose modalities in the global market place are best left to the workings of the invisible hand of the market. The neo-liberal doctrine of removing national protection measures to facilitate the deepening of a global free trade regime has enabled this policy move. As Philip McMichael explains, the reframing of food security along commodity lines serves the corporate interests of the leading global agro-business firms at the expense of local agrarian producers (2003: 180–181). The North American Free Trade Agreement, for instance, allowed '100% foreign investor rights in Mexican agriculture, Pillsbury's Green Giant subsidiary relocated its frozen food processing from California to Mexico to obtain cheap wages, minimal food safety standards, and zero tariffs on re-export to the USA' and the development also saw the involvement of Cargill and Tyson Foods in various sites of agrarian production in Mexico and others parts of Latin America (ibid.: 181).

The deepening commodification of agricultural production under the neo-liberal development project has increased food dependency for countries in the South as metropolitan states can dump their agrarian surplus in these social formations as part of the WTO's regime stipulation of the 'right to export' (ibid.) for all countries: a right that does not take into consideration the unequal power relations that mark the world trading system in agrarian products (Prempeh, 2006). Under the WTO trading regime, social formations in the North are the beneficiaries of such rights and other stipulations of this regime, for among other things, 'their commodities are cheaper on the world market because of export subsidies and economies of mechanized scale, and [their] corporations' internal transactions account for 70% of the international food trade' a reality that opens room for increased 'exports from North to South, rather than in the opposite direction' (Einarsson, 2001: 7, quoted in McMichael, 2003: 176). Commentating on the social effects of this neo-liberal agrarian strategy, Vandana Shiva notes, 'export-oriented agriculture is also creating an agricultural apartheid, with the Third World being asked to stop growing food staples and instead grow luxury products for the rich North. Production of food staples is now concentrated in the United States, and in the hands of a few multinational seed companies and grain trading companies... As countries are forced to destroy their agricultural systems to grow and export commodities, both cultural diversity and biological diversity disappear' (2006: 98). Under the rhetoric of free trade, global development partnership and human security promotion, what is occurring insidiously is the return of a colonial mode of agricultural production and global trade. For the agrarian sector in the South, this trend has significant implications for human security for it:

> symbolizes the subjection of agriculture to the commodity form, via neo-liberal institutional dictates and the corresponding privatization of food security relations. As local producers and markets are scuttled by removal of public protections, marginalized by the privileging of export cropping, and swamped by artificially cheapened food imports, the conditions of social reproduction in the countryside are reconstituted within new circuits of capital enabled by the corporate globalization project. (McMichael, 2003: 176)

Environmental sustainability

The neo-liberal export-led economic strategy has other implications and its underlying contradictions have great significance for the achievement of human security. Goal seven in the MDGs framework aims to 'ensure environmental sustainability' through the linking of 'principles of sustainable development into country policies and programs' to 'reverse the loss of environmental resources' (http://www.un.org/millenniumgoals/). The litmus test for this goal will be the reduction in the number of people living without 'access to safe drinking water' by half by 2015 and the improvement of 'the lives of at least 100 million slum-dwellers' by 2020 (ibid.). These goals for achieving environmental security and their measuring instruments conveniently forget the contributions of neo-liberal ideas and practices to environmental insecurity. The MDGs human security development supported by the TDHB ignores the social threats and other forms of human insecurity generated by the privatization of water services (see Chapter 8). Further, the neo-liberal roots of the emergence of massive slums, homelessness and internal displacement in both the North and South in an epoch marked by criminalization and de-historicization of poverty and dismantling of social protection measures do not feature in the MDGs development discourse. In addition, there is a disjuncture between this discourse's goals of ensuring environmental security and the promotion of primary commodity export-led strategy by the TDHB and their prevailing neo-liberal hegemonic development discourse. This strategy has resulted in rapid deforestation processes in countries such as Ghana as the country switched to timber production for export markets in the 1980s to increase its export earnings (Sayer et al., 1992).

The MDGs development discourses further neglect the contributions by the North to environmental insecurity globally in its depoliticized and technical approach to environmental security. Under the doctrine of free trade, dumping toxic waste from the North to the South for instance has become a significant practice in the circuit of global trade. Not only have some firms that make toxic products, such as pesticides, 'gone global' in search of production zones with limited environmental regulatory regimes, but also 'global marketing has created new outlets' in the South for most banned products in the North (Scholte, 2000: 211–212). One estimate states that 'nearly a third of pesticides exported from the North have been outlawed, unregistered or withdrawn in the country of manufacture' (ibid.: 212). In addition, the failure of previous declarations aimed at achieving environmental security crafted by institutions of global governance raises questions of where to find the political will to push for the achievement of even the minimalist environment security embodied in goal seven of the MDGs. The failure to address the environmental threats outlined in the Brundtland Report, *Our Common Future*, and the declarations that emerged at the 1992 UN Rio de Janeiro conference on the environment, leads one to conclude that the current rhetoric on securing environmental sustainability by the TDHB through the MDGs reinforces our contention that it represents old wine in new bottles.

Global partnership for development

Partnership, like other progressive-sounding phrases, such as poverty eradication and promotion of gender equality, is another concept peppering the human security development discourse. This concept,

embodied in goal ten of the MDGs, seeks to push for the establishment of a global partnership for development. A core aim of this
partnership is to push for the development of 'an open, rule-based, predictable, non-discriminatory trading and financial system' that would
enable development in the South. Nonetheless, in terms of establishing a rule-based global trading system, this idea marked the push for the
emergence of the WTO in 1994. Yet, the evolution of this trading regime
has seen the marginalization of issues that are pertinent to the majority
of countries in the South such as trade barriers and subsidies. Further,
this trading regime is contributing to poverty and other forms of human
insecurity:

> Inequalities in trade are reinforcing these wider inequalities. For every
> $1 generated through export in the international trading system,
> there are 1.1 billion people struggling to survive on $1 a day—the
> same number as the mid-1980s. Even though developing countries
> have been increasing their exports more than rich countries, large
> initial inequalities mean that the absolute gap between them is
> widening. In the 1990s, rich countries increased the per capita value
> of their export value by $1938, compared with $51 for low-income
> countries and $98 for middle-income countries. (Watkins and Fowler,
> 2002: 9–10, quoted in Prempeh, 2006: 169)

The other elements of goal ten are full of contradictions. For example, the claim that this goal aims to see the emergence of an 'enhanced
program of debt relief for Heavily Indebted Poor Countries (HIPC) and
cancellation of official bilateral debt; and more generous Official Development Assistance (ODA) for countries committed to poverty reduction'
(http://www.un.org/millenniumgoals/) disregards the limited nature of
existing practices of the TDHB on these issues. The decline of ODA
continues even after the much talked about consensus on financing
development at the UN conference on this theme held in Monterrey, Mexico in March 2002.[5] According to its advocates, the Monterrey
consensus' core mandate was to mobilize resources locally and internationally in efforts to respond to constraints facing the financing
of the global South's development. To achieve the optimum benefits
that would emerge with this development, countries in the South were
called up 'to continue their efforts to achieve a transparent, stable and
predictable investment climate, with proper contract enforcement and
respect for property rights, embedded in sound macroeconomic policies
and institutions that allow businesses, both domestic and international,

to operate efficiently and profitably and with maximum development impact' (ibid.). Thus far, the mobilization efforts have not yielded increases of financial flows from the North in the form of development aid (Bond, 2006). In addition, the stress on foreign direct investment (FDI) as a source for development finance in the Monterrey consensus ignores the nature of FDI flows in the current historical moment, which is 'skewed' against poor countries. The receipts of FDI account for 'only 0.5 percent of global FDI flows' with 86 per cent of this figure being allocated 'to ten countries and more than half goes to four oil-producing countries (Picciotto et al., 2007: 76). In the case of the African continent, which the Monterrey consensus constructs as being in much need for FDI flows, sub-Saharan countries' receipts stand at 2 per cent with the majority of this amount being allocated to places suitable for 'natural resource extraction' (ibid.).

To conclude here, the neo-liberal development discourse that underpins the contemporary world order, elements of which we incorporated in the preceding section and others discussed in Chapter 3, contradicts and limits the viability of the human security agenda embedded in its MDGs discourse. Essentially, the human security development discourse underlying the MDGs does not represent a shift from the neo-liberal core of the development ideas and practices of the TDHB. Over seven years since the launch of the MDGs, the majority of social forces in the South continue to experience social threats generated by the neo-liberal agenda. Thus, when one takes seriously the current politico-economic conditions such as neo-liberalism, the limited possibility of achieving the human security aims underpinning the MDGs is illuminated. We now turn to a discussion of the securitization of development and security and the implications of this development to the human security agenda currently invoked by the TDHB under their MDGs framework.

Securitization of development and security

In what seems to be an extremely brief interregnum following the end of the Cold War, the expansion of state security and militarism are increasingly at the forefront of political landscapes in various parts of the world polity. Of course, even in the brief interregnum, war and security issues were central to state practices as the first Gulf War in 1991 reminded those who thought an era of perpetual peace and end of history had emerged with the fall of the Berlin wall. While, the TDHB and other dominant actors in the world order, such as Multinational Corporations through their corporate social responsibility discourse, invoke their commitment to addressing poverty, environment security, gender inequality and other social realities that they consider as sources of human insecurity, the securitization of development and security is the other dominant trend in the contemporary era. In the previous section, we highlighted some of the ways in which the neo-liberal development discourse limits the viability of the human security agenda embedded in the MDGs. Here we build on that section by discussing the implications for human security development discourse given the increasing securitization of development and security in the post-Cold War era. We begin with a brief conceptual discussion followed by highlights of the implications for the TDHB's human security agenda in the context of securitization of development and security with specific reference to first, 'unending wars' (Duffield, 2007) in the age of the war on terror, and second, contemporary Africa.

Securitization

Security has emerged more overtly as a central policy preoccupation in official development circles following the horrific 9/11 terrorist attacks of 2001 in the USA. The concept of securitization emerges out of the writings of the previously discussed Copenhagen School in security studies especially in the work of Ole Wæver. To say that an issue has become securitized, means that it has not only been represented as an existential threat to a referent object such as national or international security by a securitizing agent, which could be a state or a non-state actor, but also that it has been accepted as such in the public domain (Buzan et al., 1998: 25). Securitizing agents tend to portray their 'action' as being 'on behalf of, and with reference to, a collectivity' and thus 'the referent object is that to which one can point and say: It has to survive, therefore it is necessary to...' or else (ibid.: 36). Thus, for the Copenhagen School a 'distinguishing feature of securitization' is the existence of 'a specific rhetorical structure...survival, priority of action because if the problem is not handled now it will be too late, and we will not exist to remedy our failure' (ibid.: 26). This element of securitization 'can function as a tool for finding security actors and phenomena in sectors other than the military-political, where it is often hard to define when to include new issues on the security agenda' (ibid.).

Securitization practices have significant social and political effects. Once securitizing agents present an issue as an existential threat, for example, the door is open for the introduction of measures and practices that are outside regular or pre-existing legal practices—for example, the previously highlighted state practice of extraordinary rendition. For in the securitizing processes, 'political actors tend to claim...a right to handle the issue [being securitized] through extraordinary means, to break the normal political rules of the game (e.g., in the form of secrecy, levying taxes or conscription, placing limitations on otherwise inviolable rights, or focusing society's energy and resources on a specific task). "Security" is thus a self-referential practice, because it is in this practice that the issue becomes a security issue—not necessarily because a real existential threat exists but because the issue is presented as such a threat' (ibid.: 24). For Wæver and his colleagues, securitization is a political act that state and non-state actors use to justify political projects. As such, securitization should not be deemed as 'an innocent reflection of the issue being a security threat; it is always a political choice to securitize or to accept a securitization' (ibid.: 29).

While securitization is a practice of state and non-state actors—for example, national and transnational terrorist organizations—our concern here is with the TDHB, given its current claims of being committed to implementing measures aimed at securing human security in the South. In this respect we suggest that, following the 9/11 terrorist attacks in the USA, a securitization logic, as articulated by Wæver and others affiliated with the Copenhagen School, increasingly characterizes TDHB's approach to the South. According to some analysts, following these attacks, President Bush's regime and other ruling elites such as Tony Blair in the case of the UK securitized the attacks (Smith, 2005: 34). Rather than constructing them as criminal acts, which the existing judicial structures could handle, ruling elites in the USA and elsewhere framed them as existential threats to nation-states, international security and Euro-American socio-cultural norms. To be sure, historically and currently states have the political and ethical responsibility to respond to sources of threats. However, important as it is for states to respond to threats to human security, generated by brutal terrorist attacks such as those perpetrated on 9/11, for Wæver the securitization of the latter are troublesome for they have generated 'a militarized and confrontational mind-set which defines security questions in an us-versus-them manner' (quoted in ibid.). This development we argue is increasingly contributing to the securitization of security and politico-economic geographies in the South. Further, we contend that this development is being facilitated by the resurrection of a racially coded 'representational system' (Hall, 1997) of a broad range of issues assumed as the hallmarks of the South's underdevelopment such as poverty, conflict and backward cultural and religious practices, weak state forms and many others. As we indicated in Chapters 2 and 3, a racialist representational system of the South through language—specifically that of development discourse—has been a central element in the reproduction of the coloniality of power in the post-1945 period. For Hall,

> [l]anguage... operates as a representational system. Language is one of the 'media' through which thoughts, ideas and feelings are represented in a culture. Representation through language is... central to the processes by which meaning is produced.... words... are part of our natural and material world [and] represent our concepts, ideas and feelings in such a way as to enable others to 'read', decode or interpret their meaning in roughly the same way that we do.... [Thus] representation... is conceived as entering into the very constitution of things. (1997: 5–6)

The current representational system of the South that is facilitating securitization of development and security has a long genealogy in hegemonic Euro-American social thought and practice, as examples in Chapters 1, 2 and 3 indicate. In essence, it is a re-articulation of the colonial racialist representational system for contemporary imperatives of the TDHB. As a tool for securitization of development and security, the new representational system portrays hegemonic development discourse's assumed features of underdevelopment as significant existential threats to national and international security, and thus in need of immediate attention by powerful actors in the contemporary world order. These conditions have replaced earlier securitized concerns such as communist ideology and practice discussed in Chapter 3. From the perspective of the TDHB and their partners in the war on terror in the South, development and security go hand in hand in the current juncture. For example, for President George Bush and his advisors, while poverty per se does not make individuals engage in activities that generate national, regional and global insecurity such as terrorism, its existence and 'weak institutions, and corruption can make weak states vulnerable to terrorist networks... within their boarders' (*New York Times*, 2002).[6] According to him and other members of the TDHB, the way out of this quagmire is to institute measures that will lead to security and development. In the case of the UK, its Department for international development (DFID) declares that: 'security and development are linked... Poverty, underdevelopment and fragile states create fertile conditions for conflict and the emergence of new security threats, including international crime and terrorism' (DFID, 2005: 5). For DFID, in an interdependent world where security threats easily 'spread' across national and regional borders, it is paramount that development agencies institute measures that will lead to 'progress on both security and development' (ibid.: 8).

The reproduction of a colonial representational system and the attendant trend of securitization of development and security have seen the emergence of an overtly hierarchical ordering of state forms in the world order: in the current historical moment, two dominant categories of state have emerged: 'effective' or 'ineffective' (Duffield, 2007: 122–123). In this new hierarchical ordering of states, those in the North are assumed to be effective and, further, to have the capabilities and 'political will' to ensure security not only for their citizens, but also national, regional and global security (ibid.: 122). In this schema, ineffective states have no capacity or political will to provide human security for their citizens. Given the interconnectedness that has emerged with globalization, ineffective states—which are interchangeably termed as failed, fragile or collapsed states—are considered as major sources of human insecurity for 'people everywhere' (ibid.). In the age of securitization of development and security, these states are 'associated with the criminality, breakdown and chaos that emanates from a sovereign void', a void that is now viewed 'as vulnerable to colonization by forces opposed to the West and able to grow on the poverty' that characterize the South (ibid.: 127). In this new hierarchical ordering of states which is part of contemporary manifestation of coloniality of power, effective states have constructed themselves, and are now viewed by social forces closely linked to them, as having the moral and political authority to define and intervene in political contexts that are considered to be characterized by ineffective states. Echoing such a view, the International Commission on Intervention and State Sovereignty (2002: ix, cited in ibid.: 123) claims that in the context of ineffective states that fail to provide security for citizens and hence are sources of security threats 'the principle of non-interference yields to the international responsibility to protect' by effective states in the world order.

As the preceding discussion indicates, TDHB's current development discourse of human security interlocks development and security. In its securitizing rhetorical structure, the TDHB relentlessly invokes its commitment to the achievement of human security in the South by instituting measures aimed at eliminating sources of threats to local and global security such as poverty, authoritarianism and other features of underdevelopment in its view. As our discussion will indicate shortly, we propose that TDHB's securitization of development and security in the current global conjuncture ensures and expands the security of dominant states and the institutional complexes of the current world order, and that of their collaborators in the South. Consequently, its claims notwithstanding, TDHB's contemporary practices are not laying the foundation for the achievement of a human security agenda such as that underpinning the MDGs.

Securitization, development and human (in)security, I: war on terror

TDHB's contemporary representational system of the Middle East and the Arab world in general, reproduces in an extremely insidious manner colonial imperial 'imaginative geographies' that Edward Said (1979) discusses. Said argues that ' "imaginative geography" ' from the vivid portraits to be found in the Inferno ... legitimates a vocabulary, a universe of representative discourse peculiar to the discussion and understanding of Islam and of the Orient ... underlying all the different units of Orientalist discourse—by which I mean simply the vocabulary employed whenever the Orient is spoken or written about—is a set of representative figures, or tropes' (ibid.: 70). Building on Said's arguments on imaginative geographies, Derek Gregory contends that

> These [imaginative geographies] are constructions that fold distance into difference through a series of spatializations. ... 'Their' space is often seen as the inverse of 'our' space: a sort of negative, in the photographic sense that 'they' might 'develop' into something like 'us,' but also the site of an absence, because 'they' are seen somehow to lack the positive tonalities that supposedly distinguish 'us.' We might think of imaginative geographies as fabrications, a word that usefully combines 'something fictionalized' and 'something made real,' because they are imaginations given substance. (2004: 18)

In different historical moments, then, Orientalist discourse has depended on the utilization and power of a racialist representational system that enables practices of coloniality of power including the classification of humanity. As Said contends, 'with the "Orient," ... since Napoleon's invasion of Egypt in the late eighteenth century [it] has been made and remade countless times by power acting through an expedient form of knowledge to assert that this is the Orient's nature, and we must deal with it accordingly' (ibid.: 18). In the current juncture, as the examples from the securitization practices that resulted in the launching of the wars in Iraq and Afghanistan indicate, contemporary Orientalist representational system portrays these wars as civilizing wars that will lead to the reordering of backward societal orders—economy, politics and culture—along the Euro-American trajectory. Further, the launching of these 'unending wars' as Duffield (2007) terms them, are presented by the TDHB as projects that will lead to the achievement of human security, such as those outlined in the MDGs framework. Under the new hierarchical order of state forms and the re-articulation of a colonial representational system in this securitizing age, unending wars have been launched in Afghanistan and Iraq. In the rhetorical structure marking the onset of these wars, securitizing agents defined these countries as threats to national and international security because of their ineffective states, poverty and support for terrorist groups. In the case of Iraq, President George Bush defined the country as being part of an 'axis of evil' that posed a security threat to the USA, its allies and the world in general. The representation of Iraq and Afghanistan in a securitized manner by dominant states in the world order was central to enabling the portrayal of their invasion as urgent, moral, just, necessary and as the only solution in responding to the human insecurity generated by the terrorists attacks of 9/11 and those of the future.

Securitizing agents framed the launching of these wars as necessary for the achievement of human security in these countries, because the result would be the establishment of liberal democratic states, free enterprise economic structures and other features associated with effective state forms. Further, the wars would enable the destruction of terrorist networks that had been aided by ineffective states and social conditions such as poverty and other features of underdevelopment. In addition, for advocates of these wars, the destruction of these terrorist networks would greatly enhance national and global security. Commenting along these lines in the aftermath of the launching of the war in Afghanistan, in his 29 January, 2002 State of the Union address, President Bush declared, 'we last met in an hour of shock and suffering. In four short months, our nation has comforted the victims, begun to rebuild New York and the Pentagon, rallied a great coalition, captured, arrested, and rid the world of thousands of terrorists, destroyed Afghanistan's terrorist training camps, saved a people from starvation, and freed a country from brutal oppression. . . . Terrorists who once occupied Afghanistan now occupy cells at Guantanamo Bay. (Applause.) And terrorist leaders who urged followers to sacrifice their lives are running for their own' (Bush, 2002). These declarations are of course part of the rhetorical structure of the current unending wars and their aftermath. Suffice to say that at the time of this writing (in 2007 and early 2009) contrary to these celebratory declarations, political violence continues in Afghanistan making the unending war there a major pre-occupation of Barack Obama's presidency. Increasingly, social forces committed to the Taliban and al-Qaeda projects are re-establishing themselves throughout the country. These developments do not augur well for the achievement of human security in Afghanistan. These realities make an argument put forward by Derek Gregory in 2004 stating that 'without sustained reconstruction of the Afghan economy, a concerted effort to establish the institutions of a genuinely civil society, the same matrix that supported the growth of al-Qaeda will reassert itself' disquietly farsighted (2004: 74).

Afghanistan is not the only country whereby the achievement of the MDGs and other human security projects face major obstacles because of securitization of development and security in the era of the war on terror. In the spring of 2003, the USA, Britain and other coalition part-ners launched the war in Iraq. Securitization practices triggered by the 9/11 terrorist attacks, but also the securitization of the pre-existing state apparatus lead by President Saddam Hussein, facilitated the build up to the war and its onset. Following this trend, the President of the United States declared in 2002: 'Iraq continues to flaunt its hostility toward America and to support terror. The Iraqi regime has plotted to develop anthrax, and nerve gas, and nuclear weapons for over a decade.... States like these, and their terrorist allies, constitute an axis of evil, arming to threaten the peace of the world... They could attack our allies or attempt to blackmail the United States. In any of these cases, the price of indifference would be catastrophic... all nations should know: America will do what is necessary to ensure our nation's security' (Bush, 2002). These core elements of the rhetorical structure characterizing securiti-zation practices as they pertain to Iraq have become endlessly repeated tropes, becoming extreme examples of the linguistic tropes embodying Said's argument about the lexicon of Orientalism.

Since the launching of the war, security forces captured Saddam Hussein who was later executed. Further, detailed reports have indi-cated that the intelligence data presented to the public to launch the war was faulty: there were no weapons of mass destruction. In addition, US security forces that were supposed to be enabling Iraqis to achieve their human security have contributed to their insecurity through prac-tices such as torture in Abu Ghraib prison (Byers, 2005: 132–135; Enloe, 2007: 93–98; Klein, 2007: 466–467); a practice that violates core tenets of international law.[7] Yet, the rhetorical structure leading to the war continues, even though the war has enabled the emergence of a hyper-militarized, partisan and violent space that makes the viability of human security agendas, such as the MDGs, highly unlikely. Overall, the violence generated by the war has severe consequences for individual and collective human security both for local citizens and for members of the coalition forces. The human insecurities generated in the period of President Hussein's brutal dictatorship, UN economic sanctions against his regime, compounded with those that have emerged since the war began on 20 March, 2003, make achievement of the MDGs implausible. The social and psychological trauma of violence and daily loss of life in what seems to be a protracted 'state of exception' (Agamben, 2005), in which legal norms are suspended, raises serious doubts about the feasibility of achieving any measure of human security in the country in the near future. Estimates in July 2006 indicate 34,000 Iraqi fatalities and 36,000 wounded, and in the case of the coalition forces, from 2003–2007, 3800 USA and 173 UK service members died (BBC News, 2006). Since the onset of the war, 'the risk of death from violence in the 18 months after the invasion was 58 times higher than in the 15 months before' yet 'the United States refuses to monitor or estimate the number of civilian casualties' (Millar, 2006: 52). Further, the war has also resulted in massive displacement of Iraqis with an estimated 1.9 million of them being internally displaced and 2.2 million having left the country as refugees as of April 2007 (Global Policy Forum, 2007). Weapons used in the war some of them 'banned by international convention or widely considered unacceptable and inhuman', have left an indelible human insecurity mark on the country (ibid.: ii). For example,

> The health impact of the use of depleted uranium (DU) weaponry in Iraq is yet to be known. The Pentagon estimates that U.S. and British forces used 1,100 to 2,200 tons of weaponry made from the toxic and radioactive metal during the March 2003 bombing campaign. Many scientists blame the far smaller amount of DU weapons used in the Persian Gulf War for illnesses among U.S. soldiers, as well as a seven fold increase in child birth defects in Basra in southern Iraq. (Millar, 2006: 53)

It is important to note that, in Iraq, the securitization of development and security in the context of global neo-liberal capitalism has generated more than human insecurity. These developments have generated security for some social actors. The political and economic conditions generated by the neo-liberal project and abetted by the war on terror have enabled the securing of security for elements of private authority (Strange, 1998) in this epoch of unending wars. In Iraq, the war has been a privatized affair with big private firms, such as Blackwater USA, receiving contracts to perform what has historically been the function of a national army and the state apparatus in general. Highlighting this phenomenon, Cynthia Enloe posits:

> Unlike the more familiar defense manufacturers, private military contractors actually provide, for a substantial fee, the services for-merly provided by government militaries and police forces—guarding embassies and mines, providing food for soldiers, running supply convoys. By 2006, in Iraq alone, nearly 50,000 private military and security personnel had been contracted by the U.S. government. (2007: 7; see also Klein, 2007)

Thus, securing the rights of private capital to operate has been a core feature of this war. Opportunities for major US oil firms and others engaged in the energy sector to control the modalities of the Iraqi energy industry have also been secured as a result. Donald Kagan puts it this way: 'when we [USA] have economic problems, it's been caused by disruptions in our oil supply. If we have a force in Iraq, there will be no disruption in oil supplies' (quoted in Foster, 2006: 92). As in previous imperial moments, then, in the current era of new imperialism (Harvey, 2003) in the Middle East and elsewhere 'military, political, and economic aspects are intertwined.... as well as capitalism in general' (Foster, 2006: 92). For example, the urgent calls for regime change in Iraq in the name of promoting 'freedom' and other elements of human security would most likely have remained at the level of rhetoric were the country 'the world's largest exporter of bananas or oranges' and not a leading oil producer' (Said, 1979: xx). Nonetheless, while the security of the US ruling elites and owners of capital is being secured, American citizens are paying and will continue to pay the social and economic debts generated by the war, while it is far from clear that the majority of them will benefit from the spoils of war in Iraq. Since the war began, the national debt in the USA has risen every year. In 2003–2006 the country 'spent approximately $400 billion in direct government appropriations for the conflict [and the] federal budget costs have doubled from about $4 billion per month in 2003 to more than $8,000 billion per month in late 2006' and 'total ... costs including estimates of future spending interest on the national debt, veterans' medical costs and other factors, have already passed $2 trillion' (Global Policy Forum, 2007: iii–iv).

Securitization, development and human (in)security, II: poor and 'ungovernable' Africa

As previously argued, the emergence of a new racialist representational system, is enabling the securitization of TDHB's hegemonic development discourse. In the context of Africa, the racialist colonial representation system underpins the securitized approach to the continent by the TDHB. This representation system has resulted in the construction of a new geopolitical map of Africa, which defines the continent as ' "the king" of ungoverned spaces'.[8] On the whole, in the context of Africa, the securitization of development facilitates the reproduction of what Ngugi wa Thiong'o and I (2004) have elsewhere termed as the notion of 'Africa as the land of childhood' articulated by Hegel: thus a continent in urgent need of the latest politico-economic experiment generated by organic intellectuals of the prevailing world order. As Chapter 3 indicated, the classification of Africans in racist and derogatory terms is not new. Essentially and as Achille Mbembe argues 'Africa as an idea, a concept, has historically served, and continues to serve, as a polemical argument for the West's desperate desire to assert its difference from the rest of the world. In several respects, Africa still constitutes one of the metaphors through which the West represents the origin of its own norms, develops a self-image, and integrates this image into the set of signifiers asserting what it supposes to be its identity' (2001: 2). In the era of neo-liberal and securitizing logics, the Hegelian representation of African societies is now the core frame of TDHB's development ideas and practices pertaining to the continent. For example, Tony Blair, former Prime Minister of Britain, contends that Africa is the 'the scar on the conscience of the world' (2001). Blair, of course, does not see the need to explain the historical and contemporary developments that have generated this morally troublesome situation. Blair contends that the only thing that the West, can do is to 'help Africa' so as to contain the rise of anger-infused eruptions in the continent (ibid.). The assumption underlying Blair's and those of others promoting similar ahistorical arguments, such as Jeffrey Sachs (2005), is that it is a natural condition, generated by Africa's unfavourable geographical conditions and corruption among other internal social conditions, and that the TDHB has had nothing to do with the evolution of the current situation in the African continent.

The representation of Africa in such terms has been an important tool in the rise of a securitized approach to the continent's politico-economic processes. It is interesting to note, however, the extensive use of the normative framework of human security in the new securitized development discourse. Addressing the US Congress in 2003, Blair, for instance, stated, 'there can be no freedom for Africa without justice and no justice without declaring war on Africa's poverty, disease and famine with as much vehemence as we removed the tyrant [Saddam Hussein] and the terrorists' (Blair, 2003). Overall, the Hegelian representational system of Africa enables and legitimizes securitization projects in the continent by de-historicizing and de-politicizing the latter's historical trajectory. To begin with, a dialectic of power erases the political-cultural-economic legacies of imperialism and the post-1945 coloniality of power by the TDHB in the continent. The role of the colonial legacy, and the social dislocations generated by geopolitics of the Cold War, and by over three decades of the neo-liberal development project are not only ignored by securitizing agents but replaced by a colonial mythology: that the un-governable nature of the continent, underdevelopment and poverty are results of internal dynamics stemming from the failure of African social formations to emulate the natural-linear development trajectory followed by the civilized and developed North. This selective memory is a politically useful form of historical amnesia; and embodies what Adam Hochschild (1999) has called 'Great Forgetting', which cleanses and naturalizes Europe's and other colonizing powers' practices of human insecurity and their legacies in Africa and elsewhere. In his discussion of Belgium's Great Forgetting of its brutal legacy in the Congo, Hochschild states 'the world we live in—its divisions and conflicts, its widening gap between rich and poor, its seemingly inexplicable outbursts of violence—is shaped far less by what we celebrate and mythologize than by the painful events we try to forget. Leopold's Congo is but one of those silences of history' (ibid.: 294).

From a historical perspective, acts of 'Great Forgetting', allow dominant states to repress their own contributions to the insecurity and political chaos that they claim characterize Africa and the Middle East. The works of scholars such as Mahmood Mamdani (1996) and Walter Rodney (1972), among others, seek to understand both historical and contemporary forms of imperialism in Africa thus challenging acts of Great Forgetting. In the case of Iraq and Afghanistan, various scholars have provided deeply historically-grounded work demonstrating the role of major powers, such as the USA, Britain and the former Soviet

Union, in collaboration with local allies in creating the very social realities that the TDHB consider as threats to local, regional and global security.[9] Yet, in its securitization of development and security, the TDHB's approach remains internally focused. As argued in Chapters 1, 2 and 3, an internal-centric approach to discussions of politico-economic processes in the South offers at best partial insights. Such an approach facilitates the de-politicization of contemporary practices of coloniality of power in the guise of promoting human security by the TDHB. In these ahistorical and technocratic approaches, Middle Eastern, African and other societies in the South are repeatedly reminded that 'dwelling on the depredations of empire' is a strategy meant to deflect their 'responsibility' in the emergence of their postcolonial human insecurity ridden social realities (Said, 1979: xxii). Such analyses, however, fail to recognize the reproduction of the coloniality of power in the post-1945 and the role of hegemonic development discourses in this process. Commenting on this tendency Said states:

> But what a shallow calculation of the imperial intrusion that is, how summarily it scants the immense distortion introduced by the empire into the lives of 'lesser' peoples and 'subject races' generation after generation, how little it wishes to face the long succession of years through which empire continues to work its way in the lives of, say, Palestinians or Congolese or Algerians or Iraqis. (Ibid.)

In Africa, while couched in human security terms, the contemporary ahistorical, technical and imperial representational system that portrays the continent as disorderly, insecure, poor and ungovernable is enabling the implementation of various hegemonic projects. Securitization of development and security deepens and legitimizes the involvement of the TDHB in the continent, and the expansion of the coercive powers of African allied and non-allied states in the war on terrorism, such as Ethiopia and Zimbabwe, respectively, rather than contributing to human security. For its part, the Ethiopian state's collaboration in the war on terror has seen the USA and other proclaimed promoters of human security—a core aspect of which is respect for political freedoms—ignore its manipulation of the electoral process to serve its political ends. This collaboration has led directly to the violation of the human rights of opposition party leaders and pro-democracy social activists through detention and other coercive practices (Carmody, 2007: 142–144). In Zimbabwe, the authoritarian ruler President Robert Mugabe has invoked the core features of the securitization discourse in efforts to consolidate and maintain its brutal despotism by securitizing acts of democratic dissent by members of human rights and pro-democracy movements. Essentially, in Africa and elsewhere the securitizing logic of the TDHB has generated a political scenario in which dominant actors in the world order ignore 'state terrorism' (ibid.: 220). According to Richard Falk (2003), the roots of this development took hold immediately following the terrorist attacks of 9/11 for,

> The over-generalized US response to a very specific kind of extremist trans-national violence has had the unfortunate effect of sending a green light to governments around the world to intensify their own violence against opposition and resistance activity branded as terrorism, and even to wage war against neighboring states that allegedly support anti-state forces. (Quoted in ibid.: 220)

A core effect of the securitizing of development and security in Africa is the militarization of the continent, a development that has major implications for the achievement of MDGs and other human security projects. In the case of gender inequality, this development, especially in conflict zones such as Darfur, Democratic Republic of Congo and increasingly Kenya, creates a major opening for gendered forms of violence. Further, the establishment of a securitized development institutional framework by the US government: US Africa Command (AFRICOM), which is the country's new centralized security-development apparatus in Africa, exemplifies the new militarism by the TDHB—girded by the rhetoric of promoting human security in Africa. AFRICOM is not the first or the only US military institutional structure marking the increasing militarization of contemporary Africa. Camp Lemonier, established in October 2002 in Djibouti, is the headquarters for the military activities of the US Combined Joint Task Force-Horn of Africa (Pincus, 2007). According to Carmody, US military apparatus in Djibouti has the capacity to carry out military operations in a broad range of countries in the East and Horn of Africa, and in Middle East ones such as Yemen (2007: 225). The USA also has bases, ports and military access in other countries: Tunisia, Uganda, Sao Tome and Principe, Senegal, Kenya, Mali, Morocco, Namibia, Gabon and has increased its military presence in the Gulf of Guinea (Pincus, 2007). Other US military initiatives include the Trans-Sahara Counter Terrorism Initiative which in addition to providing military training in Chad, Niger, Mauritania and Mali ensures the deepening of the country's military presence 'between oil-rich' North and West Africa and the 'encirclement of Islamic Africa' (Carmody, 2007: 226). The USA is not the only dominant state contributing to the new militarization of Africa. UK arms trade to the continent has risen sharply since the late 1990s (ibid.: 232) as has that of China (Chang, 2009).

AFRICOM operations comprise a unified command interlocking military and development activities of the USA in Africa. For advocates of this development, this new interlocked security-development complex will enable AFRICOM to provide security and facilitate the achievement of America's human security development goals such as poverty alleviation and others that are sources of existential threats. As in DFID's approach to Africa, a human security framework rings through the securitized lens through which the US views the continent. In announcing the establishment of AFRICOM, for instance, President Bush declared:

> This new command will strengthen our security cooperation with Africa and create new opportunities to bolster the capabilities of our partners in Africa. Africa Command will enhance our efforts to bring peace and security to the people of Africa and promote our common goals of development, health, education, democracy, and economic growth in Africa. We will be consulting with African leaders to seek their thoughts on how Africa Command can respond to security challenges and opportunities in Africa. (Bush, 2002)

The establishment of AFRICOM marks a heightened interest in deepening the involvement of the USA and its security apparatus in Africa. From the USA perspective and other securitizing agents, the creation of AFRICOM has been driven by the need to address Africa's multitude of problems such as poverty, insecurity, conflict, weak states and many other sources of threat to national, regional and global security. In the view of Ambassador Robert L. Loftis, for instance, 'if we don't have security in Africa' the increased levels of aid since the coming to power of President Bush 'will not be helpful' (quoted in Hanson, 2007). Further, according to American officials, since the end of World War II, the US military command in Africa has been part of its European military arrangements, a reality that has limited American capacity and involvement in the continent. For the USA, to address the myriad sources of existential threats that Africa poses to international security, new military and development arrangements need to be made; hence the calls for the establishment of AFRICOM and expansion of America's military initiatives in the continent. According to its advocates, AFRICOM will provide much needed security in Africa, thus facilitating sound development models that will lead to the achievement of a range of human security goals.

The securitization of development and security in Africa by the TDHB raises questions concerning the feasibility of achieving the human security agenda they claim to be promoting through the MDGs development discourse. The rhetorical structure of the TDHB portrays their securitized development discourse as being for the benefit of the poverty-stricken people in Africa and for the strengthening of national and international security. However, is the securitization of development and security generating enabling conditions for the achievement of human security? Our conclusion is that the rhetorical structure framing the securitized development discourse of the TDHB and their allies in Africa is geared to securing the security and other interests of this bloc and social forces closely linked to it, and not to enhancing human security for the majority of people in the continent. In the case of the establishment of AFRICOM, the political, cultural and moral panic that has emerged since 9/11 in the USA and the rise of a neo-colonial representational system is enabling not only the securitization of development and security, but also the embedding of what is fundamentally a ruling elite project aimed at creating favourable conditions for the expansion of US military, economic, ideological and bureaucratic power in Africa. Under the guise of promoting human security, AFRICOM will open a window of opportunity for the US state and American dominant interests to carve out a sphere of influence in Africa during a conjuncture in which China (see Chapter 6), India and Brazil are making headway in securing their economic and political interests in the continent. While US ruling elites continue to claim that the objective of AFRICOM is the enhancement of human security through the promotion of development, democracy, education, economic growth and the fight against terrorism, what is being secured is access to the continent's natural resources and the security interests of the USA. In the case of the oil sector, the country's contribution to the militarization of Africa will 'bolster the capacity of African military forces to protect oil production and transportation facilities' in a manner that according to one estimate 'by 2015 West Africa alone will supply 25 percent of America's imported oil' (Carmody, 2007: 225).

Securitizing of development and security, and the resulting militarization in the current conjuncture adds to the structural and political limits enveloping human security projects such as the MDGs. Further, this process is occurring in the context of a neo-liberal development discourse, a social reality that raises important questions, leading among them, whether African states have the structural capacity to meet the human security objectives embodied in the MDGs given this context. For example, in Malawi implementation of neo-liberal policies since 1979 has not resulted in the transformation of the structural base of the state. Almost three decades later, the country continues to be characterized by an 'undiversified productive base' (Adam et al., 1992: 368), geared to the production of agrarian commodities for the international market with tobacco production contributing 70 per cent to the export basket (Government of Malawi, 2006: 4). Further, these developments have resulted in rising debt levels and budgetary deficits, and thus limiting state's capacity to meet MDGs goals. In the case of budgetary deficits, the deficit in the current account has been in the range of US$ 200–500 million per year (ibid.) in the era of neo-liberalism. In Ghana, TDHB's neo-liberal narrative has shifted from a star pupil of neo-liberalism Richter (2000) to the categorization of the country as one of HIPC in 2004. Overall, the neo-liberal 'miracle' in Ghana has not resulted in the expansion of the state's material base or a fundamental shift in the country's position in the capitalist world system. Rather, what has occurred in Ghana in the name of promoting market capitalism is the consolidation of a weak agrarian economic base that has ensured increased structural dependency and debt as epitomized by the ascendancy of the country to the HIPC category of countries. Commenting on the limitations and contradictions of the neo-liberal project in Ghana, Eboe Hutchful states:

> While there was some 'structural change,' much of it was actually regressive. Services were consistently the most dynamic sector, growing at an annual rate in excess of 7% per annum and accounting for about 56% of the GDP growth in 1996. Within this sector, the strongest growth was recorded by trading and transport activities, but growth was also strong in the newer areas of financial services and communications.... The worst performance appears to have been in agriculture, which grew at barely 2% average per annum, with growth in several years actually being negative.... These marked variations in growth rates led to important—though not necessarily desirable—shifts in changes in the structural composition of GDP.... From contributing almost 16% of total GDP growth in 1990, manufacturing shrank to 7% in 1993, and to a mere 4.8% in 1996. The result of the foregoing was that, under the impact of liberalization, Ghana was progressively 'turned into a nation of shoppers

and storekeepers with very little manufacturing or industrial activity'. (Hutchful, 2002: 91)

Conclusion

This chapter offered debates concerning the notion of security in the post-Cold War and 9/11 periods. The analysis has also indicated the rise of human security development discourse, which contrary to the claims of its proponents we argued does not transform the underlying TDHB neo-liberal development discourse. A core premise of the chapter has been that, notwithstanding its ethical underpinnings, the human security development discourse neglects the ways in which the politico-economic context of neo-liberalism and securitization of development and security, which is advocated by the TDHB, limits human security inspired projects such as the MDGs. Overall, the securitization of development and security in the South by dominant actors in the world order is legitimizing contemporary forms of coloniality of power in the name of promoting human security. Nonetheless, as the next chapter highlights, counter-consensus voices, especially by movements and organizations linked to the World Social Forum, are increasingly challenging the status quo of the prevailing world order, including its development discourse.

8
World Social Forum

Since the 1980s, the evolution of neo-world order has been a twin process, with one side characterized by persistent efforts to consolidate it and another contesting it and calling for the transformation of the core ideas of this order, and their implementation at the national level. In January 1984, Tunisia's political landscape, for instance, was marked by a week of what is commonly referred to as the 'bread riot' (Zghal, 1995), an uprising that emerged following the signing of a bill dismantling the compensatory framework that had kept the prices of bread and other cereal products stable for many years. The state introduced the bill during a time of deepening economic crisis and the ascendancy of the neo-liberal development discourse. The 'bread riot' began in the village of Al-Mabrouka on 3 January, 1984 at 5.00 p.m., with 200 people marching from a European-owned textile company that had been established as part of the effort to open up the economy and create enabling conditions for foreign direct investment. The protest, led by female factory workers, saw villagers marching to various local sites representing state authority chanting 'poor, poor, people, bread now costs 170 Millimes!' (ibid.: 107). Political protests emerging out of economic crisis and the introduction of neo-liberal economic strategies embodied in structural adjustment policies (SAPS) also characterized Zambia in the 1980s. In his critique of the 'scientific capitalism' that underpins neo-liberal based SAPs in Zambia, James Ferguson argues,

> [T]he establishment of 'correct prices' and 'efficient' markets resulted, quite predictably, in a series of food riots and eventually in the fall of the government. Informants told me that the 1986 Copperbelt riots effectively had been popular uprisings in which a wide range of respectable people—including, in one account, policemen—had

177

joined. Many of those who participated in the looting were unashamed, even proud. T-Shirts were printed in the townships reading, 'Looters Association of Zambia.' For many Zambians, what was truly illegitimate was not the theft by looters, but the rise in prices itself. (2006: 81)

In South Africa, various social forces have consistently contested the neo-liberal project from the anti-privatization movements to environmental justice movements. The latter have contested the market logic that informs neo-liberal economic discourse, which at its core 'radically subordinates environmental problems.... [which] are largely disregarded or denied and externalities are placed where they will not be noticed by anyone powerful enough to make a fuss' (Hallowes and Butler, 2002: 57). The dumping of toxic waste and continuing operations of hazardous factories in poor black, coloured and Indian neighbourhoods in South Africa is an example of externalizing costs by owners of capital in spaces in which they assume they can contain challenges to their practices because of material and political power asymmetry. Protests and struggles for free water in the context of President Thabo Mbeki regime's commitment to deepening neo-liberal orthodoxy have also been a hallmark of resistance struggles in South Africa. In August 2000, for example, following various protests against the privatization of water services, the state reneged on its promise to provide 6000 litres of free water—a development that contributed to a cholera outbreak in KwaZulu-Natal in September 2000, which affected 12,000 people and caused over 48 deaths as a result of residents resorting to unsafe water sources (Bond, 2001: 218–219). From the perspective of the World Bank and its collaborating South African state, the important issue as far as provision of water was concerned was to depart from an approach that viewed water as a public good to that of a commodity like any other in the market place. From the World Bank's water discourse, the goal is 'to ensure that all countries have clearly defined policies.... Work is still needed with political leaders in some national governments to move away from the concept of free water for all.... Ensure 100% recovery of operation and maintenance costs' (ibid.: 218).

Social forces in Latin American countries, from Argentina in the early part of this century to Brazil, have also resisted the neo-liberal project. In Bolivia, from the 1990s onward, a range of social movements and organizations, including indigenous peoples' movements, organized labour, environmentalists, coca producers and *Campesinos*, and urban-based movements in cities such as El Alto, contested various aspects of the neo-liberal economic project (Kohl and Farthing, 2006). As in other social formations, then, the evolution of the neo-liberal project in Bolivia has been highly contested, with indigenous peoples' movements playing a central role in the emergence of a broad-based social movement that contributed to the election of Evo Morales as the country's President in 2005. Neo-liberal economic strategies, especially privatization, in addition to the global recession of the 1990s and the Bolivian state's project of curtailing coca production because of pressure from the US government, created a volatile economic and political context. In the case of privatization, the Bolivian government faced extensive pressure from the World Bank, the IMF and the US government since the process would 'benefit U.S. investors, create demand for equipment [and] open new markets' (ibid.: 108). As in other places, advocates of such policies ignored their social costs. The privatization process in Bolivia, for instance, led to massive job loses. The Bolivia State Oil Corporation (YPFB) 'went from a high of 9,150 workers in 1985 to around 600 by the end of 2002' (ibid.: 112). The privatization resulted in not only the crisis of legitimacy for the state because of massive job losses but also loss of revenue for the state (ibid.: 111).

In other parts of the world, resistance to neo-liberal ideas and practices has taken many forms. In France, December 1995 saw state employers lead a popular protest against neo-liberal policies, while workers in South Korea waged strikes against private capital (Leite, 2005: 45). At the transnational level, social forces have contested the global neo-liberal project at various junctures. In 1999, social movements drawn from various sectors staged protests in Seattle and managed to derail the WTO's Ministerial trade talks. Protesters presented their grievances with the neo-liberal economic doctrine through statements such as 'our world is not for sale'; 'no globalization without participation'; 'we are citizens, not only consumers'; and 'WTO = capitalism without conscience' (Della et al., 2006b: 1). Since then, social forces opposed to the neo-liberal world order have confronted WTO's trade talks in Genoa, Italy and Cancun, Mexico.

The World Social Forum process

Contestation, then, has been the other side of the coin in the rise of a world order underpinned by neo-liberalism in the 1980s and 1990s, and in the early part of the twenty-first century, this political phenomenon continues. In 2001, social forces opposed to neo-liberal economic globalization and other features of the contemporary world order congregated in Porto Alegre, Brazil, a development that marked the beginning of the World Social Forum (WSF) process. As with other national or transnational counter-hegemonic movements, the WSF did not emerge out of a historical vacuum, but rather resulted from a culmination of developments that have characterized the evolution of the neo-liberal world order, especially the resistance to the core elements of this order. The specific origins of the WSF process, though, are rooted in a proposal put forward by the Brazilian Organizing Committee (BOC) at a June 2000 meeting in Geneva. This meeting was attended by representatives of movements and organizations opposed to neo-liberal globalization and was organized to coincide with the UN 'Copenhagen +5' (Santos, 2006: 46). In envisioning the WSF, the BOC proposed:

'the World Social Forum will be a new international space for reflection and for organization of all those who counter neo-liberal policies and are constructing alternatives to prioritize human development and overcome market domination in every country and in international relations. (Leite, 2005: 80)

Various movements and organizations, such as Focus on the Global South, the French ATTAC, the French journal *Le Monde Diplomatique*, the Latin American Council of Social Sciences and many others, supported the BOC proposal. In Porto Alegre, events leading up to the inauguration of the WSF and the meeting itself received extensive support from the Brazilian Worker's Party (PT), which during this conjuncture had powerful links at various levels of the government in this region of Brazil. Since the historic meeting in Porto Alegre, the WSF has become a global process with regular, national, regional and global meetings—the latter since 2005 now held bi-annually. The first meeting of the WSF occurred in parallel with the World Economic Forum in Davos, Switzerland, an annual event that movements, participants and organizations involved in the WSF considered as representing the interests of the dominant forces in the contemporary world order. Since its inception in 2001, the WSF process has provided a space for national, global and regional organizations and movements to debate issues marking the contemporary world order, and regional and national politico-economic matters. The WSF, however, is not a permanent institution with a hierarchical organizational structure, although tensions underpin its non-hierarchical organizational architecture. Thus, while at the organizational level it has an International Council (IC), an International Secretariat (changed in 2007 to Facilitating Group) and a domestic Organizing Committee (constituted to facilitate global meetings), the WSF has from the beginning been envisioned as a space for diverse social actors to gather and debate a range of political, cultural and economic issues characterizing the current world order and to generate alternatives. As Boaventura de Sousa Santos defines it,

> The WSF is the set of initiatives of transnational exchange among social movements, NGOs and their practices and knowledges of local, national or global social struggles carried out in compliance with the Porto Alegre Charter of Principles against the forms of exclusion and inclusion, discrimination and equality, universalism and particularism, cultural imposition and relativism, brought about or made possible by the current phase of capitalism known as neo-liberal globalization (Santos, 2006: 6).

This chapter focuses on the WSF. Using Polanyi's (2001) notion of 'double-movement' as a starting point, we consider the WSF as a complex double-movement. In Polanyi's view, 'to allow the market mechanism to be sole director of the fate of human beings and their natural environment indeed... would result in the demolition of society... Robbed of the protective covering of cultural institutions, human beings would perish from the effects of social exposure; they would die as the victims of acute social dislocation through vice, perversion, crime, and starvation' (ibid.: 76). Thus, counter-consensus projects aimed at 'protecting society itself from the perils inherent in a self-regulating market system' (ibid.: 80) have characterized the promotion and expansion of global capitalism, although taking different forms in different historical conjunctures and in specific social places. As a double-movement in the Polanyi sense, the WSF focuses on the social dislocations generated by the neo-liberal ideas underlying the 'market-view' (Polanyi, 2001) of society that underpins the current world order. However, the WSF has a broader emancipatory agenda that includes contesting all forms of contemporary imperialism, the dominance of capital in the world order, destruction of the biosphere, social inequalities, war and so forth.[1]

Further, the search for alternative ideas and politico-economic practices to the core features of the current world order is a core principle of the WSF (ibid.). Along these lines, the WSF contests the notion that there is only a single universal form of economic idea and practice as espoused by leading organic intellectuals of the neo-liberal world order such as Lawrence Summers—a dominant member of President Barack Obama's administration—who has stated that: 'Spread the truth—the laws of economics are like the laws of engineering. One set of laws works everywhere' (Summers, 1991, quoted in Hedlund, 1999: 112).

Our underlying premise is that the WSF is a complex double-movement that has the potential of establishing a foundation for the emergence of emancipatory political, cultural and economic processes at various political levels. Despite some tensions and contradictions (highlighted later) marking the WSF, an embryonic base for such a development is evident when one considers its core features: the WSF's disruption of ideas and visions underpinning the neo-liberal world order and its expansion since the first meeting in Porto Alegre. We suggest that the WSF is disrupting the hegemony of the contemporary world order in two significant ways: demystifying ideas underpinning this order; and articulating alternatives to some of its core features. The chapter is comprised of four sections, with the first discussing the WSF's approach to ideas characterizing the current world order. The second part highlights the WSF's visions and struggles for alternatives to features of this order. The third part focuses on the expansion of the WSF beyond the first meeting. We conclude with a brief discussion of challenges and contradictions that may limit the emancipatory potential of the WSF.

WSF and world order: demystifying neo-liberalism

As argued elsewhere in this book, ideas are central to the rise, consolidation and transformation of world orders. For example, the global embedding of neo-liberal ideas as we argued in Chapter 3 has facilitated the rise of the contemporary world order. Since the 1980s, though, oppositional forces, some of which we highlighted earlier, have emerged to contest these ideas. While the WSF process continues this tradition, since its inception it has been consistent in its interrogation of the ideas underpinning the neo-liberal world order. The Charter of Principles, which governs the modalities of the WSF process, declares that the latter provides a space 'for groups and movements of civil society that are opposed to neo-liberalism' to debate and map out alternatives.[2] Increasingly, this effort is demystifying these ideas by revealing their structuring effects and thus unmasking their pretensions of neutrality.

For the various movements and organizations involved in the WSF, the neo-liberal foundations of the current world order have powerful economic, gender and political effects and are overall geared to serve the interests of dominant forces in the world order. In their view, the neo-liberal ideas governing the current world order have generated economic practices that have resulted in economic and other forms of social dislocations for the majority of people in the world, especially in the South. For example, these practices have resulted in the implementation of policies that have limited the capacity of states to meet social needs and provide public goods in general. A source of this development is the expansion of the structural power (Chapter 9) of private capital in the era of neo-liberalism. For the most part, the structural power of corporate capital, most of it based in the North, now exceeds the economic output of most countries in the South and elsewhere. According to some analysts,

> In terms of sheer scale of economic activity, the giant corporations now rival all but the largest countries. GNP, 51 of the world's top 100 economies are corporations. Royal Dutch Shell's revenues are greater than Venezuela's Gross Domestic Product. Using this measurement, Walmart is bigger than Indonesia. General Motors is roughly the same size as Ireland, New Zealand and Hungary combined. (Karliner et al., 2003: 55)

The privileging of the interests of capital permeates neo-liberal thinking and practices, but nowhere is this more obvious and potent than in the growth of the structural and, in the process, political power of financial capital in the contemporary era, as Chapter 9 argues in some detail. This development has made the world economy and national economic processes vulnerable to any shift in financial markets, given the freedom of movement that capital enjoys in the current phase of the world economy compared to the period of global Keynesianism when states had more room to manoeuvre in framing their monetary policies. This new social reality was evident, for instance, during the Asian financial crisis in 1997 and Argentina's economic crisis in the early part of the twenty-first century. For participants of the WSF process, there is a consensus on the growing power and dominance of capital and its effects. Overall,

> Despite the differences, the movements [at the WSF] are unified by several areas of agreement. One is the perception of a common adversary. Mentioned in a number of documents are the problems created by the expansion of corporate capitalism ('neoliberal globalization'). The perception is that corporate domination has been organized across global space by the most powerful Northern states in the world, in collaboration with the Southern economic and political elites. Simultaneously, this expansion is occurring in conjunction with the suppression of political, economic, cultural, racial, gendered, sexual, ecological and epistemological differences. (Ponniah and Fisher, 2003: 10)

Neo-liberal economic ideas have resulted in economic practices that have contributed to rising inequalities, and this reality has been a central concern for participants since the beginning of the WSF process. Rising levels of inequality in both the South and the North have unmasked core fundamental myths of neo-liberal doctrine's promises: the ascendancy of a new era of unlimited accumulation and freedom secured by the market and the embedding of procedural democracy. As contended by participants in the WSF, the deepening of neo-liberal economic practices has had significant material consequences and has deepened the historical inequality that has characterized the world system. In terms of the material capabilities of the current world order for instance, despite the claim of proponents of neo-liberal discourse that the ascendancy of neo-liberal economic strategies has generated economic well being for all, the historical divide between the North and the South in this arena has in fact deepened. Nevertheless, this does not stop advocates of the neo-liberal project from celebrating its promise of economic and political freedom. For example, in a recent text Deepak Lal argues that despite what commentators such as Joseph Stiglitz and 'the antiglobalization brigade' say, poverty has declined in the South since the rise of neo-liberal globalization in 1980s: 'China's opening ... India's economic liberalization in 1991, and the gradual move away from planned to market economies in Latin America has brought much of the Third World into the global economy. Outside the former Soviet empire, Africa—which has not integrated into the world economy and faces serious problems of governance—is the only region where poverty has risen' (2004: 122–123).

The notion that Africa is not integrated into the world capitalist order is not only ahistorical but also perpetuates the Hegelian view of the continent (Chapter 7). Further, the claim that poverty has decreased in China and India with the implementation of the neo-liberal development model ignores the myriad forms of social dislocations that peasants and other marginalized social forces face in both countries. It is important to note, however, that marginalized social forces in the North, like their counterparts in the South, have been significantly and adversely affected by economic and political developments generated by the neo-liberal project. For example, the income gap in USA has deepened: 'in the late 1970s, the share of national income of the top 1 per cent of income earners ... soared, to reach 15 per cent (very close to its pre-Second World War share) by the end of the century. The top 0.1 per cent of income earners in the US increased their share of the national income from 2 per cent in 1978 to over 6 per cent by 1999, while the ratio of the median compensation of workers to the salaries of the CEOs increased from just 30 to 1 to nearly 500 to 1 by 2000' (Harvey, 2005: 16). Further, and contrary to the views of Lal and other advocates of neo-liberal economic ideas, and as constantly argued at the WSF, the North's economic power continues to form the apex of global structural power, among other aspects of power. Overall, the core features of the world order as articulated by Robert Cox (1987)—production structure, hegemonic knowledge production sites, norm and policy setting institutions—remain concentrated and controlled by leading states in this order and its institutional complex. In the main, in the era of neo-liberal capitalism,

> In per capita terms, the income gap between the First World and the Third World has been continuously widening; the picture is worsened by the fact that in many Third World countries, a good portion of income is being used to pay off debts to First World creditors... The prices on primary and secondary goods have become 'uncoupled,' such that First World economic growth will no longer lead to equivalent demand for Third World goods. Exacerbating this is the shift from labor-intensive to knowledge-intensive production, which will further hurt Third World countries ... As the First World gets richer the Third World will fall richer behind. (Rapley, 2004: 88)

Further, movements linked to WSF contend that the ascendancy of a hegemonic neo-liberal world order has been facilitated by the representation and imposition of a single vision of the economy. For over 30 years, the constant refrain from organic intellectuals of the neo-liberal world order and its politico-economic facilitators has been the Thatcherite claim that 'there is no alternative' to corporate led and market-dominated economic strategies at both the national and global levels. In the main, the consolidation of the global neo-liberal project has been achieved by the concerted efforts of dominant forces in the world order through undemocratic means marked by 'constant policing and repressing of counter-hegemonic practices and agents' (Santos, 2006: 14). Even in its reformist turn in the early twenty-first century, as we saw in our discussion of the rise of the human security development discourse, the marketization of the economy and other aspects of social life remains the backbone of the neo-liberal world order. From the perspective of those participating at the WSF, the insistence on one economic truth amounts to a colonizing move geared towards consolidating an informal imperial project: one whose hallmark is the reproduction of 'epistemic violence' (Mignolo, 2007: 462) that has characterized the post-1945 world order and its hegemonic development discourses.

World Social Forum and world order: other visions are possible

The WSF process, however, goes beyond illustrating the strategies and effects of neo-liberal economic ideas and practices. From its inception in 2001, the WSF has insisted that, in contrast to the neo-liberal perspective, there are possible alternatives, an idea embodied in its slogan 'another world is possible'—a phrase that has come to signify the normative thread that ties the various movements and organizations of the WSF together (World Social Forum Charter of Principles, 2001). While the numerous movements involved in the WSF differ in their politics and histories, there is nonetheless a consensus among them that the contemporary order is unjust on various levels. As previously highlighted, from their perspective the current world order is marked by exclusionary economic practices that marginalize the majority of people in the world. Institutionally, this world order is underpinned by undemocratic institutions of global governance that perpetuate politico-economic marginalization of the South.

Economic processes: other visions and agents are possible

As we previously mentioned, the need to create alternatives to neo-liberal ideas has been a core feature of the WSF since the beginning of this process. Given the diversity of the movements and organizations linked to this process, the alternatives emerging from the WSF represent a wide range of practices. As Santos states:

> the alternatives range from micro-initiatives undertaken by marginalized sectors in the Global South, seeking to gain control of their lives and livelihoods, to proposals for national and international economic and legal coordination designed to guarantee respect for basic labour and environmental standards worldwide, novel forms of capital controls, revamped systems of progressive taxation and spending, and expansion of social programmes, as well as attempts to build regional economies based on the principles of cooperation and solidarity ... rather than embodying comprehensive blueprints or system-wide alternative economic agendas. (2006: 27)

In thinking about alternatives, local histories and needs inform WSF alternative proposals concerning the organization of social life broadly defined. This is a departure from the hegemonic economic vision of neo-liberalism in which the demands and workings of an abstract de-historicized market mechanism is proposed as the master blueprint of economic strategies in all societies, and local histories and priorities are considered as hindrances to the universal march to freedom. Some of the proposals by participants of the WSF stressing the importance of paying attention to local and regional needs and priorities, embrace Walden Bello's concepts of 'deglobalization' and 'decommodification'. This is a strategy geared to, among other things, the reconstitution of economic production within local contexts which evokes Karl Polanyi's (2001) vision of 're-embedding the economy in society, rather than letting society be driven by the economy' (Bello, 2003: 286)— a vision wherein economic activities are subordinated to the needs of society. Deglobalization and decommodification strategies for instance underpin various practices and objectives of social movements and social justice organizations in contemporary South Africa. These movements and organizations aim to 'turn basic needs into genuine human rights... Recent and ongoing campaigns... include: Free anti-retroviral medicines to fight AIDS (hence disempowering Big Pharma); 50 litres of free water per person per day (hence ridding Africa of Suez and other water privatizers); 1 kilowatt hour of free electricity for each individual everyday (hence reorienting energy resources from export-oriented mining and smelting, to basic-needs consumption); extensive land reform (hence de-emphasizing cash cropping and export-oriented plantations)... free education (hence halting the General Agreement on Trade in Services (GATS))' (Bond, 2007: 150–151). Such thinking further frames proposals promoting the notion of an economy based on the idea of solidary that have emerged in various places in the South such as Brazil. In his analysis of economic solidary projects in Brazil Paul Singer argues that 'a solidary enterprise rejects any separation between work and ownership of the means of production, the recognized basis of capitalism... Capital, in the solidary enterprise, is owned by those who work in it and by them alone... The company property is divided equally amongst the workers so that all have an equal voice in the decision-making process' (2007: 1). Such an approach to the economy informs the following proposal from a movement at the WSF which states: 'the past 30 years have seen the emergence of solidarity economic practices that embody, and innovate creatively on, more than a century of workers' struggles to organize.... Central to Solidarity Economics is the valuing of human labour, knowledge and creativity, rather than capital' (Quintela, 2003: 100–101).

Beyond providing a forum in which participants can share ideas about alternatives to neo-liberal ideas, the WSF opens up a space for members and participants to think of themselves as agents of their own history, while being astutely aware of the structural and political constraints marking the current world order. In doing so, the WSF foregrounds the agency of counter-hegemonic actors and thus challenges the neo-liberal world view in which only the agency of dominant forces matters in political, economic and cultural processes. That the WSF process opens political opportunity structures for social forces to make their history was evident at the WSF in Nairobi where historically marginalized groups—the landless, women farmers, gays and lesbians, and pastoral communities—in Kenya's colonial and neo-colonial politico-economic processes not only presented their grievances but also linked and shared strategies on ways to create alternative livelihoods with members of movements and organizations from other parts of the world.[3] In the case of the Kenyan women farmers association, the members viewed their linking up with women farmers from other parts of the world as a transformative development that opened up an opportunity for them not only to share knowledge and exchange agricultural produce on a fair and just basis, but also to share strategies on alternative ways of organizing agricultural production and to strengthen rural farming communities in an era that promotes contract farming and further commodification of the agricultural sector (ibid.). Generally, the WSF embrace of the idea that there is more than one way to organize the economy is not only disrupting the consolidation of the neo-liberal doctrine of one universal economic truth, but in the process it is also facilitating a process of political 'resubjectivation', which, as articulated by J. K. Gibson-Graham, involves 'the mobilization and transformation of desires, the cultivation of capacities, and the making of new iden-tifications' (2006: xxxvi), that enable the emergence of new political subjects who are open to and keen on mapping alternative ways of orga-nizing social life including new visions of the economy (ibid; see also Escobar 2008).

World Social Forum and global governance

The institutions that underpin the neo-liberal world order are deemed as playing a pivotal role in enabling the reproduction of an unjust and undemocratic world by the movements and organizations involved in the WSF process. For them, the current world order is dominated by institutions of global governance that are not accountable to the majority of people in the world. These institutions play a major role in the generation and dissemination of hegemonic development ideas which facilitate adoption of economic practices that contribute to environmental degradation, social and economic dislocation, and the marginalization of most people in the South. In the call for the democratization of institutions of global governance, participants of the WSF envision a deeper form of democracy marked by a commitment to 'deepening authority-sharing and respect for difference in the social domains' (Santos, 2006: 41). In their vision of an alternative to the current world order, the World Social Forum Charter of Principles proposes the emergence of an international order that will 'respect universal human rights, and those of all citizens—men and women—of all nations and the environment and will rest on democratic international systems and institutions at the service of social justice, equality and the sovereignty of peoples'.[4] A democratic world order through the lens of the movements and organizations of the WSF, then, goes beyond the neo-liberal vision, which promotes low-density forms of democracy at the local and global level.

WSF: Porto Alegre and beyond

With its emancipatory ideas and other features, some of which were highlighted in the previous section, WSF's expansion since the first meeting in Porto Alegre is another feature which signals the possibility of the WSF emerging as a significant counter-hegemonic political process that has the potential of contributing to the transformation of the ideas and other elements of the current world order. In terms of numbers, the first meeting was attended by over 15,000 participants from 117 countries (Leite, 2005: 84). Since then the number of participants has increased, with numbers rising to approximately 60,000 and 100,000 for the second and third World Social Forums respectively (Santos, 2006: 68). The Seventh World Social Forum, held in January 2007 in Nairobi, Kenya, documented 75,000 attendees. Further, at the organizational level, an understanding of the power asymmetry that marks the world order has seen a commitment by the IC to have the meetings in the global South (Smith et al., 2008: 58). In terms of the WSF's organizational structure, the push for the establishment of a permanent IC since 2002, has strengthened the WSF potential to continue interrupting the hegemony of neo-liberal ideas and also its emergence as a long-time political process that acts as a counter to the hegemonic projects of the contemporary world order. As argued by members of the IC, this development 'reflects the concept of the WSF as a permanent, long-term process, designed to build an international movement to bring together alternatives to neoliberal thinking in favour of a new social order, one that will foster contact among a multiplicity and diversity of proposals'.[5]

Along with the increasing numbers at its global meetings, the WSF is also extending its reach with the emergence of city, national, regional and polycentric meetings.[6] As of 2008 the WSF had a presence in Asia, Africa, Europe, North America and Latin America. The US National Social Forum was held for the first time in June 2007 in Atlanta. The growing worldwide reach of the World Social Forum presents a political opportunity structure that could enable the emergence and embedding of a planetary critical consciousness that disrupts the hegemony of neo-liberal ideas and other elements of the contemporary world order. Such a development is opening up a mental and political space, however fragile, for reimagining ways to organize, economic, cultural and economic life. As some analysts of the World Social Forum have argued,

> 'Prefigurative politics'—or the enactment of the world we envision— encapsulates the WSF [World Social Forum] process as a dynamic global entity. Social Forum events are attempts to create miniworlds, models the forum process hopes to export around the globe. If thousands of committed activists from diverse movements with multiple visions of social change are able to come together and interact during and between forum events, the WSF is building a new model of global governance and civil society. (Smith et al., 2008: 134)

WSF: challenges

As we have suggested here, the WSF is contributing to ongoing efforts to transform the main features of the current world order including its attendant development discourse. This development is opening up the possibility for the rise of a planetary counter-hegemonic political process. That being said, the WSF is faced with challenges that may derail this process. For example, the WSF faces constraints from dominant structures and political forces. From the beginning, for instance, the dominant media outlets have questioned the relevance of the WSF, given supposedly its inability to provide alternatives to neo-liberal economic globalization (Santos, 2006: 39). Further, at the national level, the WSF is vulnerable to shifts in political and economic changes, as indicated by the political developments in Porto Alegre in 2003. In addition, while the rise of the WSF has, to a large measure, disrupted the intellectual power of neo-liberal ideas especially in some social formations in Latin America, the structural power of private capital and the

repackaged neo-liberal strategies especially in the arena of finance capital (see Chapter 9) remain a constraint to counter-consensus visions
of economic production. In addition, the WSF is marked by tensions
and contradictions. Overall and as scholars of civil society groups and
social movements constantly remind us, it is important not to assume
that non-state or 'bottom-up' political processes represent progressive
sites and practices (Hutchful, 1995–1996; Ferguson, 2006; Mamdani,
1996). Cautioning against such an assumption, Laura Macdonald argues
that what is needed in discussions of civil society at all scales is 'a
nuanced understanding...one that does not assume that civil society
actors are inherently progressive, inclusive, and democratic, but subjects their claims to careful analysis' (2005: 22). In the case of the WSF,
for instance, questions of exclusion and silencing have accompanied
its evolution. First, the gendered nature of the WSF process has been
contested by feminists, and a range of women's movements and organizations participating in this process. Members of women's organizations,
movements and feminists involved in this process have 'levelled strong
criticism at the sexist nature of the organization and, more fundamentally, on the absence of a feminist political economy as a framework
for understanding global capitalism', a reality that has led to a situation
whereby 'rather than offering a plurality of views, economic analyses
dominate the forum, perpetuating a monolithic vision of the methods
by which to create a just society' (Smith et al., 2008: 60).

Second, while the WSF considers hierarchies and practices based
on race as contributing to social injustice, these tendencies, whether
intended or not, persist in its domain. In the case of the 2007 WSF in
Nairobi, for example, the backwardness of the African continent and its
social movements hung in the air and coloured post-WSF comments,
which judged the Nairobi gathering to be a failure compared to the
dynamism and excitement of the Porto Alegre and Mumbai meetings.[7]
Overall, as in other political spaces, the politics of race loomed large
in the WSF arena in Nairobi. For instance, there were demands that
the meeting be held in a location in Kenya that represented the real
Africa rather than Nairobi city centre (Onyango, 2009). In the case of the
feminist dialogue space at the Nairobi WSF, there was the oft-repeated
comment about African women's movements as not having quite 'got-
ten it'—feminism—when compared to their counter-parts from Latin
America and Asia. This inference troubled African feminists and some
feminists from other parts of the world for it contradicted one of the normative foundations of the WSF, which is respect for differences and specific histories: in essence a commitment to find common ground within

multiple forms of difference underpinning the WSF process. At the root of comments such as the one on African women's movements is a deeply held racialist representational system of African women as being hapless victims, docile and politically backward and thus in need of salvation and rescue by their enlightened sisters from other parts of the world.

Overall, the specific conditions and histories that influenced the WSF process in these other locations seem to have been forgotten or considered irrelevant in discussions about the Nairobi Forum. Take for instance, the meetings in Porto Alegre. The earlier mentioned support by the local public authority, given the strong political presence and legitimacy of the Brazilian Workers' Party, clearly shaped the modalities of the WSF gathering there and it is not difficult to imagine that had the meeting occurred in other parts of Brazil dominated by neo-liberal political forces, the modalities and the results of the gathering might have been significantly different. This is clearly evident when one considers the developments in Porto Alegre in 2003. The loss of political power by the Brazilian Workers' Party in Rio Grand do Sul saw a decline in support of the WSF meeting held that year in Porto Alegre (Leite, 2005: 119). In essence, local histories of struggles and structures of domination, among other things, set the parameters of WSF global meetings in a given setting such as Nairobi, Mumbai or elsewhere. Yet, instead of historicizing local and global conditions that led to the dominance of 'development talk' at the WSF in Nairobi, the tendency was to evoke the vibrant forms of resistance in Porto Alegre and Mumbai as a litmus test for success. That comparisons of the various WSF gatherings will be made is to be expected. However, a non-critical approach that abstracts the mediating role of local histories in the various sites where these meetings are held might see the emergence of a WSF hierarchical order: with its own script of first, second and third worlds of resistance—a development that would generate a new racialized regional geography, a practice that movements and organizations involved in the WSF process associate with the hegemonic world order. While one could dismiss the racist overtones at the WSF meeting in Nairobi as being less serious given the overall practices and encounters at the WSF, it is important to note that the global left broadly defined, needs to interrogate its historical and contemporary construction of blackness in Africa and other regions with resident populations of African descent especially in Latin America. Without a critical perspective on race that acknowledges that global forces of domination do not have a monopoly on racist ideology and practices, WSF's declarations of solidarity and celebration of difference among participants will remain at the level of rhetoric. To avoid such a development and building on lines proposed by Santos, multi-faceted projects of translation of histories of movements and developments in various regions is urgently needed in the WSF process.[8] For parachuting specific experiences and expecting the same social realities from one social formation to another by WSF participants is engaging in practices of 'history by analogy' (Mamdani, 1996: 11–12), similar to those that underpin hegemonic development discourses as we argued in chapter 4.

Conclusion

The underlying premise of this chapter has been that the rise of a neo-liberal world order has been a contested process particularly since the 1980s. In addition and with a focus on the WSF process, the chapter has discussed ways in which this process is disrupting the hegemony of the current world order; a development that we suggest has the potential of laying the foundation for the rise of a planetary counter-hegemonic political process. The discussion has further highlighted some challenges that might derail the transformative possibilities of the WSF. While cognizant of challenges facing the WSF, our conclusion is that, its normative underpinnings which are embodied in its Charter of Principles, its continuing expansion, and the willingness of participants to engage in dialogue about sources of tensions (Santos, 2006) makes the rise of the WSF an important development for social forces engaged in struggles for emancipatory political, cultural and economic processes. For when contrasted to the neo-liberal spirit of Davos's World Economic Forum, that is striving to consolidate the current world order, the main aim embodying 'the spirit of Porto Alegre [WSF]' is the making of 'a more democratic and egalitarian world' (Wallerstein, 2004: 160–161).

9
Epilogue: Global Financial Crisis, Barack Obama's Presidency and World Order

As this project was in its final stages in 2008, the crisis of the global financial system underpinning the neo-liberal world order, which began in 2007, came to a head. This crisis continues at the time of writing, that is, the early months of 2009. The manifestation of this development includes, but is not limited to, the collapse of major financial firms in the core of the capitalist world system, bailouts of some of these firms by states, tightening of credit markets and collapse of the housing market as evidenced by rising foreclosures. In the USA, firms that have dominated the financial sector, such as Bear Stearns, collapsed while others filed for bankruptcy, as in the case of Lehman Brothers. The deepening of the financial crisis in the USA has seen the state bailout major banks such as Citigroup, Bank of America and the giant insurance firm American International Group. Other parts of the world are also experiencing major economic crises generated by financial capital. On 29 September, 2008 in Iceland, the country's third largest bank, Glitnir, collapsed and the state bailed it out for £ 466 million (Stoddard, 2009).[1] By 6 October, Glitnir and the Landsbanki bank (another of Iceland's three major banks) were under government control (Parker, 2009: 45). In an effort to contain the crisis, on 21 November, the country received a loan of £ 8.5 billion with contributions from the IMF and some European countries (Stoddard, 2009; see also Parker, 2009). While crises of the capitalist world economy generated by the financial sector are not new (Minsky, 1982; Strange, 1986; Kindleberger, 1989), the current one has the potential of causing a major systemic shock to the world economy because of structural-political developments that have emerged in this sector under neo-liberal conditions.

In addition to the economic crisis generated by the liberalized global financial system, 2008 saw the ascendancy of Barack Obama to the

American and world political landscape and to the Presidency on 20 January, 2009. This development has raised hopes for the possibility of transformation of national and global politico-economic processes. This chapter has two objectives. First, to provide a discussion of the historical developments that led to the rise of a liberalized global financial system and the effects of this system on, among others things, the power divide between the North and South. Second, to discuss the implications of Obama's presidency for the current world order including its liberalized financial system. The chapter has three parts, with part one discussing developments that influenced the reconfiguration of the global financial system along neo-liberal lines. In the second part, we highlight developments that characterize the era of liberalized financial markets and their effects. The third part discusses the implications of Obama's presidency to the transformation of contemporary world order. We conclude with a brief highlight of what have been the book's central concerns.

The making of a liberalized global financial system

Like in other politico-economic arenas, the ascendancy of the neo-liberal doctrine and other developments that led to shifts in core features of the world order in the 1970s did not spare the post-1945 Keynesian financial system. A discussion of developments that led to the emergence of a neo-liberal world order need not detain us here, as we highlighted some of them in Chapter 3. For our present purposes, we revisit some of these developments with a specific reference to their contribution to the making of a liberalized global financial system. Although the four developments we discuss here—ideas, states and new financial instruments and technologies—are not exclusive, we contend that they are crucial to any explanation and understanding of the rise and consolidation of liberalized financial markets and their effects.

The role of ideas in the rise and shifts in world orders has been one of the central questions in this project. Hence, a shift in ideas governing the post-1945 financial order was one of the factors that contributed to shifts in the modalities of the global financial system. While the rise of a Keynesian economic consensus following World War II did not mark the end of intellectual and policy debates informed by other schools of economic thought, for almost three decades this consensus was the reference point for economic policies for social formations under the orbit of the capitalist geopolitical alliance including those in the South. By the 1970s, the Bretton Woods financial system underpinned by the Keynesian consensus began to unravel. Key actors in the capitalist world order increasingly viewed this system of fixed but flexible exchange rates, which had advocated that states should have power to establish capital controls on the movement of capital within and across national borders, as a source of stagnation in financial and other economic sectors. From the perspective of multinational corporations and financial firms, for example, the Keynesian financial order was a constraining factor to their economic activities (Helleiner, 1994). Thus, these firms increasingly demanded 'freedom to operate offshore', a demand that yielded some results in the 1960s as evidenced by the quiet support of the USA and the UK states for the emergence of the Eurodollar market in London (ibid.; Strange, 1986; Germain, 1997; Underhill, 1997). Consequently, as neo-liberal ideas were gaining momentum in the 1970s, multinational firms and banks supported the deepening of this development and other policies aimed at dismantling capital controls, as well as policies that had governed the global financial system under the Keynesian consensus (Helleiner, 1994: 169). The pressure by dominant actors on states (and practices of states that will be discussed shortly) to liberalize financial markets, coupled with the economic crisis of the 1970s in the context of a global ascendency of neo-liberal economic thought, provided a major opening for the rise of a liberalized global financial system.

Increasingly the foregoing context heightened calls for the liberalization of financial markets by dominant actors and neo-liberal organic intellectuals such as Milton Friedman, Friedrich Hayek and, in the context of development discourse, Lal (Chapter 3). Theoretically, the neo-liberal inspired doctrine of monetarism advocated by neo-liberal scholars such as these provided the rationale for the liberalization of the global financial system (Clarke, 1988; Harvey, 2005; Filho, 2007). Monetarists advocated the dismantling of the Keynesian monetary system of fixed but flexible exchange rates and national control of financial markets. From their perspective, the liberalization of financial markets would facilitate international free trade, foreign direct investment and development in the South. Further, as per the efficient monetary theory inspired by neo-liberalism, which claims that 'the market knows best' (Davidson, 2007: 3), markets were rational and efficient when compared to states. Thus, the market mechanism had the capacity to address the modalities of the global financial system including any instability it generated by ensuring the optimal allocation of scarce resources and would promote global 'maximum economic growth' (ibid.). Monetarist intellectuals and policy makers such as Lawrence Summers, US Treasury

Secretary under the Clinton administration (and currently Obama's administration, Director of the National Economic Council), held the monetarist view of financial markets deeply. For Summers (1989: 166), financial markets' fundamental 'social functions [are] spreading risks, guiding the investment of scarce capital, and processing and disseminating the information possessed by diverse traders'. Further, in the context of liberalized markets 'prices will always reflect fundamental values' for 'the logic of efficient markets is compelling' (quoted in Davidson, 2007: 3). Through a monetarist lens, even the much-feared economic instability from the Great Depression generated by speculative capital had a restorative effective for capital accumulation under capitalism. Such a view of speculative capital was informed by Friedman's contention that economic expectations were essentially anticipatory'; a departure from Keynes who viewed them as being based on previous historical experiences and uncertainty (Clarke, 1988: 325).

Key changes to the Keynesian financial system, advocated by proponents of neo-liberal ideas included the implementation of policies that they claimed would contain inflation and ensure monetary stability to enable the workings of capitalism (ibid.: 323; Martin and Schumann, 1997; Filho, 2007: 98) globally. According to the monetarist doctrine, states could resolve the inflationary trend of the 1970s for instance by simply limiting the expansion of money (Filho, 2007: 99). Informed by Friedman's quantity theory of money, neo-liberal monetarists claimed that states could limit the money supply by raising interest rates during inflationary moments and expanding it by lowering them during a recession (Rapley, 2002: 53). Like other monetarists, Friedman departed from Keynes economic ideas by arguing that monetary rather than fiscal policy was the best policy tool to address the up and down turns of the capitalist world economy (ibid.). In the case of inflationary conditions, monetarists' view was that, while these could be 'reinforced by the wage demands of trades unions' their roots were mainly from states' monetary policies of expanding the money supply (Clarke, 1988: 323). This practice generated 'the inflationary expectations that led unions to make such demands, and made employers willing and able to meet them' (ibid.) By limiting the expansion of the money supply workers' and employers' expectations would shift leading to 'a painless restoration of price stability' (ibid.: 324). For monetarists, states' interest rates policies were crucial in such a process for,

When interest rates are high, people prefer to invest rather than spend their money, and the high cost of loans discourages people from buying on credit. Economic activity thus slows, less money chases after the same supply of goods, and prices rise more slowly or even fall. In times of recession, lower interest rates have the opposite effect: people withdraw money from savings and spend it; they even buy on credit because it is no longer expensive, and activity resumes. (Rapley, 2002: 53)

As highlighted in Chapter 3, as the decade of the 1970s evolved, neo-liberal ideas as they pertain to the financial and other economic sectors would emerge as a major element of the contemporary world order. Important as these ideas are however, without their adoption by dominant states, especially by the US given its hegemonic status in the post-1945 world order and by institutions of global governance, they would have most likely remained in the realm of academic debates. Thus, a second factor that contributed to the rise of a liberalized financial system was the adoption of neo-liberal monetarist ideas by dominant states in the world order. In the USA, changes in US monetary policies began in earnest in 1971 when President Richard Nixon dismantled the convertibility of the dollar to gold, followed by the floating of the dollar and the removal of capital controls by 1974 (Helleiner, 1994; Strange, 1986). As highlighted in Chapter 3, the emergence of the USA as a hegemonic power following World War II was a pivotal development leading to a significant shift in the world order. Given that under the 1944 Bretton Woods agreement, the US dollar emerged as the reserve currency in the world economy—an arrangement that provided the US enormous power in the global financial order—changes in the country's monetary policy such as those that occurred in the 1970s would have a ripple effect in the world capitalist system. Thus, as in other economic sectors, dominant states in the world order played a pivotal role in the dismantling of the Keynesian financial order and the liberalization of financial markets. Suggestions to contain this process were not welcomed especially by the USA.[2] For example, with the 1970s roaming financial crisis that posed serious threat to the Keynesian financial system and the world economy, a suggestion by European and Japanese interests concerning the establishment of a more controlled system was rejected by the USA (Helleiner, 1994: 166–167).

After the USA's shifts in monetary policy, then, other states instituted this process in various stages in the 1970s and 1980s (Strange, 1986, 1998; Cerny, 1993; Helleiner 1994; Martin and Schumann, 1997). Overall, from this period onwards, state after state, fortified further by the ascendancy of neo-liberal intellectual thought, liberalized their financial markets. Even centre-left states such as France joined the world of liberalized financial markets in 1983, and this policy turn coupled with an earlier one along similar lines in 1976 by a labour-led government in Britain were significant at the 'symbolic' level for they signalled both locally and internationally the dismantling of Keynesian monetary policies (Helleiner, 1994: 168). Without these developments, the new phase of globalization driven by neo-liberal ideas might have been seriously undermined:

> A decision to introduce exchange controls in either case would have set back the process considerably. Exchange controls in Britain would have been particularly significant in removing one of the central pillars of the emerging global financial order, the Eurodollar market in London...As one U.S. official noted at the time, 'It' was a choice between Britain remaining in the liberal financial system of the West as opposed to a radical change...[and] if that [the latter] had happened the whole system would come apart. (Ibid.)

Although the establishment and evolution of monetarist policies inspired by neo-liberal ideas were mediated by national conditions,— such as the agency of the state and counter-hegemonic protests such as those discussed in Chapter 8—by the 1980s what Philip G. Cerny (1993: 157) has termed as the 'new embedded financial orthodoxy' underpinned by neo-liberal ideas had occurred. In three decades, this orthodoxy has emerged as the hegemonic discourse as far as the modalities of the financial sector are concerned. During this period, diverse countries in the world order such as the USA, Russia (Chapter 6), Chile, South Africa, South Korea, Malawi, UK, India and many others have instituted these measures. In Chile, the famed Chicago boys, with the backing of the state, as well as local and global capitalists, established monetary policies inspired by the neo-liberal embedded financial orthodoxy that underpins the current liberalized financial system such as deregulation of the financial sector and deflationary measures aimed at limiting money supply and credit (Silva, 1996). In the USA, the 'Volcker shocks' of 1979 were straight from the new neo-liberal financial orthodoxy. Through a policy shift on interest rates, Paul Volcker, Chair of the US Federal Reserve Bank, further deepened the neo-liberal turn in the country's financial sector. This policy shift saw 'the real rate of interest, which had often been negative during the double-digit inflationary surge of the 1970s...rendered positive by fiat of the Federal Reserve. The nominal rate of interest was raised overnight and, after a few ups and downs, by July 1981 stood close to 20 per cent... This, Volcker argued, was the only way out of the grumbling crisis of stagflation that characterized the US and much of the global economy throughout the 1970s' (Harvey, 2005: 23).

Development in communication technologies is a third factor that has influenced the rise of a liberalized financial system. The emergence and evolution of the internet, communication technologies and mobile communications have changed the modalities of financial markets. This development has changed not only 'the physical form in which money worked as a medium of exchange' but also the ways in which money circulates in the world system and—as will be discussed shortly—shifts in power in monetary matters (Strange, 1998: 24). New communications technologies have given private financial actors, states and individuals the ability to engage in financial markets with rapid speed in a range of spatial scales. These developments have brought to centre-stage 'the significance of instantaneous international co-ordination of financial flows...This...world of high finance encloses...variety of cross-cutting activities, in which banks borrow massively short-term from other banks, insurance companies and pension funds assemble such vast pools of investment funds as to function as dominant "market makers", which industrial, merchant, and land capital become [heavily] integrated into financial operations and structures' (Harvey, 1990: 163). To sum up this section, we suggest that the preceding developments have led to emergence and consolidation of a liberalized global financial system with significant effects.

Liberalizing financial markets: effects

Shift in monetary policies coupled with the other features of the neo-liberal world order have brought about major developments in the world order. They have largely contributed to the liberalization of financial markets, a development that emerged as a hallmark of the neo-liberal world order. This development has generated new politico-economic conditions, which have major implications for the world order including the North-South power divide. These conditions are, structural dominance of finance, deepening economic integration and consolidation of the power of TDHB and private financial firms. We discuss these developments and their effects next.

Structural dominance of capital

One of the core effects of the liberalization of financial markets has been the emergence of structural dominance of finance capital in the world economy. The creation of an ever-expanding menu of new financial instruments has enabled this process. These instruments have bene-fitted from new developments in physics and financial mathematics (Nesvetailova, 2007: 20). These developments have enabled financial institutions to construct a range of 'financial portfolios, in which price and risk exposures of various assets' are 'weighted and projected into the future' (ibid.). Further, they have influenced the rise of new financial instruments such as derivatives, and debt securitization (not to be con-fused with the concept of securitization from security studies discussed in Chapter 7) packages have emerged as tools for managing financial risk and generating profits (Nesvetailova, 2007). As Cornford (1995: 345) defines them, derivatives are mainly 'contracts specifying rights and obligations which are based upon, and thus derive their value from, the performance of some underlying instrument, investment, currency, commodity or service index, right or rate' (quoted in Strange, 1998: 30). Steinherr (2000: 291) posits that securitization entails bundling of assets that in traditional financial lending practices 'would have served as col-lateral for a bank loan into securities' and once put together by financial institutions are traded in financial markets as commodities (cited in Nesvetailova, 2007: 18). Future markets such as derivatives are not new, but they have taken a new turn in the neo-liberal era. While in other historical periods, they acted as a form of insurance for trade and other productive economic sectors, currently enabled by new communication technologies the derivative market has exploded: 'Between 1989–1995, the nominal value of contracts doubled every two years and reached the unimaginable sum of $ 41,000 globally' (Martin and Schumann, 1997: 52). With the rise of derivative markets, 'the financial world has emancipated itself from the real sphere' (Thomas Fischer, cited in ibid.: 52–53).

Overall, in the last three decades, financial capital has come to dom-inate what policy makers and scholars of monetary relations consider real and productive economic sectors such as trade and manufacturing (Strange, 1986; Davidson, 2007; Nesvetailova, 2007) and the modali-ties of the capitalist world order. According to Nesvetailova (2007: 9), for example, 'the share of the financial sector in the economy as a whole surpassed 20% of the country's GDP' in the UK during the 1990s and this sector has come to dominate the country's politico-economic developments when compared to the epoch of the Keynesian consen-sus (See also generally Martin and Schumann, 1997). This development has also manifested itself at the global level. As Harvey indicates, 'total daily turnover of financial transactions in international markets, which stood at $ 2.3 billion in 1983' rose to $ 130 billion in 2001, while 'the $ 40 trillion annual turnover in 2001 compares to the estimated $ 800 billion that would be required to support international trade and productive investment flows' (2005: 161).

The structural dominance of capital has had other consequences. To begin with, financial capital has not only come to dominate other sectors, but economic sectors have also become closely integrated into it in a manner that makes it difficult to discern the boundary of each sector in reference to the financial one (Harvey, 1990; 161). This has made other economic sectors highly susceptible to the vagaries of financial capital. These days, a crisis in financial markets tends to lead to systemic shocks in the whole economy. In essence, the structural dominance of financial capital has ushered in a period in which finance capital is no longer the 'servant' of the productive and real pillars of the world economy (Heilleiner, 1994; Nesvetailova, 2007). The ongoing economic crisis in the USA, which began in the arenas of financial sectors such as the subprime mortgage business,[3] is a case in point, as is the previously mentioned economic crisis in Iceland, which originated in the banking sector. The financial crises in Argentina in 2001, Brazil and Russia in 1998 are other examples, as is the 1997 crisis in Asia. With the onset of the latter, transnational investors withdrew their investments (for instance in Thailand) and economic activities in sectors such as construction and the real estate market came to a stand still (Klein, 2007: 334). In the case of the current financial crisis, according to *The Economist* it has generated a major global crisis in the industrial sectors of various countries:

> The destructive global power of the financial crisis became clear last year.... Industrial production fell in the latest three months by 3.6% and 4.4% respectively in America and Britain (equivalent to annual declines of 13.8% and 16.4%). Some locals blame that on Wall Street and the City. But the collapse is much worse in countries more dependent on manufacturing exports, which have come to rely on consumers in debtor countries. Germany's industrial production in the fourth quarter fell by 6.8%; Taiwan's by 21.7%; Japan's by 12%— which helps to explain why GDP is falling even faster there than it did in the early 1990s... Industrial production is volatile, but the world has not seen a contraction like this since the first oil shock in the 1970s—and even that was not so widespread. Industry is collapsing in Eastern Europe, as it is in Brazil, Malaysia and Turkey. Thousands of factories in southern China are now abandoned. Their workers went home to the countryside for the new year in January. Millions never came back. (2009)

Further, the structural dominance of financial capital has shifted the power balance between public and private actors in the economy. While states continue to have agency in monetary matters, a consequence of the structural dominance of finance has been the skewing of the balance of power in finance in favour of private authority (Strange, 1986; 1998; Helleiner, 1994; Germain, 1997; Martin and Schumann, 1997; Underhill, 1997; Eatwell and Taylor, 2000; Bello, 2002; Nesvetailova, 2007). A main source of this development is the emergence of private financial institutions as major sources of liquidity and asset building for states, multinational corporations and other dominant social forces in the world economy. Overall, with the liberalization of financial markets, 'paper entrepreneurialism' (Reich, 1983 quoted in Harvey, 1990: 163) has become the norm. World wide, financial paper entrepreneurs keep searching for new ways to generate profits rather than depending on what they view as non-lucrative traditional routes such as manufacturing and other Fordist forms of economic production (Harvey, 1990; Davidson, 2007; Nesvetailova, 2007; Phillips, 2008). Under neo-liberal conditions, the liberalization of exchange rates and removal of controls of capital movements have contributed to this trend by enabling the privatization of risk. As Nesvetoilova explains, with liberalization of financial markets the 'exchange rate became a variable, and hence a risk and a product, tradable in financial markets' and therefore, 'monitoring, managing and controlling the risk quickly became a highly profitable industry in itself' (2007: 17).

The drive to generate profits and to manage financial risk through paper entrepreneurialism has seen the rise of new private financial instruments such as securities, hedge funds and the adoption by traditional banks, insurance companies, accounting firms and new financial institutions of these instruments. These institutions follow closely the modalities of global financial markets, such as changes in foreign exchange rates and other conditions, to ensure that they maximize their capacity to generate profits (Harvey, 1990: 163). Changes in foreign exchange rates, for instance, allow dominant actors in these institutions to acquire profits rapidly. In addition, these instruments have enabled owners of capital to engage in 'asset-stripping of rival or even totally unrelated corporations' (ibid.). With the liberalization of financial markets, financial paper entrepreneurs have emerged as dominant players in the arena of transnational credit markets. Historically, for the first time, transnational private institutions such as Goldman Sachs, Normura, Citicorp, Deutsche, Dai-Ichi Kangyo Bank control large amounts of mobile capital and access to credit (Germain, 1997: 105–106) when compared to states.

Currently transnational banks, insurance companies and firms engaged in the business of hedge funds, securities and other new financial instruments are the key lenders in the liberalized financial system. For example, from US$ 108 billion in 1995, 'asset-backed securities issuance' rose to US$ 1.07, US$ 1.1 and US$ 1.23 trillion in 2000, 2005 and 2006 respectively (Phillips, 2008: 62). Indicating a similar trend Davidson states: 'currently banks transact over $ 1.5 trillion daily in foreign exchange markets, almost 70 times the volume of daily international trade in goods and services' (2007: 107). The ability of these financial firms to acquire liquidity and control access to credit markets has contributed to the deepening of the structural dominance of financial capital and the decline of public authority. These developments have led to 'a new political class' (Martin and Schumann, 1997: 46) with enormous structural power. This unelected class has reconfigured democratic politics for increasingly it is its decisions and practices that shape the workings of national economies (ibid.) and the world economy. For example,

> In September 1992, when several hundred bank and fund managers followed the example of finance guru Gorge Soros and staked billions on the devaluation of the pound sterling and the Italian lira, the Bank of England and the Banca d'Italia could not prevent the fall in the exchange rate, even though they committed nearly all their dollar and Deutschmark reserves to purchases of their national currency.... In February 1994, when the Federal Reserve put up base rates and the US capital market nose-dived as a result, the Bonn government could again only watch as German companies suddenly had to pay higher interests on their loans. (Ibid.)

Basically, the structural dominance of financial capital has increased states' structural dependency on private financial institutions as states have come to depend on these institutions for access to credit markets. For example, in the USA, regardless of which political party is in power, the state has come to rely on transnational financial flows from private monetary actors including American financial firms (Underhill, 1997; Bond 2007; Davidson, 2007). To deal with its trade deficit and other financial needs, the USA has come to rely heavily on international financial flows from countries such China and others in East Asia, which have increasingly bought its Treasury bills, and its multinational firms, which have access to credit from various transnational financial institutions (Davidson, 2007). Under competitive neo-liberal conditions though, the US state is not the only one marked by deepening structural dependency on private financial institutions for its financial flows. With the liberalization of financial markets and the world economy, 'the competitive state' form (Cerny, 1990) has become the desired norm, a development that has seen states in both the North and South in different but complementary ways try to reconstitute themselves as competitive states in efforts to attract financial and investment capital. For example, an objective of the Chilean state's liberalization of the financial sector during the Augusto Pinochet regime was to make the country attractive to local and international financial capital (Silva, 1996). Further, Argentina's policy requiring the pegging of its currency against the US dollar was a strategy aimed at strengthening the country's competitive edge in a liberalized world economy. Although the dollarization of the Argentinean financial system contributed to a major economic crisis by 2001 (Davidson, 2007: 146–148), establishing polices that deepen the country's competitive capacity has been a core strategy of states in the period of global neo-liberalism. Thus, while the nature of strategies differs across the world, states have attempted to establish the most conducive environment for financial capital to operate within, in an effort to access credit and for their politico-economic projects.

Deeper economic integration

A second politico-economic condition that has emerged with the liberalization of financial markets, and which has had significant effects on the world economy, is the deepening of economic integration. New financial instruments, financial paper entrepreneurialism and new communication technologies have facilitated this process. With the liberalization of financial markets, finance capital knows no regional or national borders. This is a departure from the Keynesian financial system, in which, national and global financial markets were highly regulated. States, multinational corporations and other dominant actors in the world system can access financial markets from a range of sources in the new geography of finance. With the rapid mediation of communication technologies, 'banking' for example has increasingly become 'indifferent to the constraints of time, place and currency...an English buyer can get a Japanese mortgage...and a Japanese investor can buy shares in a London-based Scandinavian bank whose stock is denominated in sterling, dollars, Deutsche Marks and Swiss francs' (Harvey, 1990: 161). Arguing along similar lines Robert Jessop states, capital has developed strong capacities to extend its operations in time and space (time-space distantiation) and/or to compress them in these regards (time-space compression). The mutual reinforcement of these twin processes facilitates real-time integration in the world market and makes it easier to maintain its self-expansionary logic in response to perturbations... its reliance on the symbolic medium of money to facilitate economic transactions despite disjunctions in time and place, its highly developed abstract and technical codes... All of these capabilities increase capital's 'resonance capacity' [and]... The greater this capacity relative to other systems, the greater the scope for capital's ecological dominance. (2007: 77)

While opening up financial opportunities for dominant actors in the capitalist world order, the deepening of economic integration has ushered in intense volatility in the world economy. In the era of neo-liberal driven capitalism, the crisis of financial markets is increasingly becoming the norm. For example, the 1990s saw a significant 'financial crisis every two to three years: the 1992 EMS [European Monetary System] currency crisis, the 1994–5 Mexican pesos crisis, the 1997 Asian crisis, the 1998 Russian debt default, and the 1998–9 Brazilian real crisis' (Davidson, 2007: 7). In the USA, crises in the financial sector, including that of Savings and Loans between 1989 and 1992 (Phillips, 2008: 57) and the current one, are other instances of this trend. The volatility of financial markets has led Paul Davidson to conclude that in the contemporary epoch, 'we are being haunted by Minsky's (1982) frightening financial fragility question: "Can 'it' happen again" Can we have another Great Depression'? (2007: 4). Like other aspects of financial capital, the impact of a financial crisis is global. These days, a financial crisis in one country tends to spread rapidly across the world. The 1997 Asian crisis, which began in Thailand, then rapidly spread to the rest of East Asia and to the rest of the world is an example of this development (Klein, 2007). Thus, the 'contagion' (Eatwell and Taylor, 2002) problem, which has emerged as a major characteristic of liberalized financial markets, marked the Asian financial crisis. The fact is, under conditions of 'casino capitalism' (Strange, 1986; 1998) in which the structural dominance of capital is a social reality, and national economies are deeply integrated through the mechanism of a liberalized finance system, no economic sector, national economy or individual investor is immune from the conditions of financial markets in a given moment. As Strange states:

[In] the global casino of high finance...we are all involuntarily
engaged in the day's play. A currency change can halve the value of
a farmer's crop before he harvests it, or drive an exporter out of business. A rise in interest rates can fatally inflate the costs of holding
stocks for the shop-keeper. A takeover dictated by financial considerations can rob the factory worker of his job. From school-leavers
to pensioners, what goes on in the casino in the office blocks of
the big financial centres is apt to have sudden, unpredictable and
unavoidable consequences for individual lives. The financial casino
has everyone playing the game of Snakes and Ladders. (Strange,
1996: 2)

Another consequence of deepening economic integration is that it has
made national economies and the world economy vulnerable to speculative capital. This phenomenon is of course not new. In the 1920s,
speculative capital greatly contributed to the collapse of the world economy leading to the Great Depression (Keynes, 1936; Polanyi, 2001).
However, the speculative capacity of private financial institutions and
actors has expanded with the liberalization of exchange rates and verti-
cal and horizontal linkages of these institutions (Harvey, 1991; Germain,
1997; Davidson 2007). For instance, private financial institutions can
now take advantage of 'regulatory differences and assume significant
market shares of new debt issues' (Germain, 1997: 106). Consequently,
private monetary agents who with liberalization of financial markets
have found legal avenues to generate profits across national borders
closely monitor and anticipate shifts in foreign exchange rates all over
the world. In the era of neo-liberalism, assuming a given country's
currency is about to 'devalue', financial 'speculators try to move their
currency investments into dollars'—which remains the preferred currency in the world economy—and in the process tend to generate large
profits in a very short period (Stiglitz, 2002: 94). The following example
illustrates this point:

Assume a speculator goes to a Thai bank, borrows 24 billion baht,
which, at the original exchange rate, can be converted into $ 1 bil-
lion. A week later the exchange rate falls; instead of there being 24
baht to the dollar, there are now 40 baht to the dollar. He takes $ 600
million, converting it back to baht, getting 24 billion baht to repay
the loan. The remaining $ 400 million is his profit—a tidy return for
one week's work, and the investment of little of his own money...As

perceptions that a devaluation is imminent grow, the chance to make money becomes irresistible and speculators from around the world pile in to take advantage of the situation. (Ibid.: 95)

Consolidation of financial power

The consolidation of the structural power of financial capital by the dominant states, institutions of global governance and private financial institutions is a third major politico-economic condition that has emerged with the liberalization of financial markets. The reliance of new private financial institutions and other monetary actors on access to rapid and consistently updated financial data has contributed to the concentration of financial power in the 'knowledge-intensive' (Germain, 1997: 110) economic structures, which for historical and politico-economic reasons are located in the North. Further, the power imbalance between the North and the South in the capitalist world order has meant that the TDHB and private financial capital have shaped policies pertaining to the global financial system such as the liberalization of financial markets, and removal of capital controls, as examples in this chapter have indicated. In the era of a neo-liberal world order, the consolidation of power by the TDHB and private financial capital manifests itself in several ways. For example, the dominant 'principle financial centers' (see generally, Germain, 1997) and other private financial institutions are located in global cities in the industrialized core: New York, London and Tokyo (ibid.). Thus, even though all financial institutions can compete with each other in the world financial markets, the power imbalance in economic and political terms has resulted in the concentration of financial structural power in the North. Thus, the liberalized world of finance is like other sites in the world order underpinned by asymmetrical power arrangements. As Martin and Schumann argue 'even in the cyberspace of world money, the actors are people who either wield or must submit to power and its accompanying interests' (1997: 76). Further, as we indicated in Chapter 3, under conditions of disciplinary neo-liberalism, the TDHB has come to play a major role in the politico-economic processes in the South. Core countries such as the USA, Japan and Germany have the majority of votes in the most powerful institutions in the capitalist world order, the World Bank and the IMF (Black, 2001). This fact has given these states enormous structural power in their engagement with the South as far as financial arrangements in the world order are concerned.

The consolidation of financial power in the North in the era of a neo-liberal world order has had major consequences for economic processes in the South. In essence, this development has reconstituted the coloniality of power of the TDHB and other agents of global capital. This reconstitution of coloniality of power has introduced a new form of precariousness to Southern economies and new forms of structural dependency. While under conditions of casino financial capitalism (Strange, 1986; 1998) all national economies are vulnerable, the structural and political power imbalance that underpins the world order makes Southern economic structures more vulnerable. Notwithstanding the diversity of economic structures in the South, the latter are vulnerable not only to the shifts in financial policies of dominant states in the world order but also those of private transnational financial institutions. For instance, in the case of policy shifts from dominant states in the North, although the 1979 Volker shocks generated tremendous shocks in national economies including in the USA, the systemic and more prolonged shocks were felt in the South. These shocks resulted in increased interest rates (Strange, 1998; Stiglitz, 2002; Davidson, 2007) a result of which was increased debt burdens for countries in the South, who had to borrow more money for their economic survival and to service old and new debts. In Brazil, the debt rose from US$ 50 billion to US$ 100 billion in the six years following the Volker shocks while that of Nigeria increased from US$ 9 billion to US$ 29 billion during the same period (Klein, 2007: 1999).

The coloniality of power underpinning the global financial system manifests itself in other ways. For instance, when dominant social formations in the North face economic crises generated by financial markets their powerful structural and political position in the capitalist world order provides them with varied options to address such crises. Whenever the USA has been in such as a position, its politico-economic position in the capitalist world order offers it a wide range of resources to address financial crisis. Interestingly enough, contrary to the claims by neo-liberal proponents that financial and economic crises in general should be left to efficient markets, 'whenever market discipline unleashes systemic risk to the dollarized financial system of United States, three weapons are rolled out to ameliorate the otherwise disastrous effects of market discipline...the Federal Reserve acting as a LOLR, the federal government's Comptroller of the Current's "too big to fail" doctrine, and the Federal Deposit Insurance Corporation (FIDC)' (Davidson, 2007: 141). These strategies mitigate the deep consequences of liberalized markets for the US economy (ibid.). The strategies utilized by states in the North to respond to financial crisis are for historical reasons and contemporary politico-structural power realities not available to the majority of the states in the South. Further, under neo-liberal development ideas and practices, these states face disciplinary measures, such as freezing of loans, and demands for more deepening of the neo-liberal project from the IMF and the World Bank, whenever they are in a financial crisis. The responses by these institutions to the Asian financial and Argentinean crisis are cases in point (Davidson, 2007; Klein, 2007).

Further, the coloniality of power that has emerged with the rise of a global liberalized finance system and the dominance of the TDHB and private transnational financial institutions in this system manifests itself when it comes to the question of transformation of this system. For years, the dominance of these actors in this system has contained attempts to restructure it. The policy death of minimalist reform proposals such as the Tobin Tax (TT) and those contained in the Meltzer Report ordered by the US Congress are good examples of how the dominance of these actors translates to politico-structural power limiting the transformation of global financial arrangements. The origins of the TT is the work of James Tobin Eichengreen et al., 1995, (cited in Davidson, 2007), which has persistently argued that the liberalization of exchange rates has increased volatility in financial markets, and thus shifts in these markets could generate 'devastating impact on specific industries and whole economies' (cited in ibid.: 8). To address this issue, Tobin proposed raising the cost of international finance transactions by introducing a TT (ibid.: 184) on such transactions. Even though this reform was proposing a very limited constraint on the workings of financial capital in the world order, dominant actors in this order were not interested in instituting its modest aim. As Bello and Mittal (2001: 131) argue, a source of this lack of interest in reforming global financial arrangements is the 'political clout' that finance capital has achieved in the era of a neo-liberal world order. According to them, reform proposals such as the TT have faced severe roadblocks from the financial capital 'lobby' in the North especially in the USA (ibid.). As for the Meltzer Report, while full of contradictions in its approach to the financial role of the World Bank and the IMF, it nonetheless offered not only a scathing critique on the work of these institutions in the South, but also recommendations for their transformation. The Commission recommended reforms such as massive reduction in the lending role of the World Bank and the IMF (Meltzer Report, 2000) and a transformation of the World Bank to an institution that concentrates on providing public goods such as education, especially in poorest countries in the South.[4] Although the Commission was not calling for the overhauling of the neo-liberal development ideas that inform the financial policies of these institutions and those of other major actors in the international development apparatus, dominant states in the world order that hold the majority voting power in the World Bank and the IMF did not welcome its recommendations. In its critique of the World Bank, the Commission argued that while the World Bank's 'rhetoric' claimed that its financial practices in the South focused on poverty alleviation, a close examination indicated otherwise (ibid.). For example, while claiming that its financial goal is providing loans to the poorest countries in the world that have no access to private financial markets '70% of World Bank non-aid resources flow to 11 countries that enjoy easy access to the capital markets' (ibid.).

The preceding sections have examined several issues concerning the current globalized financial system. We have highlighted the role of neo-liberal ideas, states (especially dominant states in the capitalist world order), new technologies and new financial instruments and actors in the making of this system. Our conclusion is that the liberalization of financial markets coupled with structural dominance of capital, new forms of credit practices and the emergence of an integrated financial system have ushered in a new era of global capitalism. In this regard, we agree with Harvey when he suggests that 'if we are to look for anything truly distinctive (as opposed to "capitalism as usual") in the present situation, then it is upon the financial aspects of capitalist organization and on the role of credit that we should concentrate our gaze' (Harvey, 1990: 196). Understanding these developments is crucial to any explanation of the rise and modalities of the contemporary world order and in teasing out openings and limits to the transformation of its neo-liberal financial system. Departing from the hegemonic neo-liberal perspective on the liberalized financial system that underpins the contemporary world order, the foregoing section has highlighted effects of this system. Given the effects of the liberalized financial system on economic and political processes, especially the ongoing (2007–2009) global economic crisis, is the transformation of this system possible in the era of a US president who has referred to this system as broken and unsustainable, thus in urgent need of reform? We engage with the implications of Obama's presidency on the neo-liberal world order including its liberalized financial system and securitizing tendencies next.

Neo-liberal and securitizing world order in the era of Obama

For victims of racial injustices, the ascendancy to power of President Obama is an inspiration and an indication that social struggles can lead to the achievement of some measure of justice. In Iraq for example, Jalal Thiyab Thijeel, a leader of the black Iraq social movement 'Movement of Free Iraqis', states that he not only closely followed Obama's campaign, but that the latter was a source of inspiration 'politically, and personally' (Dougherty, 2009). Further, he claims that Obama's campaign has inspired him and other black Iraqis—who arrived in the country over 1000 years ago as slave labour and are still referred to as *abed*—the term for slave in Arabic—to organize and fight for political and social inclusion. For him, Obama's presidential win is 'a victory for all black people in the world' (ibid.). In France, a black musician states, 'Obama tells us everything is possible', while the newspaper *Le Monde* declares that he is 'stirring up high hopes' among black people (quoted in Kimmelman, 2009). For leading African-American voices, such as Congressman John Lewis, 'President Obama sends a strong message to Black America and especially to our children—that they must never give out, never give in, and never give up' (McKinney-Whetstone, 2009: 70) and , Constance L. Rice, a lawyer and social activist, invoking Rev. Martin Luther King, states that Obama's ascendancy to the presidency 'is the mountaintop' (ibid.: 2009: 74).

As we have suggested in other parts of this book, racial thinking and practices have been a central element in the making of the capitalist world system and its conjunctural world order. Consequently, the rise of Obama to power in the dominant social formation in the current world order is an important development historically and at the cultural-symbolic level. This is not to say that with this development we have entered a new conjuncture in the world order where racism is no longer a factor in political, cultural and economic processes and knowledge production and its dissemination. As racist attacks (Rich, 2008) on Obama's presidential candidacy show, factions of ruling elites continue to utilize racist ideas and tactics to serve their politico-economic and cultural projects and those of their constituents. Further, the heightened racialist discourse in the USA since Obama's inauguration with terms such as 'Hitler' and 'Nazi' being used to describe him, speaks to the continuing articulation of racialist tropes in the public square. Thus, while Obama's presidency marks an important achievement in the struggle for substantive human rights in the USA, the struggle for racial equality will continue at all levels of societal orders: national, regional and global.

Important as questions of racial discourse and the political economy of racism in the age of Obama and neo-liberalism are, they are beyond the scope of this final section, the focus of which is a discussion of implications of Obama's presidency to the neo-liberal and securitizing world order including its underlying financial system.

At the time of writing this section (early 2009), it is too early from a social science perspective to offer a comprehensive response to the question of the implications of Obama's presidency to the world order given that, among other things, the global financial crisis continues and the politico-economic policies of Obama's administration are still in their embryonic stages. Nonetheless, as far as the question of transformation is concerned, pre-existing politico-structural conditions and ideological and other signals from the historical bloc anchoring Obama's regime, indicate that the restoration of an ideologically modified neo-liberal and securitizing world order rather than a fundamental transformation of this order seems to be the likely possibility in the immediate future. From a dialectic approach to politico-economic processes however, such a process is not a given. World orders and other historical processes are contested processes which are marked by contradictions that make openings for transformation possible within the 'limits of the possible' (Gill, 2003), as suggested in Chapter 2. Thus, there are potential sources of challenges and constraints to the restoration of the neo-liberal and securitizing world order, even in its modified form. For example, the deepening of the current global economic crisis generated by the crisis in the financial sector could lead to a collapse of the consensus on neo-liberal capitalism among dominant elites in the world order. This crisis could see the rise of protectionism, a development that could generate intense trade wars in the world economy and ruptures on the doctrine of free trade that underpins neo-liberal economic thought. The issue of protectionism was at the forefront of debates leading to the 2009 G20 meeting in London (Hooper, 2009).

Further, various national and transnational social movements especially those linked to the World Social Forum process and those engaged in de-commodification campaigns are potential sources of challenges to projects geared to the restoration of the neo-liberal and securitizing world order. Focusing on the other side of the dialectic of the current historical moment, our objective here is to highlight factors that are likely to facilitate the consolidation of a modified neo-liberal and securitizing world order in the immediate future of Obama's presidency. We highlight four factors that could facilitate such a process: rehabilitation of the state, political-structural dominance of liberalized finance, America's 'ecological dominance' (Jessop, 2007) and the nature of the emergent multi-polarity, and Obama's patriotic-proactive cosmopolitanism. While for organizational purposes we discuss each factor separately, their interplay is what makes them a powerful means through which a restoration of core elements—albeit in a modified form—of the current world order may occur.

The rehabilitation of the state

The discussion of the ascendancy of neo-liberal discourse in Chapter 3 indicated how this discourse constructed the state as a major source of global economic crisis, inflation, economic stagnation and the self-regulating market as the guaranteed strategy to economic recovery and development. As President Ronald Reagan (1981) famously declared in his inaugural speech in 1981 at the height of an economic downturn in the USA, 'government is not the solution to our problem'. Obama's ascendancy to power is occurring in a historical moment marked by a major national and global economic crisis after over three decades of neo-liberal economic strategies. In contrast to Reagan however, Obama considers the question of the merits of the state versus the market, as far as economic processes are concerned, as misplaced. While stressing his commitment and belief in market capitalism, he has continuously declared that states are pivotal to capitalism. According to him, 'the question we ask today is not whether our government is too big or too small, but whether it works . . . Nor is the question before us whether the market is a force for good or ill. Its power to generate wealth and expand freedom is unmatched. But this [economic] crisis has reminded us that without a watchful eye, the market can spin out of control' (Obama, 2009a). For Obama, regulating private capital is the way out of the current crisis and towards future economic sustainability and prosperity.

Although Obama's approach to the state in the neo-liberal world order offers an opening for states in the South and elsewhere to, at the ideological level, reclaim their role in economic processes, it does not significantly change the neo-liberal underpinnings of the current world order. It essentially enables the restoration, albeit in an ideologically modified manner, of the neo-liberal world order. First, the approach still considers neo-liberal capitalism as the only way out of this crisis and the sole pathway to economic prosperity. As examples—provided shortly—from his administration's responses to the financial sector indicate, this approach, while presented as a major shift in neo-liberal thinking, mainly protects the interest of dominant actors in the neo-liberal world order. Thus, his historical bloc is not introducing measures geared to the overhauling of neo-liberal ideas but rather

it is utilizing the state to contain the contradictions and social dislocations generated by neo-liberal capital accumulation practices, and
providing the neo-liberal capitalist infrastructure space to stabilize without major reforms. Hence, while there is a change in the ideological
representation of states' role in the economy, Obama's historic bloc is
not fundamentally challenging the neo-liberal ideas and practices that
generated the current economic crisis.

Overall, stabilizing neo-liberal capitalism by using state power is the
main goal of Obama's historical bloc and those of other dominant elites
in the world order. While calling for regulation of financial markets at
the 2009 World Economic Forum in Davos for instance, Russia's Prime
Minister Vladimir Putin warned strongly about the dangers of extending
the role of the state in the economy. As he stated, 'instead of streamlin-
ing market mechanisms, some are tempted to expand state economic
intervention to the greatest possible extent...There is no reason to
believe that we can achieve better results by shifting responsibility onto
the state. And one more point: anti-crisis measures should not escalate
into financial populism and a refusal to implement responsible macroeconomic policies. The unjustified swelling of the budgetary deficit and
the accumulation of public debts are just as destructive as adventur-
ous stock-jobbing' (Putin, 2009). Second, Obama's modified neo-liberal
approach fails to take cognizance of the structural and political changes
that have occurred under neo-liberal capitalism, such as the structural
dominance of financial capital—discussed shortly—and the consolidation of the power of dominant states in the North in the world order.
These developments have the potential of facilitating the restoration
of the neo-liberal ideas underpinning this order and its coloniality of
power. Essentially, while dominant elites in the world order such as President Obama are rehabilitating the role of the state in the economy in
their public discourse, we suggest that this approach to neo-liberal world
order is opening a space for the normalization and depoliticization of
the core features of this order and its effects rather than transforming
them.

Structural-political dominance of liberalized finance

As previously indicated, currently a liberalized financial system is a core
feature of the neo-liberal world order. Nonetheless, calls for the transformation of this system have been persistent at least since the 1990s.
Demands for reforming this system stem from what analysts consider as
its negative effects on national economic processes and the world economy. Leading among these effects is the volatility to economic processes

that liberalized financial markets have introduced in the world economy (Martin and Schuman, 1997; Strange 1998; Bello 2002; Bond, 2007; Davidson, 2007; Phillips, 2008). This volatility has led Susan Strange to contend that liberalized financial markets embody symptoms of madness. As she states, 'why mad? Because to my mind it was, and is, "wildly foolish"... to let the financial markets run so far ahead, so far beyond the control of state and international authorities. We recognize insanity, or madness in a man or woman, by erratic, unpredictable, irrational behaviour that is potentially damaging to the sufferers themselves or to others. But that is exactly how financial markets have behaved in recent years... Their behaviour has very seriously damaged others. Their condition calls urgently for treatment of some kind' (1998: 1).

Further, the destructive effects of financial markets on economic processes in the South have been another source of calls to transform financial arrangements in the world order. Thus far, these calls have had limited success in effecting fundamental changes in the liberalized financial system that underpins the neo-liberal world order. Nonetheless, since the contemporary economic crisis came to a head in 2008, dominant ruling elites in the world order have been calling for its transformation. For instance, even as a Presidential candidate, Barack Obama was urging for reforms in the financial sector. As he stated in March 2008, 'beyond dealing with the immediate housing crisis, it is time for the federal government to revamp the regulatory framework dealing with our financial markets. Our capital markets have helped us build the strongest economy in the world. They are a source of competitive advantage for our country. But they cannot succeed without the public's trust' (Obama, 2008a: 5). For Putin, changes to the financial system are in order for the current one, 'has failed... to duly heed tremendous risks' (2009).

Obama has continued calling for reforms to the global financial system since taking office in January 2009. From his perspective: 'it is simply not sustainable to have a 21st century financial system that is governed by 20th century rules and regulations that allowed the recklessness of a few to threaten the entire economy. It is not sustainable to have an economy where in one year, 40% of our corporate profits came from a financial sector that was based too much on inflated home prices, maxed out credit cards, overleveraged banks and overvalued assets; or an economy where the incomes of the top 1% have skyrocketed while the typical working household has seen their income decline by nearly $2,000' (Obama, 2009b). For the UK's Prime Minister, Gordon Brown, 'the fragility of the global financial system must be addressed internationally. If what happens to a bank in one country can—within minutes—bring potentially devastating effects on banks in a different continent, then only a truly international response—in policy and governance—can be effective. If we all coordinate our response there will be a quicker global and therefore British recovery' (2009). Arguing along similar lines at a pre-G20 meeting, Brown called for a 'a global New Deal—a grand bargain between the countries and continents of this world—so that the world economy can not only recover but ... so the banking system can be based on ... best principles' (Hooper, 2009). It seems that dominant elites in the world order have come to the same conclusions (albeit most likely for different reasons) as Strange, that the current liberalized financial system is in urgent need 'for treatment of some kind' (1998:1). We argue that notwithstanding President Obama's rhetoric on the urgent need to reform the liberalized financial system, the possibility of such a development is limited in the immediate future because of politico-structural developments that have occurred in the epoch of a neo-liberal world order. We highlight one of these politico-structural conditions here.

A major politico-structural factor that will most likely contribute to the restoration rather than a fundamental transformation of the liberalized financial system even in the era of Obama is the rise of private authority in financial matters because of the structural dominance of financial capital. As we argued before, with the liberalization of financial markets, the balance of political and structural power has shifted towards private financial institutions and monetary actors. This is not to say that states are powerless in financial matters given that ruling elites utilized state power to usher in liberalized markets. Nonetheless, while not monolithic given the uneven nature of existing geographies of capitalism, states' structural dependency on local and transnational private institutions for financial flows to address states' responsibilities such as current budget and trade deficits, limits their willingness to introduce reforms that could transform liberalized finance markets in a significant way. In essence, because of the rise of private authority in the financial sector, states have tended to introduce measures geared to the preservation of the status quo in global financial arrangements. Regulatory measures introduced during this era of neo-liberalism such as the Financial Stability Forum, whose members include the G7 countries, the World Bank, IMF, Bank for International Settlements, members of the OECD, Hong Kong and Singapore, have mainly served to reinforce the neo-liberal financial orthodoxy (Soederberg, 2004: 2) rather than transform it. As Susan Soederberg posits, this Forum's main

aim is to 'achieve systematic stability' in the liberalized global financial system 'by ensuring that all countries, especially those that are
seen by the G7 as the main source of instability...emerging market
economies...adopt the rules and standards of the global capital markets
and G7 countries through adherence to pro-market principles' (ibid.).
Even the much-touted ascendancy of a new era of financial regulation
announced at the 2009 G20 meeting in London, where the creation
of a 'Financial Stability Board to replace' the Forum was announced,
reinforces Soerberg's conclusion, for while the Board's mandate will be
strengthened 'it will not have specific control over financial companies'
(EurActiv Network, 2009).

In the case of the USA, even in these early months of Obama's presidency, the country's agenda for reforming liberalized financial markets
indicates the continuing structural and political power of financial capital. The reforms introduced to address the financial crisis in the USA
under President Obama such as the stress tests for banks, bailouts to
major banks suggest the restoration of the neo-liberal project in financial markets rather than its transformation in any fundamental manner.
While Obama frames the regime's responses to the financial crisis as
introducing a new era of regulation in financial markets, its much-
broadcast reforms do not fundamentally challenge the ideology and
practices of either the private financial institutions that generated the
crisis in the first place or the neo-liberal doctrine of liberalized financial markets. These responses for instance fail to acknowledge a major
contradiction underlying their response to the financial crisis, that is,
the bailing out of private financial institutions, which under the neo-
liberal monetarist doctrine are supposedly rational and efficient when
compared to the state. While the bailing out of financial institutions
runs contrary to the monetarist doctrine, this contradiction does not
seem to have generated a transformative shift on USA's financial policy under Obama's historical bloc. Overall, the responses of this bloc
to the financial crisis have created opportunities for private financial
institutions and actors whose practices mainly generated the financial
crisis to benefit from what it presents as reform measures. The irony of
this development brings to light one of the contradictions of neo-liberal
thought and its emphasis on the rationality and efficiency of financial
markets. Fundamentally, financial capital has depended on state power
for its rise and survival in the midst of a crisis it generated as current
bailouts by states indicate. It seems, contrary to the neo-liberal doctrine
for the core 'result' of its call for the liberalization of financial markets has been 'the exact opposite of its ideological intentions. Instead
of freeing the private sector and the market economy from the toils of

state intervention' it has ended 'in involving the state more extensively' in the financial and other sectors (Strange, 1986: 58; see also Harvey, 2005).

On the whole, the Obama administration seems to be focused on instituting 'plumbing solutions' (Davidson, 2007) aimed at stabilizing the current status quo in the operations of financial markets rather than fundamentally changing their structural dominance and their logics so that they can serve the public interest both in the North and the South. An example of his administration's approach to reforms in the derivatives market and what it terms as 'toxic assets' in the US banking system illustrates this point. In the case of derivatives, the proposed reform for this '$ 600 trillion shadow market' is a two-pronged approach: public and private (Partnoy, 2009: 1) categorization of derivatives. In this approach the derivatives market would have 'standardized instruments, which would be traded on regulated exchanges and privately negotiated contracts, customized deals (often called 'swaps') that are made between two financial organizations and would not be publicly traded or regulated. Rather, such transactions would be reported privately to a 'trade repository', which apparently would make only limited aggregate data available to the public' (ibid).

In the main, the current administration has not instituted measures that would signal a commitment to significant reforms to the liberalized global financial system and thus it is facilitating the reconstitution of its politico-structural power. In the case of America's liberalized banking system, its politico-structural power is manifesting itself even in the midst of the current financial crisis. Mainly, as a USA Senator Richard Durbin has stated, it is 'hard to believe in a time when we're facing a banking crisis that many of the banks created [they] are still the most powerful lobby on Capitol Hill ... they frankly own the place' (quoted in Doster, 2009).

While introducing some measure of regulation, the Obama administration's approach to financial instruments such as derivatives—which contributed to financial crises in Orange County, Enron and Long-Term Capital Management, as well as the current global financial crisis—does not significantly transform the workings of the liberalized financial system (Partnoy, 2009: 1). As the Editorial in *New York Times* (2009: 1) declared, the approach does not 'go far enough. In apparent deference to those who have made major profits from unfettered derivatives trading, the proposal stops shy of creating a fully transparent market'. In terms of the 'toxic assets' in the banking sector, while his administration portrays its reform proposal 'as a win-win' situation, it will mainly benefit private financial actors:

The administration's plan is based on letting the market determine the prices of the banks' 'toxic assets'—including outstanding house loans and securities based on those loans. The reality, though, is that the market will not be pricing the toxic assets themselves, but options on those assets. The two have little to do with each other. The government plan in effect involves insuring almost all losses. Since the private investors are spared most losses, then they primarily 'value' their potential gains... What the Obama administration is doing is far worse than nationalization: it is ersatz capitalism, the privatizing of gains and the socializing of losses. It is a 'partnership' in which one partner robs the other. And such partnerships—with the private sector in control—have perverse incentives, worse even than the ones that got us into the mess. (Stiglitz, 2009: 1–2)

America's ecological dominance

For many analysts, USA's power in the world order is in serious decline. Analysts tend to cite developments such as the growing economic power of countries such as China, Brazil, Russia, India and the ongoing projects of expanding membership to the European Union and the struggle to achieve deeper politico-economic integration of this Union as signals of this trend. While these developments and the responses to 9/11 attacks by the Bush regime have to some extent eroded America's power in the world order, our premise is that USA's 'ecological dominance' (Jessop, 2007) in key spheres, which has emerged due to politico-economic and military developments in the post-1945 world order, while not hegemonic, remains. This social reality opens the possibility for the USA to institute measures aimed at restoring an ideologically modified neo-liberal and securitizing world order, although potential sources of challenge to such a development exist. Moreover, countries that might have emerged as potential rivals to such dominance such as Russia and China have introduced strategies underpinned by neo-liberal economic thought. Further, as discussed in Chapter 6, while declaring their commitment to the making of a multi-polar world order, ruling elites in these countries have stressed that it is not in their national interest at this juncture to challenge the neo-liberal and American dominated world order.

As some examples in Chapter 3 and the current one have indicated, the USA has been a pivotal player in the rise of a neo-liberal world order. Even with the rise of other economies, the country's dominance has continued—albeit differently from its hegemonic form following World

War II to the 1980s. This form of dominance we suggest is one of the factors that can contribute to the restoration of core features of the current world order. In his articulation of the concept of 'ecological dominance' of a given social system, Robert Jessop argues that a hallmark of such a system is its high capacity to bring about harm to other systems when compared to the capabilities of such systems to do the same to it (2007: 82). For our present purposes, we deploy the concept of ecological dominance to indicate America's dominance in two systems: economic and military. A principal way in which America's ecological dominance in these systems can contribute to the restoration of the neo-liberal and securitizing world order is the structural and political agency that this dominance accords the USA in the political and economic workings of this order when compared to other social formations and non-state political actors. Brief discussions of the two systems embodying USA's ecological dominance in the world order and their particular implications for the restoration of the neo-liberal and securitizing world order follows.

Fundamentally, at the economic level, while the USA has become dependent on countries such as China for the sustaining of its debt and balance of trade deficit, the country 'still retains the (destructive) power of ecological dominance, i.e., it still causes more problems for other economies than they can cause for it' (ibid.: 83). While China and other countries, through massive reserves of US dollars, have emerged as key players in the USA's growing debt, China's economic modernization project for instance is highly dependent on access to the American market. Thus, 'if the USA market collapses then the economies that look to that market as a sink for their excess productive capacity will go down with it. The alacrity with which the central bankers of countries like China, Japan, and Taiwan lend to cover US deficits has a strong element of self-interest: They thereby fund the US consumerism that forms the market for their products' (Harvey, 2003: 72). Further, because of its ecological dominance in economic matters in the world order, the USA 'is better able to displace and defer the contradictions of neo-liberalism onto other spaces and times than other varieties of capitalism in other spaces can displace their problems into the American economy' (ibid.). The ability of the USA to address the contradictions of capitalism through 'spatial-fix' (Harvey, 1990; 2003) has enabled it to remain dominant in the world economy even when its economic futures are in a crisis. As far as the ecological dominance of the US economic system is concerned, previously discussed examples, such as the effects of the Nixon regime's floating of the dollar and 1979 Volcker shocks, are further illustrations of its capacity to generate more crises for other economies than they can to the American economy. Further, the fact that the dollar remains the reserve currency in global trade reinforces the ecological dominance of the USA on other economies in the world order. Shifts in the exchange rates of the US dollar tend to have significant effects on other economies when compared to other currencies. Generally, the USA's ecological dominance at the economic level, at this historical moment characterized by a major financial crisis, means that in terms of reforms to the global financial system underpinning the world order, its agenda has the potential of prevailing.

The ecological dominance of the US military system, which began in the interwar period and deepened through Reagan's military Keynesianism in the 1980s, continues in the first decade of the twenty-first century even though China may emerge as 'a peer competitor' (Bajoria, 2009) in the future. This form of US dominance, however, faces tensions given the rise of non-state and securitizing networks such as al-Qaeda and the Taliban. Nonetheless, even with these developments—and the growing military power of emerging 'great powers' such as Russia, China, Japan and the European Union the USA's 'superpower' status in the international security infrastructure remains (Buzan, 2005: 177–183). For example, the USA 'generates 55 percent of all defense spending and 80 percent of military research and development among the world's seven power states' (Wohlforth, 2002: 104). The country's dominance in the global military system is reinforced by its extensive links with regional military-industry-political complexes (Buzan, 2005: 180), and in Africa with the establishment of AFRICOM (Chapter 7). Even with the end of the Cold War, in Europe and East Asia the USA has maintained the 'arrangements and institutions' such as NATO and its alliance with Japan that emerged during that period and it is a major player in military and political processes in Latin America (ibid.). Further, Obama has declared his commitment to ensuring that the USA continues its military ecological dominance: 'we're investing in the capabilities and technologies of tomorrow—the littoral combat ships, the most advanced submarines and fighter aircraft—so that you have what you need to succeed. In short, we will maintain America's military dominance and keep you the finest fighting force the world has ever seen' (Obama, 2009d).

The ecological dominance of America's military system means that it has expansive capacity to destroy the military systems of other social formations while the latter have limited capacity to do the same to its

military system. The destruction of Iraqi military systems since the invasion is an example of this capacity and the ability of the USA to ignore
international norms, for instance in the launching of its unending wars,
signals the ecological dominance of its military system. The threat that
this form of ecological dominance poses to other military systems offers
the US significant room to manoeuvre in its contemporary securitizing
projects in Afghanistan and elsewhere. This dominance is one of the
core factors that has enabled the intertwining of neo-liberal capitalism,
securitization and unending wars as examples in Chapter 7 demonstrated. It also has the tremendous capacity to facilitate the restoration
of the current neo-liberal and securitizing world order in the immediate future of Obama's presidency as the continuing war with increased
troops in Afghanistan under his watch indicates.

Obama's patriotic-proactive cosmopolitanism

A core argument of this project is that ideas play a central role in
politico-economic processes such as shifts in world orders and the
nature of states' engagement with core features of a prevailing order. In
the case of Obama, even in these early days of his administration, signals
from his presidential campaign and beyond indicate the influence of
cosmopolitan ideas on his approach to the world order. Ideas steeped in
cosmopolitan thought underlie his various speeches, as a candidate and
as President, and in his writing (2004). His life history, which he invokes
often has been underpinned by transcultural experiences in the USA,
Indonesia and Kenya and indicates a 'rooted' (Appiah, 1996) form of
cosmopolitanism. The underlying premise of cosmopolitan thought is
the idea that individuals belong to overlapping communities: local and
global. Thus for the Stoics—considered early advocates of cosmopolitan and global citizenship—'human beings', because of their capacity
for reason, are 'members or "citizens" of a more fundamental human
community than that of their particular city, state or empire of which
they might be politically citizens: the latter citizenship was an accident
of birth and circumstance' (Dower, 2003: 6).

In addition, for Stoics and contemporary cosmopolitan thinkers,
human beings have moral obligations to others beyond their immediate family and boundaries of their town and nation. According to
Martha Nussbaum, 'it is this [human] community that is, fundamentally, the source of our moral obligations. With respect to the most basic
values, such as justice, "we should regard all human beings as our fellow citizens and neighbours" (Plutarch, On the Fortunes of Alexander).
We should regard our deliberations as, first and foremost, deliberations

about human problems of people in particular concrete situations, not problems growing out of a national identity that is altogether unlike that of others' (1996: 7). For Andrew Linklater, cosmopolitan philosophy provides a normative framework that enables individuals to extend their moral obligations beyond their immediate communities and this school of thought 'obliges all human beings to extend hospitality to strangers as fellow 'citizens of a universal state of humanity ' (Kant, 1970: 206, quoted in Linklater, 1999: 39). Thus, for cosmopolitan thinkers, moral obligations to other citizens, foreigners within and beyond national borders, should not be considered as acts of charity but rather as a morally driven political practice that can facilitate the emergence of 'universal frameworks of communication' as articulated in the works of Jürgen Habermas (cited in ibid.: 37). Overall, the cosmopolitan view of humanity considers all human beings as having 'a global status as the ultimate unit of moral concern' (Pogge, 1992: 49). In essence, for advocates of cosmopolitan ethics, the normative underpinning of cosmopolitan philosophy opens up the possibility of eradicating ideas and politico-economic practices that have led to the emergence of what the philosopher Achille Mbembé (2005) terms as an 'international division of life'; a view of the world and practice that has historically and in the contemporary resulted in some lives being considered as more important than others.

In his reflections on what he terms as 'cosmopolitan patriots', Kwame Anthony Appiah continues the cosmopolitan philosophical tradition with a specific focus on tensions underpinning liberalism, cosmopolitanism and patriotic ideas (1996). From his perspective, an individual can adopt and promote patriotic as well as cosmopolitan ideas and practices. Drawing on insights from his father's life, who was among other things, a Ghanaian nationalist leader in the age of British imperialism in Africa, he argues that individuals can be patriots who 'accept the citizen's responsibility to nurture the culture and politics of their homes' and cosmopolitans who engage and are involved in the world beyond immediate borders of family and nation. For Appiah, a cosmopolitan patriot is open to 'the possibility of a world in which everyone is a rooted cosmopolitan, attached to a home of his or her own, with its own cultural particularities' and also to 'taking pleasure from the presence of other, different, places that are home to other, different, people' (ibid.: 22). Further, rooted cosmopolitans have moral obligations to contribute to struggles for social justice wherever they are, as Appiah's father reminds his children (ibid.: 21).

Signs of Obama's patriotic cosmopolitanism are evident in various speeches during his presidential campaign and since his taking office in January 2009. In 2008 for instance, Obama declared in a speech, 'I come to Berlin as so many of my countrymen have come before. Tonight, I speak to you not as a candidate for President, but as a citizen— a proud citizen of the United States, and a fellow citizen of the world' (Obama, 2008b). Like Appiah's father, in Obama's worldview there is no contradiction between being a proud US citizen and a citizen of the world. Obama's cosmopolitanism, however, goes beyond patrio- tism and includes an element of what Taylor (1999) terms as 'proactive cosmopolitanism'. His cosmopolitan vision embodies an attempt to construct America as a cosmopolitan political and cultural space and building on Taylor's insights we suggest that it also endeavours to reha- bilitate the country's image in the eyes of what he envisions as a global 'cosmopolitan community' (ibid.: 540). In his construction of America as a cosmopolitan community he states, 'I love America. I know that for more than two centuries, we have strived—at great cost and great sacrifice—to form a more perfect union; to seek, with other nations, a more hopeful world. Our allegiance has never been to any particu- lar tribe or kingdom—indeed, every language is spoken in our country; every culture has left its imprint on ours; every point of view is expressed in our public squares' (Obama, 2008b).

Obama's patriotic-proactive cosmopolitan vision endeavours not only to rehabilitate America's image in a global cosmopolitan community but also 'attempts to create consensus about values and behaviour' among 'diverse communities' that make up the world (Taylor, 1999: 540). His patriotic-proactive cosmopolitanism has seen his administra- tion introduce key measures aimed at restoring America's image in his envisioned global cosmopolitan community. His signing of Executive Orders on January 22, 2009, one ending torture and another calling for the closing of the Guantánamo Bay detention centre are some of the efforts aimed at enabling the reconstitution of America's place in Obama's envisioned global cosmopolitan community after years of growing anti-American sentiments generated by political and economic practices during the regime of President George W. Bush.[5] In addition, his speech in Turkey (2009c) where he reiterated his administration's commitment to transforming USA's relationship with the Muslim world and his speech in Cairo in which he declared 'America is not—and never will be—at war with Islam' and called for 'a new beginning' marked by a dialogue driven by mutual interests and respect (Obama,

2009e), are efforts aimed at restoring his country's image in the cosmopolitan world community. Further, his form of cosmopolitanism has seen him invoke a sense of shared values and vision in addressing contemporary global issues that are sources of political, cultural and economic human insecurities. Concerning the global environmental crisis for instance, he has stated, 'this is the moment when we must come together to save this planet. Let us resolve that we will not leave our children a world where the oceans rise and famine spreads and terrible storms devastate our lands. Let us resolve that all nations—including my own—will act with the same seriousness of purpose as has your nation, and reduce the carbon we send into our atmosphere... This is the moment to stand as one' (Obama, 2008b). Commenting on economic, racial, religious and ethnic sources of conflict he invoked a cosmopolitan vision of equal humankind in which 'the walls' of divisions and hatred come down (ibid.). Further, echoing a constant theme in cosmopolitan thought Obama has argued that individuals and nations have responsibilities to others beyond their borders. Regarding the responsibilities of the dominant and wealthy nations in the world order he has stated, 'to those nations like ours that enjoy relative plenty, we say we can no longer afford indifference to the suffering outside our borders, nor can we consume the world's resources without regard to effect. For the world has changed, and we must change with it' (Obama, 2009a).

A core element of Obama's patriotic-proactive cosmopolitanism is a comprehensive-power approach to American foreign policy. Rather than relying solely on force and securitizing logic, the current administration considers drawing on all forms of American power, military, cultural, diplomatic, ideological and so forth in its engagement with allies and perceived threats as the best strategy. In the case of its defence policy, Obama has declared, 'we reject as false the choice between our safety and our ideals. Our Founding Fathers... faced with perils that we can scarcely imagine, drafted a charter to assure the rule of law and the rights of man—a charter expanded by the blood of generations. Those ideals still light the world, and we will not give them up for expedience sake' (ibid.). A comprehensive-power approach to perceived security threats to the USA, such as Iran's continuing objective of developing nuclear and ballistic missile capability, and North Korea's nuclear program, seems to be an emerging thread in his administration's foreign policy.[6] Such an approach to foreign policy is noticeable in his administration's engagement with Latin American countries especially those that it considers problematic such as Venezuela. The approach also informs his administration's approach to Afghanistan. For Obama, 'now, we also know that military power alone is not going to solve the problems in Afghanistan and Pakistan. That's why we plan to invest $ 1.5 billion each year over the next five years to partner with Pakistanis to build schools and hospitals, roads and businesses, and hundreds of millions to help those who've been displaced. That's why we are providing more than $ 2.8 billion to help Afghans develop their economy and deliver services that people depend on' (Obama, 2009e).

From an ethical perspective, the normative underpinnings of the cosmopolitan thought that informs Obama's patriotic-proactive cosmopolitanism are a welcome relief from his predecessor's approach to the world order and other countries. As Dan Skinner argues (2004), during Bush's presidency, American foreign policy was driven 'by a preoccupation with destruction of the Other. Who we are as Americans—at least in W's America—is determined by who we are not. Once we determine who we are not, then the task at hand becomes to destroy who we are not. The paradox inherent in this formulation is even scarier than it might first appear, for this ontological system is incapable of envisioning a world without enemies'. Welcomed as Obama's patriotic-proactive cosmopolitanism is, our argument is that it has the potential of providing a major opening for the restoration of core features of the current world order. Like other ideas, his cosmopolitanism is not neutral and neither is it occurring in a politico-economic vacuum. In terms of current politico-economic conditions, his articulation of a cosmopolitan worldview is occurring at a time when American hegemony is in crisis. Further, this worldview is emerging in a conjuncture in which there is a rise of centre-left regimes in several Latin American countries. In addition, it is a period marked by the emergence of non-state securitizing networks such as al-Shabaab in the Horn of Africa and many others. Further, counter-hegemonic movements such as those linked to the World Social Forum are challenging the neo-liberal and securitizing world order. Finally, the global economic crisis has put into question the viability of the American dominated neo-liberal world economy.

In the context of these preceding conditions and others, a core manner in which Obama's cosmopolitan worldview might open a possibility for the restoration of core features of the current world order is by it enabling the American state to construct and gain consent (Gramsci, 1971) for its vision of the politico-economic modalities of this order at home and at the global level. At the national level, for example, his patriotic-proactive cosmopolitanism is already contributing to the containment of calls to end securitizing logics that led to unending wars among progressive members of the social forces that brought Obama's historical bloc to power. In the case of the anti-war movement within American civil society and Congress, elements of it are giving the Obama administration consent for its unending wars. As Rep. William Lacy Clay, D-Mo, has posited following consultations in his district on a pending vote in Congress pertaining to the passing of a spending bill for the unending wars in Iraq and Afghanistan, 'we have a lot of anti-war sentiment in the district, and I thought people would provide me cover to vote against the bill...It was just the opposite. Lots of callers told me they trust the president, and we should give him a chance' (cited in Lightman, 2009). Economically, while framing the ongoing crisis as one that has affected every American and one requiring responses and sacrifices from every citizen, the measures that the Obama administration has introduced thus far indicate a commitment to restoring American neo-liberal capitalist order, rather than transforming it to benefit the majority of Americans. In taking such an approach, he is not far from the democrat ruling elites who now control both the Congress and Senate but who after years of blaming their Republican colleagues for economic dislocations generated by neo-liberal capitalism and President Bush's unending wars are not interested in fundamentally transforming the status quo. Overall, once in power, the democrats seem keen on introducing cosmetic changes to America's neo-liberal capitalism and not challenging it and the power of social forces closely linked to its core sectors, who have benefited and continue to benefit from the global neo-liberal project and who are pushing for its restoration. Commenting along these lines Howard Zinn states,

> We can be sure that the Democratic Party, unless it faces a popular upsurge, will not move off center...None of this should surprise us. The Democratic Party has broken with its historic conservatism, its pandering to the rich, its predilection for war, only when it has encountered rebellion from below, as in the Thirties and the Sixties. We should not expect that a victory at the ballot box in November will even begin to budge the nation from its twin fundamental illnesses: capitalist greed and militarism. (Quoted in Estabrook, 2009)

At the global level, while invoking a cosmopolitan vision of a world order, it seems that building consent for America's hegemony in this order is the core goal of Obama's presidency. While portraying America as equal to other nations, he has often indicated that restoring the USA to its leadership role in the world order is a core aim of his administration (2009a). Obama nonetheless embeds this agenda in a representational system enveloped by cosmopolitan ideas. As he stated in his inaugural speech, 'to all the other peoples and governments who are watching today, from the grandest capitals to the small village where my father was born, know that America is a friend of each nation, and every man, woman and child who seeks a future of peace and dignity. And we are ready to lead once more' (ibid.). When he declares, that his country is 'ready to lead again' the question of who benefits from America's leadership in the capitalist world order is neglected in this representation of his country's dominance in this order as benign and essentially in the interest of members of a universal cosmopolitan humankind. Thus, by neglecting the power dynamics that underpin the world order, Obama's presidency opens the door for the domestication of his administration's efforts to restore a neo-liberal and securitizing world order along modified lines, and American's hegemony in this order. At the level of the restoration of core elements of neo-liberalism, as we discussed earlier, this is already occurring as examples of his administration's responses to the current economic crisis and its view of market capitalism demonstrates.

In terms of securitization, while the Obama administration has introduced new policies, and a cosmopolitan worldview peppers its foreign policy, and the hyper-securitizing tone of the Bush era has been restrained, other practices such as extraordinary rendition and denial of due process for 'enemy combatants' continues (Savage, 2009). Further, the unending war continues in Afghanistan and, while 31 August, 2010 is the scheduled end of combat in Iraq, for the Obama administration, the country remains 'an unusual and extraordinary threat to the national security and foreign policy' as his recent signing of the Executive Order[7] signed by his predecessor on 22 May, 2003 contends. Moreover, the defiant nationalist pronouncements that were characteristic of the securitizing projects of President Bush, while tamed to some extent by Obama's cosmopolitan language, have not disappeared. In Obama's patriotic-proactive cosmopolitan worldview, nationalist ideology and cosmopolitan liberal internationalist (Chapter 5) ideas stressing the need for cooperation in the world order go hand in hand. For example, he has stated,

Recall that earlier generations faced down fascism and communism not just with missiles and tanks, but with the sturdy alliances and enduring convictions. They understood that our power alone cannot protect us, nor does it entitle us to do as we please... We are the keepers of this legacy. Guided by these principles once more we can meet

those new threats that demand even greater effort, even greater cooperation and understanding between nations... We will not apologize
for our way of life, nor will we waver in its defense. And for those
who seek to advance their aims by inducing terror and slaughtering
innocents, we say to you now that our spirit is stronger and cannot
be broken—you cannot outlast us, and we will defeat you. (Obama,
2009a)

Essentially, by invoking the cosmopolitan notion that all nations
have the responsibility of working together to ensure global security—a
departure from his predecessor's unilateralist approach—Obama con-
ceals America's continuing securitizing practices, militarist approach to
unending wars, American's ecological dominance in the world order and
his administration's commitment to restoring America's hegemony in
the world order. The patriotic-proactive bend of his cosmopolitanism
reassures the world and Americans who support him of the need for
cooperation on global issues and the shared humanity of all peoples.
Notwithstanding his articulation of cosmopolitan ideas, our conclusion is that underlying them is a political project. This project is aimed
at shifting America's dominance in the neo-liberal capitalist and securitizing world order from one based on force—which was the trend
under President Bush—to one that balances consent and force (Gramcsi,
1971). This serves the interests of Obama's historical bloc at home and
abroad, and in the process it opens up the possibility for America to
regain its hegemony in the world order. Overall, in different but complementary ways, his patriotic-proactive cosmopolitanism coupled with
previously highlighted current structural-political conditions have significant potential to enable the restoration of a modified neo-liberal and
securitizing world order in the immediate future of his presidency rather
than its transformation.

Conclusion

To conclude here, this chapter marks the end of this project. The centrality of ideas generated in the process of shifts in the post-1945 world
order has been one of the central concerns of the project. Building on
insights from the neo-Gramscian and Quijano's coloniality of power
analytical and ethical frameworks, we have highlighted the role and
effects of hegemonic ideas and other features of shifting world orders
in the post World War II period on political and economic processes
in the South. With a focus on Malawi and South Korea, we have also

demonstrated the analytical limitations of dominant approaches in the field of IDS in the study of socio-political processes in the South such as the role of the state in the economy. In addition, discussions concerning the question of the possibility for the transformation of the current world order, and the 'limits of the possible' (Gill, 2003) in this respect given actual existing structural, political and ideological conditions, have been other objectives of the project. In this regard, we have interrogated the nature of Russia and China's approach to the contemporary world order, the nature of China's role in contemporary Africa, the transformative potential of debates concerned with the transformation of institutions of global governance, human security development discourse and the World Social Forum process. The question of transformation of the current neo-liberal and securitizing world order has also been the focus of this last chapter in light of the ongoing global financial crisis and the ascendency to power of President Obama.

While various parts of the project focused on dominant structures of power and their effects, the underlying approach to its central concerns has been dialectical. Overall, an underlying premise of the project has been that even in the context of the manifestations of coloniality of power, the possibility for people in the South to make their own histories within the 'limits of the possible' (Gill, 2003) exists for a dialectical 'struggle among social forces is the principal dynamic of change in societies' (Cox, 2002: 185) and world orders. Currently, 'the one-civilization vision', which underpins the neo-liberal and securitizing world order, 'has the preponderance of military, economic and communications power behind it. But its dialectical contradiction is alive and active in the vision shared by less powerful of a more decentred and plural world of coexisting... civilizations [and] of alternative ways to live' (ibid.: 191). Thus, while constrained, processes geared to the transformation of the core features of the current world are 'latent within the structures' (ibid.: 192) as indicated by our discussion of the WSF process in Chapter 8.

Notes

1 Introduction

1. For details on Millennium Development Goals, see http://www.un.org/
   millenniumgoals/ and Chapter 7.
2. These scholars provide detailed discussions on the nature and implications of
   positivist methodologies, see Cox (1981) and Gill (1993).
3. We offer an extended discussion of this question in Eunice N. Sahle
   (forthcoming) 'TGNP's feminist-decolonial project in Tanzania'.

2 Analytical Framing

1. While focusing on different historical conjunctures, Gramsci (1971) and
   Harvey (2005) offer interesting discussions on the role of consent in politico-
   economic processes.
2. For a detailed discussion of the factors that led to calls for a New International
   Economic Order (NIEO) and the limits and contradictions of this project see,
   Augelli and Murphy (1988).
3. See for instance the extensive discussion by Mignolo (2000).
4. While not exhaustive, here is a list of other scholars who have used the concept of hegemony to analyse global political and economic processes: Cox
   (1987), Robinson (1996), Cox (1993), Gill (2003) and Agnew (2005).
5. For discussions of peripheral structural dependency see Gill and Law (1988),
   Frank (1969) and Cardoso and Faletto (1979).
6. Scholars in the field of collective action and social movements have elab-
   orated extensively on the concept of 'political opportunity structures'. The
   concept highlights the ways in which political movements seize openings
   generated by, for instance, economic, moral and legitimacy crises of the
   state, shifting ideologies, transnational developments and so forth. For further discussions see McAdam, McCarthy and Zald (1996) and Della and Diani
   (2006a).
7. For an excellent and detailed discussion, see Gregory (2004), especially
   pp. 5–12.

3 World Orders, Development Discourse and Coloniality

1. For a detailed discussion see Shoup and Minter (1977), pp. 11–187.
2. Parsons posited the pattern variables as, particularism vs. universalism, ascrip-
   tion vs. achievement, diffuseness vs. specificity. For a detailed discussion of his
   theory of social change, see Parsons (1951).
3. Huntington argues that India's liberal democracy is an exceptional case in
   the developing world and attributes this exceptionality to the existence of

an old political party, the Congress Party, and a well-established institutional framework, specifically the civil service, before the country's independence in 1947 (1967: 227–228).

4. In terms of aid conditionality, in the 1980s the focus was on the demonstration by states in the South that they were making concerted efforts in implementing the neo-liberal market development model. From the latter part of the decade, the TDHB extended conditionality to include the twin agenda of establishment of multiparty democracy and free markets. For detailed discussion on the broadening of conditionality measures by the TDHB, see Killick et al (1998), especially pp. 1–18, and Stokke (ed.) (1995), pp. 1–87.

5. See Robinson (1996) for a detailed examination of America's policy of promoting democracy in the post-Cold War era.

6. See especially Chapters 3 and 4, Toye (1993).

7. For detailed discussion of colonial forms of violence and their effects, see Fanon (2004; 2008).

8. See Polanyi 2001, especially Chapters 6, 7 and 8.

9. For a detailed discussion of colonial forms of dispossession, see Rodney (1972) Part V and Quijano (2007 and 2008).

4 State, World Order and Development: Malawi and South Korea

1. For a detailed discussion of these strategies and their political and institutional legacies see generally Mamdani (1996) particularly Chapters 2–4.

2. For extensive discussions of the variety of pre-colonial political arrangements see generally (Davidson, 1984a; Mamdani, 1996; Schraeder, 2004: 23–32).

3. Views expressed by various imperial interests during this period signal the determination of European imperial powers to push for cotton production in the colonies in the context of a deepening global 'cotton famine'. As Isaacman and Roberts state, 'From the outset European officials were confident that their newly acquired territories would fuel the metropolitan textile revolution. In an 1885 speech to the Reichstag, Bismarck predicated that colonial output would reduce his nation's unhealthy dependence on the United States, which supplied almost 80 percent of Germany's raw cotton. Twenty years later BCGZ representatives declared that production in northern Nigeria alone would satisfy all the needs of Lancashire. In 1906, a spokesman for the Portuguese Industrial Association assured prospective investors that the initiatives in Angola and Mozambique would surpass the levels of cotton production in other colonial nations.... these expectations rested on the assumption that African rural societies enjoyed abundant leisure' (1995: 14).

4. For an extensive examination of the nature and evolution of the 1915 Chilembwe anti-colonial movement led by John Chilembwe, a Christian intellectual and community leader, see Shepperson and Price (1958).

5. For a detailed discussion of the September 1964 cabinet crisis see McMaster (1974).

6. Interview, Dr Vera Chirwa, Blantyre, Malawi, July 2006. She was a leading member of the nationalist movement and is the widow of the late Orton

Chirwa, a founder of the Malawi Congress Party and one of the Ministers who was forced into exile following the 1964 cabinet crisis.

7. Details of these estates, for instance names and sizes, are available at the Malawi National Archives, Zomba, 19/3/5/V/117.

8. For further details see Peattie (1984: photograph 8), and generally his chapter.

9. For a detailed discussion of the emergence of a manufacturing sector and other industrial developments during colonialism, see Ho (1984), particularly Table 3 'Growth and Composition of Manufacturing, Korea, Taiwan, and Kwantung'.

10. See especially Chapters 3–8.

5 Global Governance

1. See generally, Duffield (2001) especially Chapters 3 and 4.

2. See the following text for arguments along similar lines: Späth (2005).

6 Russia, China, Africa and Multi-polarity

1. For a detailed discussion of a sample of modes of transition from periphery to semi-periphery to core status in the world economy, see Wallerstein (1979), especially Chapter 5.

2. China is not the only social formation in the historical global South to engage with multilateralism to meet its strategic aims. As Cooper and Shaw (2009) indicate, in the context of the current phase of globalization, even 'smaller states' in the world order are increasingly competing with each other in the multilateral arena; a process that is leading to differentiation among these states in this sphere.

3. In the case of revolutionary movements, China considered Africa and other parts of the South as the epicentre for revolutionary change against the dominant super powers especially following its split with the Soviet bloc in the late 1950s. China's support for revolutionary movements—in Africa and elsewhere—was informed by Mao Zedong's conceptualizing the world as comprising three worlds, the Soviet and Western bloc forming the first world; an intermediately zone or second world of countries in North America and Europe that belonged to the first world but were also 'exploited' and consequently could be convinced to join the struggles against the two global hegemonic powers; and Africa, Asia and Latin America forming the Third World (Kim, 1989: 7). Building on this theory Mao contended that the Third World was the 'the focus of world contradictions' and the 'storm center of the world revolution' in the context of the geopolitics of the Cold War and dominance of capitalist social formations in the world system (Harris, 1985: 31). The support for revolutionary movements in independent Africa generated tensions between the Chinese and African states. For these newly independent states, the Chinese state's commitment to revolutionary struggle was deemed as a source of political instability and a significant departure from its Five Principles especially that of non-interference.

7 Human Security, Neo-liberalism and Securitization of Development

1. See the following texts for examples: Truong et al. (2007); Kaldor (2007); Maclean et al. (2006); and Picciotto et al. (2007).
2. Hobbes, T. and Gaskin, J. C. (1996) offers an extended discussion on these ideas.
3. See particularly Buzan et al. (1998); Buzan and Wæver (1997) and Buzan (1983 and 1991) for detailed analysis.
4. For extended discussion of United Nations Millennium Development Goals, see http://www.un.org/millenniumgoals/.
5. See United Nations, http://www.un.org/esa/ffd/monterrey/Monterrey-Consensus.pdf, for a detailed discussion of the core themes of this conference.
6. See, *New York Times*, National Security Strategy of United States of America, 2002 http://www.nytimes.com/2002/09/20/politics/20STEXT_FULL.html.
7. Enloe (2007) provides insightful analysis of human rights abuses in Abu Ghraib, Guantánamo and Bagram prisons, from a critical feminist perspective.
8. For further discussion, see Garamone (2007), http://www.defenselink.mil/ http://www.defenselink.mil/. See also Lewis (2007).
9. See Gregory (2004) especially Chapters 3 and 7.

8 World Social Forum

1. For extensive details see, World Social Forum Charter of Principles, http://www.forumsocialmundial.org.br/main.php?id_menu=4&cd_language=2.
2. For more details on the Charter of Principles see: http://www.forumsocialmundial.org.br/main.php?id_menu=4&cd_language=2.
3. Author's observations at the WSF Nairobi, 2007.
4. For more details, see World Social Forum, http://www.worldsocialforum.org.
5. This development and the nature of the IC is discussed in 'IC—Nature, responsibilities, composition and functioning', http://www.worldsocialforum.org.
6. See, 'Social Forums Around the World', http://www.forumsocialmundial.org.br/quadro_frc.php?cd_forum=9, for extensive details of regional and other WSF meetings.
7. My discussion of the 2007 World Social Forum in Nairobi has greatly benefitted not only from my participation at the Forum, but also ongoing discussions with Oloo Onyango, who was the National Coordinator for the Kenya Social Forum in 2006 and was a member of the National Organizing Council for the World Social Forum in Nairobi in 2007. I am very grateful for his insights on this matter.
8. For an extended discussion, see Chapter 7, Santos, 2006.

9 Epilogue: Global Financial Crisis, Barack Obama's Presidency and World Order

1. For an extended discussion of the nature and evolution of the economic crisis in Iceland, see Stoddard (2009) and Parker (2009).

2. See Panitch and Konings (2008) for a detailed discussion of USA's influence in the evolution of the global financial system and its attendant contradictions and crises.
3. For a detailed analysis of 'varieties of residential capitalism' in various parts of the world and their link to financial crisis and economic instability, see Schwartz and Seabrooke (2009).
4. The complete report is available at http://www.house.gov/jec/imf/meltzer.htm.
5. See President Barack Obama, 22 January, 2009, Executive Order—Ensuring Lawful Interrogations, http://www.whitehouse.gov/the_press_office/Ensuring-LawfulInterrogations/, Executive Order—Review and Disposition of individuals detained at the Guantánamo Bay Naval Base and closure of detention facilities, http://www.whitehouse.gov/the_press_office/closureofguantanamo-detentionfacilities/.
6. Obama's administration uses the concept of 'smart power' to describe its foreign policy approach, which we suggest is underpinned by a comprehensive-power approach to foreign policy matters and contemporary global issues. Highlights and up to date developments of this administration's approach to foreign policy and global issues including global security are available at http://www.whitehouse.gov/issues/foreign_policy/.
7. For more details and history of this Executive Order see, http://www.whitehouse.gov/the_press_office/Message-from-the-President-and-Notice-of-Continuation-regarding-Iraq/.

Bibliography

Adam, C., Cavendish, W. and Mistry, P. S. (1992) *Adjusting Privatization* (London: James Currey).

Adler, E. and Hass, P. M. (1992) 'Conclusion: epistemic communities, world order, and the creation of a reflective research program', *International Organization*, 46 (1): 367–390.

Agamben, G. (2005) *State of Exception* (Chicago: The University of Chicago Press).

Agnew, J. A. (2005) *The New Shape of Global Power* (Philadelphia: Temple University Press).

Aiguo, L. (2000) *China and the Global Economy since 1840* (London: Macmillan Press Ltd.).

Alden, C. (2005) 'China in Africa', *Survival*, 47 (3): 147–64.

Almond, G. T. (1970) *Political Development: Essays in Heuristic Theory* (Boston: Little Brown).

Alvares, C. (1992) 'Science', in W. Sachs (ed.), *The Development Dictionary: A Guide to Knowledge as Power* (London: Zed Books): 219–232.

Amin, S. (1976) *Unequal Development: an essay on social formations of peripheral capitalism, translated by Brian Pearce* (Brighton, Sussex: The Harvester Press Limited).

—— (2006) 'The millennium development goals: A Critique from the south', translated by James H. Membrez, in *Monthly Review*, 57 (10): 1–15.

Appiah, K. A. (1996) 'Cosmopolitan patriots', in Cohen, J. (ed.), *For Love of Country* (Boston: Beacon Press): 21–29.

Armijo, L. E. (2007) 'The BRICs Countries (Brazil, Russia, India and China) in the Global System', *Asian Perspective* 30 (4): 7–42.

Arrighi, G. (2005) 'Global governance and hegemony in the modern world system', in Ba, A. D. and Hoffmann, M. J. (eds), *Contending Perspectives on Global Governance: Coherence, Contestation and World Order* (London and New York: Routedge): 20–30.

Augelli, E. and Murphy, C. (1988) *America's Quest for Supremacy and the Third World* (London: Pinter Publishers, London).

Bagchi, A. K. (1982) *The Political Economy of Underdevelopment* (Cambridge: Cambridge University Press).

Bajoria, J. (2009) 'China's Military Power', *Council on Foreign Relations*, February 4, 2009, http://www.cfr.org/publication/18459/chinas_military_power.html.

Baker, P. and Donadio, R. (2009) 'Obama Wins More Food Aid but Presses African Nations on Corruption', *New York Times*, http://www.nytimes.com/2009/07/11/world/europe/11prexy.html?_r=1&scp=1&sq=obama%20on%20kenya%20and%20south%20korea&st=cse.

Baker, P. and Glasser, S. (2005) *Kremlin Rising Vladimir Putin's Russia and the End of the Revolution* (New York: A Lisa Drew Book/Scribner).

Banda, K. H. (1965) *Hansard*, 4 April 1965.

—— (1968) *Speech at the Chiradzulu Agricultural Show*, 27 July, 1968.

—— (1969) *The President Speaks, Malawi Congress Party Convention*, September (Blantyre: Department of information).

Barfield, C. and Groombridge, M. (2003) 'Avoiding deadlock', in Ostry, S., Alexandroof, A. S. and Gomez, R. (eds), *China and the Long March to Global Trade* (London: Routledge): 30–43.

Bates, R. H. (1981) *Markets and States in Tropical Africa* (Berkeley: University of California Press).

—— (1989) *Beyond the Miracle of the Market: The Political Economy of Agrarian Development in Kenya* (Cambridge: University Press).

Bauer, P. T. (1984) *Reality and Rhetoric: Studies in the Economics of Development* (Cambridge: Harvard University Press).

BBC News Online. (2006a) 'China and Nigeria Agree Oil Deal', http://news.bbc.co.uk/2/hi/business/4946708.stm.

—— (2006b) 'China's Hu Urges More Africa Ties', April 27, 2006 http://news.bbc.co.uk.

—— (2006c) April 28 and 29, 2006, http://news. bbc.co.uk.

—— (2006d) 'China's Ambitions in Africa', November 25, 2006 http://news.bbc.co.uk.

—— (2006e) 'Iraq Violence: Facts and figures', November 29, 2006 http://news.bbc.co.uk/2/hi/5052138.stm.

Bello, W. F. and Mittal, A. (2001) *The Future in the Balance: Essays on Globalization and Resistance* (Oakland: Food First Books).

—— (2002) *Deglobalization: Ideas for a New World Economy* (London: Zed Books).

—— (2003) 'The international architecture of power: International organizations and the architecture of world power', in William F. Fisher and Thomas Ponniah (eds), *Another World is Possible: Popular Alternatives to Globalization at the World Social Forum* (Nova Scotia, Fernwood Publishing Ltd, SIRD, Selangor, David Philip, Cape Town and London & New York, Zed Books): 285–289.

Black, S. (2001) *Life and Debt*, http://www.lifeanddebt.org/.

Blair, T. (2003) 'Text of Blair's speech', *BBC News*, http://news.bbc.co.uk/2/hi/uk_news/politics/3076253.stm.

—— (2001) *Speech, Labour Party Conference*, October, http://www.guardian.co.uk/politics/2001/oct/02/labourconference.labour6.

Bond, P. (2001) *Against Global Apartheid: South Africa Meets the World Bank, IMF and International Finance* (Lansdowne: University of Cape Town Press).

—— (2006) 'Global governance campaigning and MDGs: From top-down to bottom-up anti-poverty work', *Third World Quarterly*, 27 (2): 339–354.

—— (2007) 'Volatile, uneven and combined capitalism', in Robert Albritton, Robert Jessop and Richard Westra (eds), *Political Economy and Global Capitalism: The 21st Century, Present and Future* (London; New York: Anthem Press): 127–157.

—— (2008) 'World bank and the IMF in Africa', in Peter N. Sterns (ed.), *The Oxford Encyclopedia of the Modern World* (Oxford: Oxford University Press) 8: 60–64.

Booth, K. (1991) 'Security and emancipation', *Review of International Studies*, 17 (4): 313–326.

—— (2005) 'Critical explorations', in Ken Booth (ed.), *Critical Security Studies and World Politics* (Boulder and London: Lynne Rienner Publishers).

Breslin, S. (2007) *China and the Global Political Economy* (Basingstoke: Palgrave Macmillan).

Broadman, H. G. (2007) *Africa's Silk Road: China and India's New Economic Frontier* (Washington: World Bank).

Brodie, J. (1994) 'Shifting the boundaries: Gender and the politics of restructuring', in Isabella Bakker (ed.), *The Strategic Silence: Gender and Economic Policy* (London: Zed Books in Association with the North-South Institute/Institut Nord-Sud): 46–60.

Brown, G. (2009) *The Guardian*, January 26, http://www.guardian.co.uk/politics/2009/jan/26/gordon-brown-economic-policy/print.

Brown, L. R. (2001) 'Who will feed China?', in James D. Torr (ed.), *China: Opposing Viewpoints* (San Diego: Greenhaven Press).

Bush, G. (1991) 'Address to the 46th Session of the United Nations General Assembly', New York City, The American Presidency Project, http://www.presidency.ucsb.edu/george_bush.php.

Bush, W. G. (2002) *State of the Union Address*, 29 January, 2002 http://www.whitehouse.gov/news/releases/2002/01/20020129-11.html.

Buzan, B. (1983) *People, States and Fear: The National Security Problem in International Relations* (Chapel Hill: The University of North Carolina Press).

—— (1991) *People, States and Fear: An Agenda for International Security Studies in the Post-Cold War Era* 2d ed. (New York: Harvester Wheatsheaf).

—— and Wæver, O. (1997) 'Slippery? contradictory? Sociologically untenable? The Copenhagen school replies', *Review of International Studies*, 23: 241–250.

—— Wæver, O. and Wilde, J. De (1998) *Security: A New Framework for Analysis* (Boulder and London: Lynne Rienner Publishers).

—— (2005) 'The security dynamics of a 1 + 4 World', in Ersel Aydinli and James N. Rosenau (eds), *Globalization, Security, and the Nation-State: Paradigms in Transition* (New York: State University of New York Press): 117–133.

Byers, M. (2005) *War law* (London: Atlantic).

Cammack, P. (2005) 'The governance of global capitalism: A new materialist perspective', in Rorden Wilkinson (ed.), *The Global Governance Reader* (London and New York: Routledge): 156–173.

Cardoso, F. H. and Faletto, E. (1979) *Dependency and Development in Latin America* (Berkeley: University of California Press).

Carlson, A. (2006) 'More than just saying no: China's evolving approach to sovereignty and intervention since Tiananmen', in Alastair Iain Johnston and Robert S. Ross (eds), *New Directions in the Study of China's Foreign Policy* (Stanford: Stanford University Press): 217–241.

Carmody, P. (2007) *Neoliberalism, Civil Society and Security in Africa* (Basingstoke [England]: Palgrave Macmillan).

Cartier, C. L. (2001) *Globalizing South China* (Oxford: Blackwell Publishers).

Castells, M. (1998) 'Paths and problems of the integration of post-communist Russia into the global economy: A concept paper', in Stephen S. Cohen, Andrew Schwartz and John Zysman (eds), *The Tunnel at the End of the Light: Privatization, Business Networks, and Economic Transformation in Russia* (Berkeley: International and Area Studies University of California at Berkeley).

Cerny, P. G. (1990) *The Changing Architecture of Politics: Structure, Agency and the Future of the State* (London and Thousand Oaks, CA: Sage).

—— (1993) 'American decline and the emergence of embedded financial orthodoxy', in Philip G. Cerny (ed.), *Finance and World Politics: Markets, Regimes and States in the Post-Hegemonic Era* (Aldershot and Brookfield: Edward Elgar): 155–185.

Chan, S., Clark, C. and Lam, D. (1998) *Beyond the Developmental State: East Asia's Political Economies Reconsidered* (Houndsmills: St. Martin's Press).

Chang, A. (2009) 'China Expanding African Arms Sales', UPI Asia.com, http://www.upiasia.com/Security/2009/01/26/china_expanding_african_arms_sales/1148/.

Changhe, S. (2007) 'China in the world and the world in China: The domestic impact of international institutions on China's politics, 1978–2000', in David Zweig and Zhimin Chen (eds), *China's Reforms and International Political Economy* (New York: Routledge, 2007): 62–76.

Chau, L. C. (2001) 'South Korea: Government-led development and the dominance of giant corporations', in Kwong Kai-Sun, Chau Leung-Chuen, Francis T. Lui and Larry D. Qui (eds) *Industrial Development in Singapore, Taiwan, and South Korea* (New Jersey: World Scientific): 118–200.

Chen, C. C. (1984) 'Police and community control systems in the Empire', in Ramon H. Myres and Mark R. Peattie (eds), *The Japanese Colonial Empire, 1895–1945* (Princeton: Princeton University Press): 213–239.

China.org.cn (2003a) 'Chinese leaders on Sino-African relations', 10 December, 2003 http://www1.china.org.cn/english/features/China-Africa/82054.htm.

———— (2003b) 'China's African Policy', http://china.org.cn/english/features/China-Africa/82055.htm.

Christiansen, R. E. (1984) 'Financing Malawi's Development Strategy', in *Malawi, An Alternative Pattern of Development*, Proceedings of a Seminar Held in the Centre of African Studies, University of Edinburgh: 409–470.

———— and J. G. Kydd (1986) 'The Political Economy of Agricultural Policy Formulation in Malawi 1960–80.' Paper prepared for the Managing Agriculture Development in Africa (MADIA) Study (Washington, DC: World Bank).

Clarke, S. (1988) *Keynesianism, Monetarism and the Crisis of the State* (Aldershot: Edward Elgar).

———— (2007) *The Development of Capitalism in Russia* (London and New York: Routledge).

Clegg, J. (2009) *China's Global Strategy: Towards a Multipolar World* (London: Pluto Press).

Cohen, S. F. (2000) *Failed Crusade: America and the Tragedy of Post-Communist Russia* (New York: Norton).

Commission on Global Governance. (1995) *Our Global Neighbourhood: The Report of the Commission on Global Governance* (Oxford and New York: Oxford University Press).

Commission of Inquiry into the Actions of Canadian officials in Relation to Maher Arar (2006), http://www.fedpubs.com/subject/govern/arar.htm.

Cook, J. and Roberts, J. (2000) 'Towards a gendered political economy', in Joanne Cook, Jennifer Roberts, and Georgina Waylen (eds), *Towards a Gendered Political Economy* (New York: St. Martin's Press in Association with Political Economy Research Centre the University of Sheffield): 3–13.

Cooper, A. F. and Shaw, T. M. (eds) (2009) *The Diplomacies of Small States: Between Vulnerability and Resilience* (Basingstoke [England]: Palgrave Macmillan).

Cord, R. (2007) *Keynes* (London: Haus Publishing).

Cowen, M. and Shenton, R. W. (1995) 'The invention of development', in Jonathan Crush (ed.), *Power of Development* (London and New York: Routledge).

———— (1996) *Doctrines of Development* (London and New York: Routledge).

Cox, R. W. (1981) 'Social forces, states, and world orders: Beyond international relations theory', *Millennium: Journal of International Studies*, 10 (2): 126–155.

—— (1986) 'Social forces, states, and world orders: Beyond international relations theory', in Robert, R. O (ed.), *Neorealism and its Critics* (New York: Columbia University Press): 204–254.

—— (1987) *Production, Power, and World: Social Forces in the Making of History* (New York: Columbia University Press).

—— (1993) 'Gramsci, Hegemony and International Relations: An Essay in Method', in Stephen Gill (ed.), *Gramsci, Historical Materialism and International Relations* (Cambridge: University Press): 49–66.

—— (2002) with Michael G. Shechter, *The Political Economy of a Plural World: Critical Reflections on Power, Morals and Civilization* (London and New York: Routledge).

Crush, J. (1995) 'Introduction: Imaging development', in Jonathan Crush (ed.), *Power of Development* (London and New York): 1–23.

Cummings, B. (1984) 'The legacy of Japanese colonialism in Korea', in Ramon H. Myres and Mark R. Peattie (eds), *The Japanese Colonial Empire, 1895–1945* (Princeton: Princeton University Press): 478–496.

Davidson, B. (1984a) *Kings and Cities*.

—— (1984b) *This Magnificent African Cake*.

Davidson, P. (2007) *Interpreting Keynes for the 21st Century* (Basingstoke, Hampshire: Palgrave Macmillan).

Dean, M. (1999) *Governmentality: Power and Rule in Modern Society* (London: SAGE Publications).

Della, P. D. and Diani, M. (2006a) *Social Movements: an Introduction* (Malden, MA: Blackwell Publishing).

—— Andretta, M., Mosca, L., and Reiter, H. R. (2006b) *Globalization From Below: Transnational Activists and Protest Networks* (Minneapolis and London: University of Minnesota Press).

Deng, Y. (2005) 'Better than power: "International Status", in Chinese foreign policy', in Yong Deng and Fei-Ling Wang (eds), *China Rising* (Lanham: Rowman & Littlefield Publishers): 51–72.

Department for International Development. (2005) *Fighting Poverty to Build a Safer World: A Strategy for Security and Development*, March, http://www.dfid.gov.uk/Media-Room/Press-releases/2005-completed/Safety-and-security-must-be-at-the-heart-of-development/.

Dequin, H. (1969) *Agricultural Development in Malawi* (Munchen: Institut Fur Wirtschaftsforschung).

Doster, A. (2009) 'Durbin on Congress: The Banks "Own the Place"', http://progressillinois.com/2009/4/29/durbin-banks-own-the-place.

Dougherty, J. (2009) 'Black Iraqis make Obama a model to follow', CCN, http://www.cnn.com/2009/WORLD/meast/01/19/obama.black.iraqis/index.html.

Dower, N. (2003) *An Introduction to Global Citizenship* (Edinburgh: Edinburgh University Press).

Duffield, M. R. (2001) *Global Governance and the New Wars: The Merging of Development* and Security (London and New York: Zed Books).

—— (2007) *Development, Security and Unending War: Governing the World of Peoples* (Cambridge, UK and Malden, US: Polity).

Dussel, E. D. (1996). *The Underside of Modernity: Apel, Ricoeur, Rorty, Taylor, and the Philosophy of Liberation*, translated and edited by Mendieta, E. (Atlantic Highlands, NJ: Humanities Press).

Eatwell, J. and Taylor, L. (2002) *Global Finance at Risk* (Oxford: Polity Press).

Economic Planning Board (1982) *Economic Policies of the Development Era: The Twenty Year History of the Economic Planning Board* (Seoul: Economic Planning Board).

Einarsson, P. (2001), 'The Disagreement on Agriculture', www.grain.org/publications/mar012-en.cfm.

Eisenman, J. (2007) 'China's post-cold war strategy in Africa: Examining Beijing's methods and objectives', in Joshua Eisenman, Eric Heginbotham, and Derek Mitchell (eds), *China and the Developing World: Beijing's Strategy for the Twenty-First Century* (New York: M. E. Sharpe).

Enloe, C. (1990) *Bananas, Beaches and Bases: Making Feminist Sense of International Politics* (Berkeley: University of California Press).

—— (1993) *The Morning After: Sexual Politics at the End of the Cold War* (Berkeley: University of California Press).

—— (2007) *Globalization & Militarism: Feminists Make the Link* (Lanham: Rowman & Littlefield Publishers).

Escobar, A. (1995a) *Encountering Development, The Making and Unmaking of the Third World* (Princeton, NJ: Princeton University Press).

—— (1995b) 'Imagining a Post-development Era', in Jonathan Crush (ed) *Power of Development* (London and New York: Routledge).

—— (1997) 'The making and unmaking of the third world through development', in Majid Rahnema with Victoria Bawtree (eds), *The Post-Development Reader* (London & New Jersey: Zed Books, Dhaka: University Press, Ltd., Halifax & Nova Scotia: Fernwood Publishing, and Cape Town: David Philip): 85–93.

—— (2008) *Territories of difference: Place, movements, life, redes* (Durham: Duke University Press).

Estabrook, C. G. (2009) 'Obama the war manager: Minion of the long war', in Alexander Cockburn and Jeffrey St. Clair (eds), *Counterpunch*, May, http://www.counterpunch.org/estabrook05012009.html.

EurACtiv Network. (2009), 'Obama asked for it and got it: Unity at G20', April 3, 2009 http://www.euractiv.com/en/euro/obama-asked-got-unity-g20/article-180954.

Falk, R. (2003) *The Great Terror War* (Gloucestershire: Arris Books).

Fanon, F. (2004) *The Wretched of the Earth*, translated by Richard Philcox (New York: Grove Press).

—— (2008) *Black Skin, White Masks*, translated by Richard Philcox (New York: Grove Press).

Ferguson, J. (1994) *The Anti-Politics Machine: "Development," Depoliticization, and Bureaucratic Power in Lesotho* (Minneapolis, USA and London, UK: University of Minnesota Press).

—— (2006) *Global Shadows: Africa in the Neoliberal World Order* (Durham [NC]: Duke University Press).

Ferguson, N. (2003) *Empire: How Britain Made the Modern World* (London: Allen Lange/Penguin).

Filho, A. S. (2007) 'Monetary policy in the neo-liberal transition: A political economy critique of Keynesianism, monetarism and inflation targeting', in Robert

Albritton, Robert Jessop and Richard Westra (eds) *Political Economy and Global Capitalism: The 21ˢᵗ Century, Present and Future* (London; New York: Anthem Press): 89–119.

Fishman, T. C. (2005) *China, Inc.: How the Rise of the Next Superpower Challenges America and the World* (New York: Scribner).

Foster, J. B. (2006) *Naked Imperialism: The U.S. Pursuit of Global Dominance* (New York: Monthly Review Press).

Foucault, M. (2003) *Society Must Be Defended* (New York: Picador).

Francis, M. and N. Francis. (2006), *Black Gold*, http://www.blackgoldmovie.com/.

Frank, A. G. (1969) *Capitalism and Underdevelopment in Latin America: Historical Studies of Chile and Brazil* (New York: Monthly Review Press).

Freedman, L. (1998) 'International security: Changing targets', in *Foreign Policy*, 110: 48–63.

Friedman, M. (1988) 'Capitalism and Freedom', in Michael A. Walker (ed.), *Freedom, Democracy, and Economic Welfare: Proceedings from an International Conference* (Vancouver: Fraser Institute): 47–57.

Fukuyama, F. (1992) *The End of History and the Last of Man* (New York: Avon Books).

Garamone, J. (2007) Department of Defense, 'Pace: Military, Other Agencies to Forge New Relations in Africa', http://www.defenselink.mil/news/NewsArticle.aspx?ID=3020.

Germain, R. D. (1997) *The International Organization of Credit: States and Global Finance in the World-Economy* (Cambridge: Cambridge University Press).

Ghai, D. and Radwan, S. (1983) 'Growth and inequality: Rural development in Malawi, 1964–78', in Dharam Ghai and Samir Radwan (eds), *Agrarian Policies and Rural Poverty in Africa* (Geneva: International Labour Organisation): 71–97.

Gibbon, P. and Ponte, S. (2005) *Trading Down: Africa, Value Chains, and the Global Economy* (Philadelphia: Temple University Press).

Gibson-Graham, J. K. (2006) *A Postcapitalist Politics* (Minneapolis and London: University of Minnesota Press).

Gill, S. (1993) 'Epistemology, ontology, and the "Italian school"', in Stephen Gill (ed.), *Gramsci, Historical Materialism and International Relations* (Cambridge: University Press).

———— (2003) *Power and Resistance in the New World Order* (Basingstoke [England]: Palgrave Macmillan).

Gill, S. and Law, D. (1988) *The Global Political Economy: Perspectives, Problems and Policies* (Baltimore: The Johns Hopkins University Press).

Global Policy Forum. (2007) *War and Occupation in Iraq*, June, http://www.globalpolicy.org.

Goldman, M. I. (2008) *Petrostate: Putin, Power, and the New Russia* (Oxford: Oxford University Press).

Goldman, M. (2005) *Imperial Nature: The World Bank and Struggles for Social Justice in the Age of Globalization* (New Haven and London: Yale University Press).

Goldstein, A., Nicolas Pinaud, Helmut Reisen and Xiaobao Chen (2006) *The Rise of China and India: What's in it for Africa?* (Paris: OECD).

Gorbachev, M. (1989) 'Perestroika', in Ernest W. Lefever and Robert D. Vander Lugt (eds), *PERESTROIKA How New Is Gorbachev's New Thinking* (Lanham, University Press of America, Inc.).

Government of Malawi. (1965) *The 1965 Land Act*.

———— (1966) *The Republic of Malawi Constitution*.

―――― (1967a) *The Customary Land (Development) Act.*

―――― (1967b) *The Registered Land Act.*

―――― (1967c) *The Local Land Boards Act.*

―――― (1967d) *The Malawi Land (Amendment) Act*, No. 8.

―――― (1970) *Industrial Development in Malawi—A Guide for Prospective Investors.*

―――― (1987) *Statement of Development Policies 1987–1996* (Zomba: Government Printer).

―――― *Hansard*, April 2, 1993 (Zomba: Government Printer).

―――― (2006) 'Ministry of industry, trade and private sector development', *Private Sector Development in Malawi*, July 2006.

Gramsci, A. (1971) *Selections from the Prison Notebooks*, translated and edited by Quintin Hoare and Geoffrey Nowell Smith (New York: International Publishers).

Gregory, D. (2004) *The Colonial Present: Afghanistan, Palestine, Iraq* (Malden, USA, Oxford UK and Victoria, Australia: Blackwell Publishing).

Gurley, J. G. (1976) *China's Economy and the Maoist Strategy* (New York: Monthly Review Press).

Hall, R. B. and Biersteker, T. J. (eds), (2002) *The Emergency of Private Authority in Global Governance* (Cambridge: Cambridge University Press).

Hall, S. (1997) 'Introduction', in Stuart Hall (ed.), *Representation: Cultural Representations and Signifying Practices* (London: Sage in association with The Open University).

Hallowes, D. and Butler, M. (2002) 'Power, poverty, and marginalized environments: A conceptual framework', in David A. McDonald (ed.), *Environmental Justice in South Africa* (Athens: Ohio University Press and Cape Town: University of Cape Town Pres): 51–78.

Halliday, H. (1989) *Cold War, Third World: An Essay on Soviet-US Relations* (London: Hutchinson Radius).

Hamilton, P. (1986) 'Editor's foreword: The concept of hegemony', in Robert Bocock (eds), *Hegemony* (Chichester, Sussex: Ellis Horwood Limited): 7–9.

Hanson, S. (2007) 'The pentagon's New Africa command', *Council on Foreign Relations*, February 6, http://www.cfr.org/publication/13255.

Harcourt, W. (2004) *The Road to the UN Millennium Development Goals: Some insights into the International Debate* (Amsterdam: NCDO).

Harris, L. C. (1985) *China's Foreign Policy Toward the Third World* (New York: Praeger).

Hart-Landsberg, M. (1993) *The Rush to Development: Economic Change and Political Struggle in South Korea* (New York: Monthly Review Press).

―――― and Paul Burkett (2005) *China and Socialism: Market Reforms and Class Struggle* (New York: Monthly Review Press).

Harvey, D. (1990) *The Condition of Postmodernity* (Cambridge MA & Oxford UK: Blackwell).

―――― (2003) *New Imperialism* (Oxford: Oxford University Press).

―――― (2005) *A Brief History of Neoliberalism* (New York: Oxford University Press).

―――― (2006) *Spaces of Global Capitalism: Towards a Theory of Uneven Geographical Development* (London: Verso).

Hedlund, S. (1999) *Russia's Market: A Bad Case of Predatory Capitalism* (London: University College).

Park, C. H. (1971) *To Build a Nation* (Washington, DC: Acropolis Books).

Hegel, W. F. (1956) Trans. J. Sibree, *The Philosophy of History* (New York: Dover).

Held, D. (1995) *Democracy and the Global Order: From the Modern State to Cosmopolitan Governance* (Stanford, Calif.: Stanford University Press).

Helleiner, E. (1994) 'From Bretton Woods to global finance: A world turned upside', in Richard Stubbs and Geoffrey R. D. Underhill (eds), *Political Economy and the Changing Global Order* (Toronto: McClelland & Steward Inc.): 163–175.

Hevia, J. L. (2003) *English Lessons: The Pedagogy of Imperialism in Nineteenth-Century China* (Durham and London: Duke Press, and Hong Kong: Hong Kong University Press).

Hobbes, T. and Gaskin, J. C. (1996) *Leviathan* (Oxford: Oxford University Press).

Hochschild, A. (1999) *King Leopold's Ghost: A Story of Greed, Terror, and Heroism in Colonial Africa* (Boston: Houghton Mifflin).

Ho, S. P. S. (1984) 'Colonialism and development: Korea, Taiwan, and Kwantung', in Ramon H. Myers and Mark R. Peattie (eds), *The Japanese Colonial Empire, 1895–1945* (Princeton: Princeton University Press): 347–398.

Holslag, J. (2006) 'China's New Mercantilism in Central Africa', *African and Asian Studies*, 5 (2): 133–169.

Hooper, S. (2009) 'Financial crisis dominates G-20 agenda', CNN, http://www. cnn.com/2009/WORLD/europe/03/30/g20.summit.explainer/index.html.

Howell, J. (1991) 'British aid to agriculture, Tanzania, and Kenya', in Uma Lele (ed.), *Aid to African Agriculture: Lessons from Two Decades of Donors' Experience* (Baltimore: The Johns Hopkins University Press): 418–475.

Huntington, S. P. (1967) 'Political Development and Political Decay', in Claude Welch Jr. (ed.), *Political Modernization* (Belmont: Wadsworth Publishing Company): 126–145.

—— (1968) *Political Order in Changing Societies* (New Haven: Yale University Press).

Hutchful, E. (1995–96) 'The civil society debate in Africa', *International Journal*, 51 (1): 54–77.

—— (2002) *Ghana's Adjustment Experience: The Paradox of Reform* (Geneva: UNRISD and Oxford: James Currey).

Isaacman, A. and Roberts, R. (1995) 'Cotton, colonialism, and social history in sub-Saharan Africa', inAllen Isaacman and Richard Roberts (eds), *Cotton, Colonialism and Social History in Sub-Saharan Africa* (Portsmouth: Heinemann and London: James Currey): 1–39.

Jaggar, A. M. (1983) *Feminist Politics and Human Nature* (Totowa, NJ: Rowman & Allanheld).

Jain, D. (2005) *Women, development, and the UN: A sixty-year quest for equality and justice* (Bloomington: Indian University Press).

Jessop, R. (2007) 'What follows neo-liberalism? The deepening contradictions of US domination and the struggle for a new global order', in Robert Albritton, Robert Jessop and Richard Westra (eds), *Political Economy and Global Capitalism* (London, New York, Delhi: Anthem Press): 67–88.

Johnson, J. J. (1964) *The Military and Society in Latin America* (Stanford: Stanford University Press).

Johnston, H. H. (1897) *British Central Africa* (London: Methuen & Co).

Jones, R. W. (1999) *Security, Strategy, and Critical Theory* (Boulder and London: Lynne Rienner Publishers).

Kagarlitsky, B. (2002) *Russia Under Yeltsin and Putin Neo-Liberal Autocracy* (London, Sterling, Virginia: Pluto Press).

Kahn, J. (2003) 'China's workers risk limbs in export drive', *New York Times*, April 7.

Kaldor, M. (2007) *Human Security* (Cambridge: Polity).

Kaluwa, B. (1992) 'Malawi Industry: Policies, Performance and Problems', in Guy Mhone (ed), *Malawi at the Crossroads: The Postcolonial Political Economy* (Harare: SAPES).

Kandawire, K. J. A. (1979) *Thangata: Forced Labour or Reciprocal Assistance?* (Zomba, University of Malawi).

Karliner, J. and Aparicio, K. (2003) 'Transnational corporations: Issues and pro-posals', in William F. Fisher and Thomas Ponniah (eds), *Another World is Possible: Popular Alternatives to Globalization at the World Social Forum* (Nova Scotia, Fernwood Publishing Ltd, SIRD, Selangor, David Philip, Cape Town and London & New York, Zed Books): 55–61.

Keohane, R. O. (2002a) 'Governance in a Partially Globalized World', in David Held and Anthony McGrew (eds), *Governing Globalization: Power, Authority and Global Governance* (Cambridge: Polity Press): 325–347.

—— (2002b) *Power and Governance in a Partially Globalized World* (London: Routledge).

—— and Nye, J. S. Jr. (2002a) 'Governance in a globalizing world', in Robert O. Keohane (eds), *Power and Governance in a Partially Globalized World* (London: Routledge): 193–218.

—— (2002b) 'The club model of multilateral cooperation and problems of democratic legitimacy', in *Power and Governance in a Partially Globalized World* (London: Routledge): 219–244.

Kettlewell, R. W. (1965) 'Agricultural change in Nyasaland: 1945–1960', *Studies in Tropical Development, Food Research Institute Studies*, 5 (3)(: 220–285.

Keynes, J. M. (1936) *The General Theory of Employment Interest and Money* (New York: Harcourt, Brace and Company).

Killick, T., Gunatilaka R., and Marr, A. (1998) *Aid and the Political Economy of Policy Change* (London: Routledge).

Kim, E. M (1997) *Big Business, Strong State: Collusion and Conflict in South Korean Development, 1960–1990* (New York; State University of New York Press).

—— (2000) 'Globalization of the South Korean Chaebol', in Samuel S. Kim (ed.), *Korea's Globalization* (Oxford: Cambridge University Press): 102–125.

Kim, K. J. (2006) *The Development of Modern South Korea: State formation, Capitalist Development and National Identity* (London and New York: Routledge).

Kim, S. S. (1989) *The Third World in Chinese World Policy* (Princeton, NJ: Center of International Studies Woodrow Wilson School of Public and International Affairs, Princeton University).

—— (1999) 'China and the United Nations', in Elizabeth Economy and Michael Oksenberg (eds), *China Joins the World: Progress and Prospects* (New York: Council on Foreign Relations Press): 42–89.

—— (2006) 'Chinese foreign policy faces globalization challenges', in Alastair Iain Johnston and Robert S. Ross (eds), *New Directions in the Study of China's Foreign Policy* (Stanford: Stanford University Press): 276–306.

Kimmelman, M. (2008) 'For blacks in France, Obama's rise is reason to rejoice, and to hope', *New York Times*, http://www.nytimes.com/2008/06/17/

arts/17abroad.html?scp=1&sq=Michael%20Kimmelman,%20Blacks%20in%20 france&st=cse.

Kindleberger, C. P. (1989) *Manias, Panics, and Crashes: A History of Financial Crisis* (New York: Basic Books, Inc).

Klein, N. (2007) *The Shock Doctrine: The Rise of Disaster Capitalism* (New York: Picador).

Kohl, B. H. and Farthing, L. C. (2006) *Impasse in Bolivia: Neoliberal Hegemony and Popular Resistance* (London and New York: Zed Books).

Kohli, A. (1999) 'Where do high-growth political economies come from? The Japanese lineage of Korea's "development state"', in Meredith Woo-Cumings (ed.), *The Developmental State* (Ithaca: Cornell University Press): 93–136.

Kong, T. Y. (2000) *The Politics of Economic Reform in South Korea: A fragile Miracle* (London and New York: Routledge).

Kornberg, J. F. and Faust, J. R. (2005) *China in World Politics* (Boulder: Lynne Rienner).

Kothari, U. (2005) *Radical History of Development Studies* (Cape Town: David Philip and London and New York, Zed Books).

Kuppens, J. (2006), *Fieldwork interview,* Lilongwe, Malawi.

Kydd, J. (1984) 'Malawi in the 1970s: Development policies and economic change', *Malawi, An Alternative Pattern of Development,* Proceedings of a Seminar Held in the Centre of African Studies (Edinburgh: University of Edinburgh): 295–380.

Lal, D. (1985). *The Poverty of 'Development Economics'* (Cambridge: Harvard University Press).

—— (2004) *In Praise of Empires: Globalization and Order* (Houndmills: Palgrave Macmillan).

Landes, D. (1965) 'Japan and Europe: Contrasts in industrialization', in William W. Lockwood (ed.) *The State and Economic Enterprise in Japan* (Princeton: Princeton University Press): 93–182.

Lane, D. (2000) 'The transformation of state socialism in Russia: From "Chaotic" economy to state-led cooperative capitalism', in Michel Dobry (ed.), *Democratic and Capitalist Transitions in Eastern Europe Lessons for the Social Sciences* (Dordrecht: Kluwer Academic Publishers): 181–196.

Larraín, J. (1989) *Theories of Development: Capitalism, Colonialism and Dependency* (Cambridge: Polity Press).

Laslett, R. (1984) 'An account of Malawi's economy and economic policies in the 1970s', *Malawi, Alternative Patterns of Development,* Proceedings of a Seminar Held in the Centre of African Studies (Edinburgh: University of Edinburgh): 381–406.

Leite, J. C. (2005) *The World Social Forum: Strategies of Resistance* (Chicago: Haymarket Books).

Lele, U. (1991) 'The MADIA Countries: Aid, Inflows, Endowments, Policies, and Performance', in Uma Lele (ed.) *Aid to African Agriculture: Lessons from Two Decades of Donors' Experience* (Baltimore: The Johns Hopkins University Press): 14–106.

—— and Jain, R. (1991) 'The world bank's experience in MADIA countries: Agricultural development and foreign assistance', in Uma Lele (ed.), *Aid to African Agriculture: Lessons from Two Decades of Donors' Experience* (Baltimore: The Johns Hopkins University Press): 107–167.

Lewis, A. (2007) 'Africa's ungoverned spaces', *On the Map*, Canadian Broadcasting Corporation, June 28.

Leys, C. (2001) *Market-driven Politics: Neoliberal Democracy and the Public Interest* (London: Verso).

Lie, J. (1998) *Han Unbound: The Political Economy of South Korea* (Stanford, Calif.: Stanford University Press).

Lightman, D. (2009) *Even with Obama in Charge, Anti-War Democrats Powerless*, McClatchy Newspapers http://www.mcclatchydc.com/homepage/story/68306.html.

Linklater, A. (1999) 'Cosmopolitan citizenship', in Kimberly Hutchings and Roland Dannreuther (eds), *Cosmopolitan Citizenship* (New York: Macmillan Press): 35–59.

Lippit, V. D. (1987) *The Economic Development of* China (Armonk, NY: M. E. Sharpe).

Lipset, S. M. (1981) *Political Man: The Social Bases of Politics* (Baltimore: Johns Hopkins University Press).

Low, L. (ed.) (2004) 'Introduction and overview', *Developmental States: Relevancy, Redundancy or Reconfiguration?* (New York: Nova Science Publishers, Inc.): 3–27.

Lynch, A. C. (2005) 'General patterns of Russian foreign policy', in Julie Wilhelmsen (ed.), *Putin's Russia Strategic Westernisation?* (Oslo, Norway: Norwegian Institute of International Affairs): 15–29.

Macdonald, L. (2005) 'Gendering transnational social movement analysis: Women's groups contest free trade in the Americas', in Joe Bandy and Jackie Smith (eds), *Coalitions Across Borders: Transnational Protest and the Neoliberal Order* (Lanham: Rowman & Littlefield Publishers, Inc): 21–41.

Maclean, S. J., Black, D. R. and Shaw, T. M. (eds), (2006) *A Decade of Human Security: Global Governance and New Multilateralisms* (Aldershot: Ashgate Publishing House).

Malawi Development Corporation, *Annual Report*, 1979.

Malawi National Archives. Central region: Estates Acquired by Press Farming Limited, 1971, M19/3/5/V/117, Zomba.

Malia, M. E. (1994) *The Soviet Tragedy A History of Socialism in Russia*, 1917–1991 (New York: The Free Press).

Mamdani, M. (1996) *Citizen and Subject* (Princeton, NJ: Princeton University Press).

Marchand, M. H. (1994) 'The political economy of north-south relations', in Richard Stubbs and Geoffrey R. D. Underhill (eds), *Political Economy and the Changing Global Order* (Toronto: McClelland & Stewart Inc.): 289–301.

Matlock, J. F. (2004) 'Rebellion in the hinterland', in Head, T. (ed.), *Mikhail Gorbachev* (Farmington Hills: Greenhaven Press).

Martin, H. P. and Schumann, H. (1997) *The Global Trap: Globalization and the Assault on Prosperity and Democracy* (London and New York: Zed Books).

Mbembé, M. (2001) *On the Postcolony* (Berkeley and Los Angeles, University of California Press).

—— (2005) Public Lecture, University of North Carolina at Chapel Hill, April, 2005.

McAdam, D., McCarthy, J. D. and Zald, M. N. (eds), (1996) *Comparative Perspectives on Social Movements: Political Opportunities, Mobilizing Structures, and Cultural Framings* (Cambridge: Cambridge University Press).

McGregor, R. (2003) 'Thriving U.S. companies ignore China trade surplus issue', *Financial Times*, August 7.

McGrew, A. G. (1997) *The Transformation of Democracy?: Globalization and Territorial Democracy* (Cambridge: Polity Press in association with Open University).

McKinney-Whetstone, D. (2009) 'Celebrating the Dream', *Essence*, http://www.essence.com/news_entertainment/news/articles/insidethisissuejanuary2009.

McMaster, C. (1974) *Malawi-Foreign Policy and Development* (London: Julian Friedmann Publishers Ltd).

McMichael, P. (2003) 'Food security and social reproduction: Issues and contradictions', in Isabella Bakker and Stephen Gill (eds), *Power, Production and Social Reproduction* (Basingstoke, Hampshire: Palgrave Macmillan): 169–189.

McNamara, D. L. (1990) *The Colonial Origins of Korean Enterprise 1910–1945* (Cambridge, [England]: Cambridge University Press).

Meltzer Commission Report. (2002) http://www.house.gov/jec/imf/meltzer.htm.

Mignolo, W. D. (2000) *Local Histories/Global Designs: Coloniality, Subaltern Knowledges, and Border Thinking* (Princeton, NJ: Princeton University).

—— (2007) 'DELINKING: The rhetoric of modernity, the logic of coloniality and the grammar of de-coloniality', in *Cultural Studies* (London: Routledge, Taylor & Francis Group): 21 (2–3): 449–514.

Miller, J. (1993) *Mikhail Gorbachev and the End of Soviet Power* (Houndmills, Basingstoke, Hampshire; New York, NY: St Martin's Press).

Millar, K. (2006) 'A human security analysis of the war in Iraq', *Human Security Journal*, 2: 47–63.

Minsky, H. (1982) *Can 'It' Happen Again?: Essays on Instability and Finance* (New York: M. E. Sharpe).

Millennium Development Goals, http://www.un.org/millenniumgoals/.

Mitchell, T. (2002) *Rule of Experts: Egypt, Techno-Politics, Modernity* (Berkeley: University of California Press).

Moore, T. G. (2005) 'Chinese foreign policy in the age of globalization', in Yong Deng and Fei-Ling Wang. (eds), *China Rising* (Lanham: Rowman & Littlefield Publishers): 121–158.

Murphy, C. N. (2005) 'Global governance: Poorly done and poorly understood', in Rorden Wilkinson (ed.), *The Global Governance Reader* (London and New York: Routledge): 90–104.

Murray, S. S. (1932) *A Handbook of Nyasaland* (London: C.A.C.).

Mwakasungura, A. K. (1984) *The Rural Economy of Malawi: A Critical Analysis* (Bergen, Norway: Development Research and Action Programme, Working Paper A309, 1984).

Myers, R. H. and Saburo, Y. (1984) 'Agricultural development in the empire', in Ramon H. Myres and Mark R. Peattie (eds), *The Japanese Colonial Empire, 1895–1945* (Princeton: Princeton University Press): 420–452.

Naughton, B. (2007) *The Chinese Economy: Transitions and Growth* (Cambridge, Mass.: Massachusetts Institute of Technology).

Nelson, L. and Kuzes, I. (1995) *Radical Reform in Yeltsin's Russia: Political, Economic, and Social Dimensions* (Armonk, NY: M. E. Sharpe).

Nesvetailova, A. (2007). *Fragile Finance: Debt, Speculation and Crisis in the Age of Global Credit* (Basingstoke [England]: Palgrave Macmillan).

Neve, A. (2007) 'Extraordinary rendition, the Canadian edition: National security and challenges to the global ban on torture', in Judith Blau and Alberto

Moncada (eds), *Societies Without Borders* (Leiden and Boston: Brill) 2 (1): 117–130.

New York Times (2002) *National Security Strategy of United States of America* http://www.nytimes.com/2002/09/20/politics/20STEXT_FULL.html.

—— (2009) 'New Rules for Derivatives', 14 May, http://www.nytimes.com/ 2009/05/15/opinion/15fri1.html.

Nolan, P. (2004) *China at the Crossroads* (Cambridge, UK: Polity).

Nussbaum, M. C. (1996) 'Patriotism and cosmopolitanism', in Joshua Cohen (ed.), *For Love of Country* (Boston: Beacon Press): 2–17.

Nyasaland government (1962) *Development Plan, 1962–1965* (Zomba: Government Printer).

Nye, J. S. (2004) *Soft Power: The Means to Success in World Politics* (New York: Public Affairs).

Obama, B. (2004) *Dreams from My Father: A Story of Race and Inheritance* (New York: Three Rivers Press).

—— (2008a) 'Renewing the American Economy', *USA Today*, http:// www. usatoday.com/news/politics/election2008/2008-03-27-economy-speech_ N.htm.

—— (2008b) 'Obama's Speech in Berlin', *New York Times*, http://www. nytimes.com/2008/07/24/us/politics/24text-obama.html.

—— (2009a) 'President Barack Obama's Inaugural Address', http://www. whitehouse.gov/blog/inaugural-address/.

—— (2009b) 'Remarks on the Economy', Georgetown University, http://www. whitehouse.gov/the_press_office/Remarks-by-the-President-on-the-Economy-at-Georgetown-University/.

—— (2009c) 'Remarks by President Obama to the Turkish Parliament', April 6 http://www.whitehouse.gov/the_press_office/Remarks-By-President-Obama-To-The-Turkish-Parliament/.

—— (2009d) 'Remarks by the President at the United States Naval Academy Commencement', The White House, May 22, http://www.white house.gov / the_press_office / Remarks-by-the-President-at-US-Naval-Academy-Commencement/.

—— (2009e) 'Remarks by the President on a new beginning', Cairo, http:// www.whitehouse.gov/the_press_office/Remarks-by-the-President-at-Cairo-University-6-04-09/.

Pachai, B. (1978) *Land and Politics in Malawi, 1875–1975* (Kingston: The Limestone Press).

Packenham, R. A. (1973) *Liberal America and the Third World; Political Development Ideas in Foreign aid and Social Science* (Princeton, NJ: Princeton University Press).

Panitch, L. and Konings M. (2008) *American Empire and the Political Economy of Global Finance* (Basingstoke [England]: Palgrave Macmillan).

Parker, I. (2009) 'Lost: After financial disaster, Icelanders reassess their identity', *The New Yorker*, March 9.

Parsons, T. (1951). *The Social System* (Glencoe, Ill.: Free Press).

Partnoy, F. (2009) 'Danger in Wall Street's Shadows', *New York Times* http://www.nytimes.com/2009/05/15/opinion/15partnoy.html.

Peattie, M. R. (1984) 'Introduction', in Ramon H. Myres and Mark R. Peattie (eds), *The Japanese Colonial Empire, 1895–1945* (Princeton: Princeton University Press): 3–26.

Petras, J. (1978) *Critical Perspectives on Imperialism and Social Class in the Third World* (New York: Monthly Review Press).

Phillips, K. (2008) *Bad Money: Reckless Finance, Failed Politics, and the Global Crisis of American Capitalism* (New York: Viking).

Phiri, K. (1998) *Interview*, University of Malawi, Zomba, 5 May.

Picciotto, R., Olonisakin, F. and Clarke, M. (2007) *Global Development and Human Security* (New Brunswick and London: Transaction Publishers).

Pigg, S. L. (1992) 'Inventing social categories through place: Social representations and development in Nepal', *Comparative Studies in Society and History*, 34 (3) (Cambridge, UK: Cambridge University Press): 491–513.

Pike, J. (1968) *Malawi: A Political and Economic History* (London: Praeger).

Pincus, W. (2007) 'U.S. Africa command brings new concerns: Fears of militarization on continent', *The Washington Post* http://www.Washingtonpost.com/WP_dyn/content/article/2007/05/27/AR2007052700978.html.

Pogge, T. W. (1992) 'Cosmopolitanism and sovereignty', *Ethics*, 103 (1): 48–75.

Polanyi, K. (2001) *The Great Transformation: The Political and Economic Origins of Our Time* (Boston: Beacon Press).

Pollock, N. H. (1971) *Nyasaland and Northern Rhodesia: Corridor to the North* (Pittsburgh: Duquesne University Press).

Ponniah, P. and Fisher, W. F. (2003) 'The World Social Forum and the Reinvention of Democracy', in William F. Fisher and Thomas Ponniah (eds) *Another World is Possible: Popular Alternatives to Globalization at the World Social Forum* (Nova Scotia, Fernwood Publishing Ltd, SIRD, Selangor, David Philip, Cape Town and London & New York, Zed Books): 1–20.

Prempeh, E. O. K. (2006). *Against Global Capitalism: African Social Movements Confront Neoliberal Globalization* (Aldershot, England: Ashgate).

Press Corporation Limited. (1995) *Press in the 1990s: Questions and Answers* (Blantyre: Press Corporation Limited).

Pryor, F. L. (1990) *The Political Economy of Poverty, Equity, and Growth: Malawi and Madagascar* (*Oxford* [England]; New York: Oxford University Press).

Putin, V. (2009) 'The World is Facing the First Truly Global Economic Crisis', *Centre for Research on Globalization*, http://www.globalresearch.ca/index.php?context=va&aid=12087.

Quijano, A. (2007) 'Coloniality and modernity/rationality', in *Cultural Studies* (London: Routledge, Taylor & Francis Group): 21 (2–3): 168–178.

—— (2008) 'Coloniality of power, eurocentrism, and social classification', in M. Moraña, M., E. Dussel, and C. A. Jáuregui (eds), *Coloniality at Large: Latin America and the Postcolonial Debate* (Durham and London: Duke University Press): 181–224.

Quintela, S. (2003) 'A solidarity economy', in William F. Fisher and Thomas Ponniah (eds), *Another World is Possible: Popular Alternatives to Globalization at the World Social Forum* (Nova Scotia, Fernwood Publishing Ltd, SIRD, Selangor, David Philip, Cape Town and London & New York, Zed Books): 97–105.

Rai, S. M. and Waylen, G. (eds) (2008) *Global Governance: Feminist Perspectives* (Basingstoke: Palgrave Macmillan).

Rangeley, W. H. J. (1957) 'A brief history of the tobacco industry in Nyasaland', *The Nyasaland Journal*, 10 (1): 62–83.

Rapley, J. (2002) *Understanding Development: Theory and Practice in the Third World* (Boulder: Lynne Rienner Publishers).

――― (2004) *Globalization and Inequality: Neoliberalism's Downward Spiral* (Boulder: Lynne Rienner Publishers).

Reddaway, P. and Glinski, D. (2001) *The Tragedy of Russia's Reforms: Market Bolshevism Against Democracy* (Washington, DC: United States Institute of Peace).

Regan, R. (2009) *President Ronald Regan's First Inaugural Address*, 20 January, http://reagan2020.us/speeches/First_Inaugural.asp.

Republic of Malawi. (1994) *Commission of Inquiry: Mwanza Road Accident Report* (Limbe: Civic Offices).

Rich, F. (2008) 'The Terrorist Barack Hussein Obama', *New York Times,* http://www.nytimes.com/2008/10/12/opinion/12rich.html?_r=1&scp=4&sq=racism%20 and%20obama%27s%20campaign&st=cse.

Richter, R. (2000) *The Money Lenders: Update.* http://www.richtervideos.com/TheMoneyLendersUpdate2000/.

Rist, G. (2004) *The History of Development: From Western Origins to Global Faith* (London and New York: Zed Books).

Robinson, W. I. (1996) *Promoting Polgarchy, Globalization, US Intervention and Hegemony* (Cambridge: Cambridge University Press).

Rodney, W. (1972) *How Europe Underdeveloped Africa* (London: Bogle-L'Ouverture).

Rosenau, J. N. (1997) *Along the Domestic-Foreign Frontier: Exploring Governance in a Turbulent World* (Cambridge: Cambridge University Press).

――― (2002) 'Governance in a new global order', in David Held and Anthony McGrew (eds), *Governing Globalization: Power, Authority and Global Governance* (Cambridge: Polity Press): 70–86.

――― (2005) 'Governance in the twenty-first century', in Rorden Wilinson (ed.), *The Global Governance Reader* New York: Routledge): 45–67.

Rostow, W. W. (1990) *The Stages of Economic Growth: A Non-Communist Manifesto* (Cambridge [England]: Cambridge University Press).

Sachs, J. (2005) *The End of Poverty: Economic Possibilities for our Time* (New York: Penguin Press).

Sahle, E. N. (2008) 'Gender, states, and markets in Africa', in Joseph Mensah (ed.), *Neoliberalism and Globalization in Africa: Contestations on the Embattled Continent* (New York: Palgrave Macmillan): 72–92.

Said, E. (1979) *Orientalism* (New York: Random House).

Santos, B. S. (2006) *The Rise of the Global Left: The World Social Forum and Beyond* (London, New York: Zed Books).

――― and Rodríguez-Garavito, C. A. (2007) 'Introduction: Expanding the economic canon and searching for alternatives to neoliberal globalization', in Boaventura de Sousa Santos (ed.), *Another Production Is Possible: Beyond the Capitalist Canon* (London and New York: Verso): xvii–lxii.

――― Nunes, J. A and Meneses, M. P. (2008) 'Introduction: Opening up the canon of knowledge and recognition of difference', in Boaventura de Sousa Santos (ed.) *Another Knowledge is Possible: Beyond Northern Epistemologies* (London and New York: Verso): xvix–lxii.

Savage, C. (2009) 'Obama's war on terror may resemble Bush's in some areas', *New York Times*, http://www.nytimes.com/2009/02/18/us/politics/18policy.html.

Sayer, J. A., C. S. Harcourt and N. M. Collins (eds) (1992) *The Conservation Atlas of Tropical Forests in Africa* (Basingstoke: Macmillan Publishers).

Schechter, M. G. (1999) 'Our global neighborhood: Pushing problem-solving theory to its limits and the limits of problem-solving theory', in Martin Hewson and Timothy J. Sinclair (eds), *Approaches to Global Governance Theory* (New York: State University of New York Press): 239–257.

Scholte, A. J. (2000) *Globalization: A Critical Introduction* (New York: St. Martin's Press).

Schraeder, P. J. (2004) *African Politics and Society: A Mosaic in Transformation* (Belmont: Thomson Wadsworth).

Schwartz, H. M. and Seabrooke, L. (eds), (2009) *The Politics of Housing Booms and Busts* (Basingstoke: Palgrave Macmillan).

Shepperson, G. and Price T. (1958) *Independent Africa: John Chilembwe and the Origins, Setting and Significance of the Nyasaland Native Rising of 1915* (Edinburgh: Edinburgh University Press).

Shin, K. Y. (1998) 'The political economy of economic growth in East Asia: South Korea and Taiwan', in Eun Mee Kim (ed.), *The Four Asian Tigers: Economic Development and the Global Political Economy* (San Diego: Academic Press): 3–31.

Shiva, V. (2006) 'War against Nature and the People of the South', in Marina Della Giusta, Uma S. Kambhampati, and Robert Hunter Wade (eds), *Critical Perspectives on Globalization* (Cheltenham: Edward Elgar Publishing Limited): 279–312.

Shoup, L. H. and Minter, W. (1977) *The Imperial Brain Trust: The Council on Foreign Relations and United States foreign policy* (New York: Monthly Review Press).

Silva, E. (1996) *The State and Capital in Chile: Business Elites, Technocrats, and Market Economics* (Boulder, Colo.: Westview Press).

Singer, P. (2007) 'The recent rebirth of the solidary economy in Brazil', in Boaventura de Sousa Santos (ed.), *Another Production is Possible* (London and New York: Verso): 3–42.

Skidelsky, R. (1996) *Keynes* (Oxford and New York: Oxford University Press).

Skinner, D. (2004) 'Calling Bush's Views Manichean Is an Insult to the Manicheans', *George Mason University's History News Network*, http://hnn.us/articles/7202.html.

Smith, S. (1991) 'Mature anarchy, strong states and security', *Arms Control*, 12 (2): 325–339.

―――― (2005) 'The Contested Concept of Security', in Ken Booth (ed.), *Critical Security Studies and World Politics* (Boulder and London: Lynne Rienner Publishers): 27–62.

Smith, J., Karides, M., Becker, M., Brunelle, D., Chase-Dunn, C., Donatella, D. P., Garza, R. I., Juris, J. S., Mosca, L., Reese, E., Smith, P. J., and Vázquez, R. (2008) *Global Democracy and the World Social Forums* (Boulder: Paradigm Publishers).

Soederberg, S. (2004) *The Politics of the New International Financial Architecture: Reimposing Neoliberal Domination in the Global South* (London : Zed Books).

Späth, K. (2005) 'Inside global governance: New borders of a concept', in Markus Lederer and Philipps Müller, S. (eds), *Criticizing Global Governance* (New York: Palgrave Macmillan): 21–44.

Steinherr, A. (2000) *Derivatives – The Wild Beast of Finance: A Path to Effective Globalisation?* (New York: John Wiley and Sons).

Stiglitz, J. E. (2002) *Globalization and its Discontents* (New York and London: W. W. Norton & Company).

―――― (2009) 'Obama's Ersatz capitalism', *New York Times*, March 31, http://query.nytimes.com/search/sitesearch?query=stiglitz%2C+2009&x=13&y=7&type=nyt.

Stoddard, K. (2009) 'How Iceland's financial crisis unfolded', http://www.guardian.co.UK/world/2009/jan/26/iceland-crisis-timeline.

Stokke, O. (1995) (ed.) *Aid and Political Conditionality* (London: Frank Cass).

Stoler, A. L. (1995) *Race the Education of Desire: Foucault's History of Sexuality and the Colonial Order of Things* (Durham, NC and London: Duke University Press).

Strange, S. (1986) *Casino Capitalism* (Oxford: Basil Blackwell).

—— (1996) *The Retreat of the State: The Diffusion of Power in the World Economy* (Cambridge: Cambridge University Press).

—— (1998) *Mad Money: When Markets Outgrow Governments* (Ann Arbor: The University of Michigan Press.

Taylor, I. (2006a) *China and Africa: Engagement and Compromise* (London and New York: Routledge).

—— (2006b) 'China's oil diplomacy in Africa', *International Affairs*, 82 (5): 937–959.

Taylor, P. (1999) 'The United Nations in the 1990s: Proactive cosmopolitanism and the issue of sovereignty', *Political Studies* XLVII: 538–565.

The Economist. (2002) 'A dragon out of puff', June 13, 2002.

—— (2009) 'The collapse of manufacturing', May 19, http://www.economist.com/printedition/PrinterFriendly.cfm?story_id=13144864.

Thiong'o, N. and Sahle, E. N. (2004) 'Hegel in Africa literature: Achebe answer', *Diogenes*, 51 (2): 63–67.

Thomas, S. (1975) 'Economic developments in Malawi since Independence', in *Journal of Southern African Studies*): 30–51.

Tickner, J. A (1992) *Gender in International Relations: Feminist Perspectives on Achieving Global Security* (New York: Columbia University Press).

Toye, J. (1993) *Dilemmas of Development* (Oxford: Blackwell).

Truong, T. D. Wieringa, S. and Chhachhi, A. (eds), (2007) *Engendering Human Security: Feminist Perspectives* (London: Zed Books).

Tsikata, D. and J. Kerr (2000) *Demanding Dignity: Women Confronting Economic Reforms in Africa* (Ottawa: The North-South Institute).

Tsygankov, A. P. (2004) *Whose World Order? Russia's Perception of American Ideas after the Cold War* (Notre Dame: University of Notre Dame Press).

Tucker, R. C. (1978) *The Marx-Engels Reader* (New York: W. W. Norton & Company).

Tull, D. M. (2006) 'China's engagement in Africa: Scope, significance and consequences', *Journal of Modern African Studies*, 44 (3): 459–479.

Underhill, G. R. (1997) 'The making of the European financial area: Global market Integration and the EU single market for financial services', in Geoffrey R. Underhill (ed.), *The New World Order in International Finance* (Houndmills, England: Macmillan Press Ltd): 101–123.

United Nations Development Programme. (1994) *Human Development Report* (New York and Oxford: Oxford University Press).

—— (2002) *Report of the International Conference on Financing for Development*, Monterrey, Mexico, http://www.globalpolicy.org/socecon/ffd/conference/.

—— (2003) *Commission on Human Security*, http://www.humansecurity-chs.org/finalreport/English/FinalReport.pdf.

Vail, L. (1983) 'The state and the creation of colonial Malawi's agricultural economy', in Robert I. Rotberg (ed.), *Imperialism, Colonialism, and Hunger: East and Central Africa* (Lexington, Mass.: Lexington Books): 39–87.

Vohra, R. (ed.), (1994) 'Deng Xiaoping's modernization: Capitalism with Chinese characteristics!', in Dhirendra K. Vajpeyi (ed.), *Modernizing China* (Leiden: E. J. Brill): 46–58.

Wade, L. L. and B. S. Kim (1978) *Economic Development of South Korea: The Political Economy of Success* (New York and London: Praeger Publishers).

Wallerstein, I. (1979) *The Capitalist World-Economy* (Cambridge [Eng.]: Cambridge University Press).

—— (2000) *The Essential Wallerstein* (New York: The New Press).

—— (2004) *Alternatives: The United States Confronts the World* (Boulder and London: Paradigm Publishers).

Walt, S. M (1991) 'The renaissance of security studies', *International Studies Quarterly*, 35 (2): 211–239.

Waltz, K. (1979) *Theory of International* Politics (New York: Random Hourse).

Wang, F.-L. (2006) 'Beijing's incentive structure: The pursuit of preservation, prosperity, and power', in Yong Deng and Fei-Ling Wang (eds), *China Rising: Power and Motivation in Chinese Foreign Policy* (Lanham: Rowman & Littlefield Publishers): 19–49.

Wang, Y. (2003) *China's Economic Development and Democratization* (Aldershot: Ashgate Publishing).

Watkins, K. and Fowler, P. (2002) *Rigged Rules and Double Standards: Trade, Globalisation, and the Fight Against Poverty* (Oxford: Oxfam).

Weil, R. (1996) *Red Cat, White Cat: China and the Contradictions of "Market Socialism"* (New York: Monthly Review Press).

Weitz, R. (2009) 'Strategic review: Russia resurgent?', *World Politics Review*, http://www.worldpoliticsreview-digital.com/wpr/20090102/?pg=66.

White, S. (2002) 'Thinking race, thinking development', *Third World Quarterly*, 23 (3): 407–419.

Whitworth, S. (1994) *Feminism and International Relations: Towards a Political Economy of Gender in Interstate and Non-Governmental Institutions* (Houndmills, Basingstoke, Hampshire: Macmillan Press Ltd).

—— (2005) 'Militarized masculinities and the politics of peacekeeping', in Ken Booth (ed.), *Critical Security Studies and World Politics* (Boulder and London: Lynne Rienner Publishers).

Wohlforth, W. C. (2002) 'U.S. strategy in a unipolar world', in Ikenberry, J. G. (ed.), America *Unrivaled: The Future of the Balance of Power* (Ithaca: Cornell University Press): 98–118.

Wolf, E. R. (1982) *Europe and the People Without History* (Berkeley: University of California Press).

Wollstonecraft, M. and Poston C. H. (1975 *A Vindication of the Rights of Woman: An authoritative text, backgrounds, criticism,* (New York: W. W. Norton).

Woods, N. (2002) 'The role of institutions', in David Held and Anthony McGrew (eds), *Governing Globalization: Power, Authority and Global Governance* (Cambridge: Polity Press): 25–45.

World Bank. (1989) *Sub-Saharan Africa, From Crisis to Sustainable Growth* (Washington: The World Bank).

—— (1990) *Trends in Developing Economies* (Washington, DC: World Bank).

—— (2002a) *World Bank Report 2002: Building Institutions for Markets* (New York: Oxford University Press).

—— (2002b) *China: National Development and Sub-national Finances* (Washington, DC: World Bank).

World Social Forum, http://www.worldsocialforum.org.

—— 'IC – Nature, responsibilities, composition and functioning', http://www.worldsocialforum.org.

Worth, O. (2005) *Hegemony, International Political Economy and Post-Communist Russia* (Aldershot, Hants, England: Ashgate).

Xinhua News Agency, (2003) 'China-Africa Cooperation Forum Not Talking Shop: Ethiopia FM', http://www.china.org.cn/english/features/China-Africa/82631.htm.

Yongming, F. (2007) 'How reform drove China's integration into the international community', in David Zweig and Chen Zhimin (eds), *China's Reforms and International Political Economy* (New York: Routledge): 97–111.

Zedong, M. (1977) 'On the cooperative transformation of agriculture', *Selected Works of Mao Zedong, Vol. 5* (Beijing People's Publishing House).

Zhimin, C. (2007) 'Soft balancing and reciprocal engagement: International structures and China's foreign policy choices', in David Zweig and Chen Zhimin (eds), *China's Reforms and International Political Economy* (New York: Routledge): 42–61.

Zghal, A. (1995) 'The "Bread Riot" and the crisis of the one-party system in Tunisia', in Mahmood Mamdani and Wamba-dia-Wamba (eds), *African Studies in Social Movements and Democracy* (Dakar: CODSRIA): 99–133.

Index